Powering Apollo

New Series in NASA History

Before Lift-off: The Making of a Space Shuttle Crew
by Henry S. F. Cooper, Jr.

The Space Station Decision:
Incremental Politics and Technological Choice
by Howard E. McCurdy

Exploring the Sun: Solar Science since Galileo
by Karl Hufbauer

Inside NASA: High Technology and Organizational Change
in the U.S. Space Program
by Howard E. McCurdy

Powering Apollo: James E. Webb of NASA
by W. Henry Lambright

POWERING APOLLO

James E. Webb of NASA

W. Henry Lambright

The Johns Hopkins University Press
Baltimore and London

© 1995 The Johns Hopkins University Press
All rights reserved. Published 1995
Printed in the United States of America on acid-free paper
04 03 02 01 00 99 98 97 96 95   5 4 3 2 1

The Johns Hopkins University Press
2715 North Charles Street
Baltimore, Maryland 21218-4319
The Johns Hopkins Press Ltd., London

Library of Congress Cataloging-in-Publication Data will be found
at the end of this book.
A catalog record for this book is available from the British Library.

ISBN 0-8019-4902-0
"paperback edition 1998"
"0-8018-6205-1"

To my family

CONTENTS

Preface and Acknowledgments   ix

Introduction   1

1. The Making of a Public Executive   11

2. Directing the U.S. Budget   30

3. Managing the Department of State   47

4. The Oklahoma Years   69

5. NASA: From Appointment to Apollo   82

6. Launching a Stronger NASA   102

7. The Struggle to Maintain Momentum   132

8. The Apollo Fire   142

9. From Crisis to Recovery   165

10. Last Hurrah at NASA   189

11. The Moon and After   206

12. Legacy   214

Notes   219

An Essay on Sources   255

Index   265

PREFACE AND ACKNOWLEDGMENTS

In the mid-1980s, I had the opportunity to become involved with a group of scholars, drawn from throughout the country, who were concerned with issues of administrative leadership. Led by Jameson W. Doig of Princeton and Erwin C. Hargrove of Vanderbilt, this group was examining whether leaders of agencies and departments of the federal government made much difference in public policy and, if so, how they did. There was a school of thought in the academic literature that they did not, and the Reagan administration was fanning the widespread conventional wisdom that "bureaucrats" were hopelessly ineffectual. Supported by the Sloan Foundation, this group studied a number of individual administrators who were believed to have been capable leaders—indeed, were considered innovative and entrepreneurial. I was asked to prepare an essay on James Webb, head of NASA in the era of Apollo. That essay became a chapter in the book edited by Doig and Hargrove, *Leadership and Innovation: A Biographical Perspective on Entrepreneurs in Government* (Baltimore: Johns Hopkins University Press, 1987; reissued in an abridged edition, 1990).

Doig and Hargrove encouraged me to think about a book-length study of Webb. They did not have to push very hard. I had encountered Webb as a student in the turbulent 1960s when he was still NASA administrator. Later in the decade, as an assistant professor of political science at the Maxwell School, Syracuse University, I had the opportunity to interview him. He had a reputation for being quite a formidable individual—a political animal who was dynamic and intelligent and who projected an intense can-do attitude that was infectious. He was all of that and more.

Genuinely interested in the theory as well as practice of public management, he wanted to improve both of them through the interaction of practitioners and academics. He talked with me because he wanted NASA used as a laboratory, especially by young public administration scholars. He believed that both NASA and the university would benefit from the interaction. I found him a fascinating and intriguing man.

I suppose I began contemplating a book on Webb after this meeting. Then came the Doig-Hargrove project. I needed additional resources to research and write a book, and the NASA History Program provided funds and promised me total freedom as to content; it lived up to that understanding.

The book I had in mind would fill a critical gap in the literatures of space history and public management. There was, of course, an existing literature on space and Project Apollo. But there was nothing that looked at the enterprise from the vantage point of the individual in charge. Between the scientists, engineers, astronauts, and contractors who performed the work of space and the politicians who provided the funds stood James Webb, a man in the middle of often conflicting forces. Until someone looked at Apollo through the administrator's eyes, something would always be missing from writings on this epic adventure.

While filling a gap in the literature on space history (and indeed the history of the 1960s), I also sought to contribute to the continuing debate about the role of administrative leaders. Particularly important was the question of "match" among leader, organization, and times, a matter Webb presented an unusual opportunity to illuminate because he had three significant and different federal executive positions in his career: budget director, under secretary of state, and NASA administrator. Indeed, within NASA, Webb faced exceptionally different environments in the first half of the 1960s, when NASA was a dominant national priority, and the second half, when the Great Society and the Vietnam War caught NASA in a budgetary vise.

The biographical approach can be a source of strength for many fields: history, political science, management. It shows us the conditions that allow for leadership, how a person gets to a particular key position, and the mix of personality and experience that causes a particular leader to master the position or become its victim.

In researching and writing this manuscript, I have had the help of many. First were Jameson Doig, Erwin Hargrove, and the Sloan Foundation, who got me started. Second was the NASA History Office, led initially by Sylvia D. Fries and then by Roger D. Launius. Sylvia Fries helped me obtain funding, and Roger Launius and his colleague John "Dill" Hunley provided additional encouragement and constructive critiques of the manuscript as it evolved. Martin Collins and his colleagues at the National Air and Space Museum shared their interviews of Webb and other NASA officials and were also "talking partners" about Webb and NASA along the way. A multitude of interviewees—family, friends, associates of Webb in government and the private sector—graciously spent time with me and shared their recollections of relevant events and decisions. Robert Seamans, NASA general manager and then Webb's deputy, was especially accommodating. I was able to interview James Webb himself, although he often could speak only for minutes before his energy—once so overwhelming—completely left him. I will be forever thankful that I was able to get his unique perspective on several occasions before he died. I appreciate the help of Nina Scrivener, his secretary, and of Patsy Webb, his wife, for making it possible for me to see him.

I am grateful to numerous archivists who assisted me at presidential libraries and other repositories of documents. Many individuals aided me through research tasks of one kind or another: Michelle A. Crew, then a graduate student, performed admirably in obtaining pertinent information, as did Rosemary O'Leary, then a graduate student and now on the faculty of Indiana University. Thanks are due also to Robert A. Divine, who read my manuscript for Johns Hopkins and provided useful guidance for its improvement. Robert Brugger and Bobbe Hughey, Johns Hopkins editors, made numerous valuable suggestions to streamline the book.

I also want to express my gratitude to Kathleen E. Morezak, a superb administrative assistant, who lived with the Webb project from start to finish. Her professionalism in typing numerous drafts and her eye for editorial excellence were tremendous assets.

Finally, I wish to thank my sons, Dan and Nat, for their encouragement, and my wife, Nancy, who read portions of the manuscript and gave me her usual excellent advice on how to strengthen it. She was also a constant source of inspiration, always reminding me, when pressures built, that finishing the Webb book was truly important—not just to me, but to others.

To all who helped, I am truly grateful. Any errors in the book are my responsibility alone.

Powering Apollo

INTRODUCTION

On *May 25, 1961*, President John F. Kennedy addressed Congress and, in a now classic national challenge, declared his belief that the United States "should commit itself to achieving the goal, before this decade is out, of landing a man on the moon and returning him safely to the earth."[1]

A little more than eight years later, in an explosion of fire and cacophony of sound, the 3,817-ton Saturn rocket lifted the *Apollo 11* space capsule off the ground. Its destination, 238,000 miles away, was the moon. On board were three astronauts: Edwin Aldrin, Jr., Neil A. Armstrong, and Michael Collins.

Four days later, July 20, 1969, Armstrong climbed down the ladder of his landing craft, placed his foot on the moon, and took "one small step for [a] man, one giant leap for mankind."

On July 24, the small remnant of the once mighty space machine broke through the earth's atmosphere, ablaze from the friction of entry. Parachutes erupted, and the capsule gradually splashed down into the Pacific Ocean. The three astronauts; all safe, were soon aboard the recovery aircraft carrier. On a large screen at Mission Control in Houston, where the National Aeronautics and Space Administration (NASA) had been tracking the entry flight, the words of President Kennedy appeared, followed by "TASK ACCOMPLISHED, July 1969."[2]

In Washington, D.C., a private citizen named James Edwin Webb breathed a deep sigh of relief. His own personal mission to the moon was at last over. The national celebrations that followed *Apollo 11*'s triumphant success did not glorify Webb. He stayed largely on the sidelines, while others owned the spotlight, for he no longer held a position at NASA. But for most of NASA's journey to the moon, from 1961 to 1968, he had been the man in charge. As administrator of NASA in the 1960s, he had been the power behind Apollo. When he died on March 27, 1992, and was buried in Arlington National Cemetery, his special role at the helm of NASA was widely acknowledged. The *New York Times* obituary cited his reputation as "an extraordinary manager." The *Washington Post* wrote that he was "hard charging and immensely capable." Not a scientist, Webb was chosen as NASA administrator "for his management skills and political sophistication." Though he left NASA before Neil Armstrong walked on the moon, "he was universally credited with laying the groundwork for that epic event."[3]

It took approximately $24 billion to place a man on the moon (over $100 billion in current dollars), and the effort required the talents of twenty thousand industrial firms, two hundred university labs, and a team of four hundred thousand public and private workers.[4] Leading NASA in the 1960s was one of the greatest administrative and political challenges any individual has ever faced.

Who was James Webb? What did he do? How did he do it? What difference did he make as leader of NASA?

The Puzzle of Bureaucratic Leadership

Few questions are more important to ask or difficult to answer than those concerning governmental leadership. With our eyes focused on political leaders, few of us even know the names of the men and women who lead the large public organizations under them. They are part of the vast bureaucracy—that fourth branch of government about which little complimentary is said. Our color for bureaucracy is grey, our bureaucrats faceless. Many of us view *leadership* and *bureaucracy* as mutually exclusive terms, and a great deal of scholarly writing reinforces the conventional wisdom. In Herbert Kaufman's theory of organizational change, executive leadership plays little or no role. According to Kaufman, organizations that fail to adapt to shifts in their environment wither and die; organizations that prosper do so less because of leaders than of luck. In his extreme theory of environmental determinism, leaders have little impact on policy and programs.[5]

The other view, of course, is the "great man" theory, in which history is painted on canvas by outstanding individuals. Declares Thomas Carlyle, the nineteenth-century historian: "They were the leaders of men . . . the modelers, patterns, and in a wide sense creators, of whatsoever the general mass of men contrived to do or to attain."[6] In this view, organizations are extensions of their leaders.

Truth, as in most cases, lies somewhere in between. For the most part, individuals at the top of organizations likely have only marginal impact, especially if they happen to be there for but a brief time. But once in a while, when the context is right, an individual can make a difference in the success of an organization. And when that happens, the achievement is worth noting and attempting to understand, especially in U.S. public administration. For in the United States not only do great constraints prevent one from placing one's mark on a public organization but also a widespread belief holds that an individual bureaucrat should not have too much room in which to maneuver. After all, bureaucrats are not supposed to make policy. That is the task of elected officials in the United States, at least in theory.

Again, reality is often different. Ample evidence suggests that certain bureaucratic executives are major players in policy, and that an informal and unofficial reality requires them to play significant roles if American democracy is to function. Policy means little if it is not implemented, and the agencies and departments of government must lead this implementation. The way they lead is often deliberately obfuscated, however. Effective administrators in government often employ the strategy attributed to President Dwight D. Eisenhower—"hidden-hand leadership."[7]

Indeed a fourth branch of government, the U.S. bureaucracy consists of a multitude of agencies, departments, commissions, and government corporations. While exercising their authority under legislative and constitutional mandates, they inevitably have a degree of autonomy. Some individual agency executives use their discretion effectively, and some do not. Once in a while, an individual uses the position of public executive with such exceptional force that he or she is noticed—even remembered. As is J. Edgar Hoover, longtime chief of the Federal Bureau of Investigation, they are more often remembered for their abuse of power in office than for its use in the public interest.

Yet, if government is to work well, administrators must be willing and able to provide positive leadership. They must motivate followers, raise the performance level of their organizations, and accomplish the purposes for which their organizations were established and funded. Most leaders, able to maintain their organizations, are "transactional" leaders, in the words of

James MacGregor Burns. Those who create new possibilities, "transforming" leaders, change organizations and imbue them with values that last beyond their tenure.[8]

This administrative biography of James Edwin Webb, who played a "transforming" role in American public administration, tells the story of the man who built NASA in a few years from a new, small, vulnerable agency into an organization capable of taking America to the moon.

Webb's NASA has subsequently been cited as a model of "excellence in management of large-scale public enterprises." According to one observer, "Webb's tenure at NASA set the standard by which all subsequent administrators have been judged. He was called the quintessential manager."[9] Still, Webb's record at NASA was not perfect: he was administrator when three astronauts died in a fire that should not have happened; he left NASA with no firm post-Apollo goal; and he launched a mammoth effort to reform universities and regional economies that some regarded as ill-advised and that did not achieve the goals he set.

Nevertheless, NASA got to the moon on time and within the general costs projected, a monumental achievement by government and its private-sector partners. Project Apollo, the key NASA program, was one of the most impressive demonstrations of technological prowess in history. For most of it Webb was ultimately responsible. While Apollo had its critics then and now, it stands as a symbol of what the United States can do when it decides on a course and puts the necessary resources behind it.

Operating in the Cold War context of his times, Webb made the most of the opportunity his place as head of NASA presented him by influencing the Apollo decision, forcefully and skillfully seeing to its implementation, and even affecting the management of Apollo after he left. He pulled together the scientific, engineering, personnel, budgetary, political, and governmental efforts required. Apollo represented a Cold War technological victory, and he was the general who guided that victory.

Webb's administration of NASA culminated a series of major public assignments: director of the Bureau of the Budget (BOB) and under secretary of state in the administration of President Harry S. Truman. In every role, he tried to leave his mark, effectively in the cases of BOB and NASA, less so at the State Department, where his frustration illuminates the limits of administrative leadership in a particular context.

The son of a North Carolina county school superintendent, Webb worked his way through the University of North Carolina, was elected to Phi Beta Kappa, and graduated in 1928. After serving first a member of

Congress and then a leading New Deal Washington lawyer, Webb joined Sperry Gyroscope Company in 1936, rising to vice-president in seven years. In 1946, President Truman chose him for director of the budget, then for under secretary of state from 1949 to 1952. During the Eisenhower years, Webb served as president of Republic Supply Company and assistant to the president of Kerr-McGee Oil Industries.

When President John F. Kennedy appointed him NASA administrator at age fifty-four, Webb looked and acted the successful man he was. Standing five feet nine inches, he dressed impeccably, was always well-groomed, and typified the midcentury executive who moved easily among corporate and governmental elites.[10] He had thick, wavy, dark-brown hair, "graying smartly, and combed straight back." Every strand seemed "nailed in."[11] Although stocky, he did not look overweight. Invariably polite, he had a disarming southern accent, but his square jaw matched the forcefulness that usually led him to dominate conversations. Said one NASA official, "Trying to make conversation with Jim Webb is like trying to drink out of a fire hydrant." "A man with a florid complexion and an intense manner that gave his blue eyes a permanently pleading, worried look," he was known for his "memorable, gesticulating, humorless volubility, with frequent interjections of a tic-like rhetorical question: Do you follow me?" His intensity was sometimes overwhelming. "If you ask [him] a question," said a top executive of one government agency, "you get fifty facts when two or three would do, but he has the knack of getting large numbers of people moving. I'm damned if I can understand how he does it."[12]

Perhaps it was the sheer energy of the man that made him such a memorable leader. Perhaps beyond the strong personality lay a set of management techniques he understood and practiced. Without a doubt, Webb believed in a Holy Grail of management, and that he had found it at NASA.[13]

Webb's Disputed Legacy

While not widely known to the general public, Webb is, among professionals in government and close students of government, a Washington legend. President Lyndon B. Johnson called him his best administrator, and bureaucratic veterans look to Webb for lessons in how to accomplish great deeds through public policy.[14] Accorded innumerable awards, testimonials, and honorary degrees (at least thirty-two from universities across the country), Webb had a special fund and lectureship for Excellence in Public Service established in his name. He has been featured in various lists of "giants" in management in the twentieth century and among the top "public entrepreneurs" the United States has produced.[15] A leading business management scholar, Leonard Sayles, called Webb a manager of "heroic" proportions:

> No one has ever adequately pointed out that, under Jim Webb, NASA was a magnificently managed program. As a society, we went from almost zero knowledge of man in space to a fully operational space program in less than ten years. I've seen a company take that long to build a new plant or get a new process working. Webb achieved an enormous accomplishment in organizational leadership. He contributed more than one can easily say to our national welfare. In the process, he showed himself to be an extraordinary human being. Yet the accomplishments of NASA are not associated in our minds with leadership or administrative ability, but with the courage of some superb astronauts and with the new technology of rockets and space capsules. Hardly ever, if ever, do we hear that this was management at its finest.[16]

Similar views of Webb abound. A reviewer of a book on space policy referred to him as an administrative "genius" who was able to build and control "NASA's vastly intricate structure, while never forgetting for a moment his need for full congressional support."[17] Webb had been called an administrative genius before—by Dean Acheson, whom he served as under secretary of state in a difficult, sometimes strained relationship.

If ever a man thought and talked about administrative leadership, especially in the public sector, it was James Webb. He read books about it, engaged scholars in debate on issues in the field, provided funds for university fellowships linking science, technology, and management, served as president of the American Society for Public Administration, wrote a book about the management of "large-scale endeavors," and helped found the National Academy of Public Administration to honor administrators as national academies honor scientists and engineers. Yet, some of the factors that made Webb so remarkable a public executive caused him also to have his detractors. For them he was a "combative bureaucrat who guarded his turf with canine ferocity,"[18] a "slippery, corny, insincere opportunist" whose championing of space was because it gave him "a bureaucratic empire." At the time of the Apollo fire, his stonewalling thoroughly exasperated the *New York Times* and such liberal Democratic critics as Senator Walter F.

Mondale. The *Times* questioned Webb's "candor" and called for his ouster, as other media and congressional observers quipped that NASA stood for "never a straight answer."[19] His principles of large-scale management, celebrated by management scholars Leonard Sayles and Margaret Chandler, have been questioned by historian Walter McDougall, who labels Webb a "Big Operator" and a "technocrat."[20]

In his award-winning history of the space program, McDougall paints a rather unflattering picture of Webb as a man who saw NASA not just as an agency of government but as "a model of integration, a team effort drawing confidently on government, industry, and university," and Apollo not as a race with the Soviet Union but as an all-purpose engine mobilizing the country toward a range of larger ends. NASA, organization, technology—these were instruments for Webb.[21]

While McDougall speaks of Webb's surpassing ability and service-oriented motives, he is wary of state-funded and state-directed technological and social change, a view that others have shared. In the 1960s, admirers of Webb marveled at NASA's mobilization skills and agreed with him that NASA was a "wave of the future," an alternative to the "military-industrial complex," a dynamic, positive aggregation of public and private power that could serve in the public interest. If the nation could integrate government, industry, and universities to go to the moon, it could do the same for a host of other civilian problems. Then, as later, however, Webb's detractors said that NASA simply augmented the existing "contract state" and was on its way toward creating the administrative means to turn government into "Big Brother."[22]

Webb, therefore, represented a threat to critics of big government, because he exemplified the superbureaucrat, the man who makes the "megamachine" of government operate, seemingly oblivious to the dangers of concentrated power. That Webb himself wrote about the need to make such aggregated power accountable to elected officials made him no less worrisome to social critics of government-sponsored large-scale technology.

Was James Webb a "heroic figure" or a "big operator"? The question cannot be avoided because he was, in truth, something of both. To unravel his many aspects is to deal with the ambiguities and complexities of bureaucratic power in American democracy.

Webb thought of himself as an administrator, and he consciously sought to create in NASA a "perfect organization." But what virtually everyone else also saw in him was a skilled administrative politician, "supremely capable," at NASA particularly, in the art of "power brokering."[23] The

American people and the system of government they created are suspicious of power. The Constitution explicitly separates power among institutions to ensure slow, deliberate decision making. Checks and balances abound to make it difficult for any one person or group to wield too much influence. Yet to accomplish certain public purposes, power has to be focused. Institutions have to converge. Although political parties play a role in aggregating interests, slack party discipline and the geographical orientations of party members limit their influence. Administrators, responsible to the president and Congress, find they must build coalitions to be effective. Here lay Webb's true genius: his understanding of the relation of administration to power in Washington. To get America to the moon, he exercised governmental power in a way that provided NASA the resources and autonomy it needed. Whether his means were beneficial or harmful in the long run depends on one's view of both bureaucratic power and the Apollo program, but their effectiveness was undeniable.

Norton Long, in a classic statement, wrote that power "is the lifeblood of administration." He went on to say that

> its attainment, maintenance, increase, dissipation, and loss are subjects the practitioner and student can ill afford to neglect. Loss of realism and failure are almost certain consequences. This is not to deny that important parts of public administration are so deeply entrenched in the habits of the community, so firmly supported by the public, or so clearly necessary as to be able to take their power base for granted and concentrate on the purely professional side of their problems. But even these islands of the blessed are not immune from the plague of politics. . . . To stay healthy one needs to recognize that health is a fruit, not a birthright. Power is only one of the considerations that must be weighed in administration, but of all it is the most overlooked in theory and the most dangerous to overlook in practice.[24]

Whatever else can be said about him, Webb did not overlook power in his practice of public management. He built, in and through NASA, a power base of huge proportions. It is in part because he did so that NASA was successful, and it is also because he succeeded that he had adversaries. Power is a concept about which there is great ambivalence—especially bureaucratic power. Aware of this, Webb frequently noted that there was a "line" the responsible public executive had to walk.

The story of James Webb is as much a story of administrative power as of administrative accomplishment, because one made the other possible.

Moreover, while Webb built power for himself and his agency, he also recognized its limits. Because he knew failure as well as success in his career, he sensed when power had been lost. At NASA, he sought to create a bureaucratic momentum that could last beyond his tenure.

In doing so, he defended the distinctive competence of his organization against the Defense Department and other agencies that challenged NASA's quest to lead in space policy. He pressed the disparate, competitive parts of NASA to work together in a more cohesive whole. He built coalitions involving Congress, president, media, and more. He fashioned an alliance embracing industry, universities, and others on whom NASA depended. He fused administration with science and technology. He used the financial resources of NASA to reward and punish. He employed rhetoric and other intangible resources to accomplish his ends. He was both administrator *and* politician.

Tom Wolfe, author of *The Right Stuff,* called Webb one of the "ablest and most distinguished of the off-the-ballot politicians," "a valuable breed well known in Washington." He described Webb as "the sort of man of whom a congressman or senator was likely to say: 'He speaks my language.'" But more than a politician, Wolfe noted, Webb was an administrator "known as a man who could make bureaucracies run."[25] Armed with a national goal set by the president, as well as a personal agenda set by himself, in order to succeed he used every legal and legitimate means at his disposal—with guile, against influential opponents. The congressional consensus behind Apollo lasted barely two years. By 1963, NASA's requested budget was heatedly debated, and while NASA received more than in 1962, it obtained far less than Webb had sought. In the mid-1960s, the country turned to the Great Society, which substantially expanded social programs and federal spending, and by the late 1960s, the overriding priority, Vietnam, was tearing the country apart. The wind shifted steadily against Webb as priorities changed and rose sharply against him in 1967, when the Apollo fire killed three astronauts. The way Webb handled that crisis highlighted his strengths and weaknesses. In the view of some, he allowed his end to justify his means, violating proper administrative accountability in a democracy. Webb's conduct then in defense of NASA helped make him the issue.

His reputation diminished by the experience, Webb survived the Apollo fire and its aftermath, drew even more power to himself within the agency, and propelled NASA toward a full recovery where Apollo was concerned. But when he could not sell a post-Apollo program, he largely abandoned the task, casting aside most of the items on his personal agenda, such as using universities to strengthen regional economies and moving the United States toward what McDougall called a "Space Age America." In the end, Webb used his diminishing political capital to give NASA one last push toward the moon, finally sacrificing his own position on the altar of Apollo.

As astronauts walked the moon, Webb proclaimed to all who would listen that Apollo's real achievement lay in demonstrating that a democratic nation could outmanage an authoritarian state. He said that if the United States could go to the moon, it could solve its other public problems. Few listened. Richard M. Nixon, president in 1969 when the moon landing took place, ushered in a lengthy conservative era. Rather than an engine for problem solving, government was depicted as part of the problem. Even Democrats—among them President Jimmy Carter—cast aspersions against government, especially government bureaucracy. Big technology, which Webb embraced, was also suspect in the wake of Vietnam, a counterculture movement, and the rise of environmentalism. The longstanding partnership between federal officials and scientific and technical experts, forged in World War II, was shattered. Apollo seemed the end of an era rather than the prototype for a future civilian science and technology relationship.

Webb continued a productive life after NASA, but his message was increasingly out of touch with the times. He died at eighty-five, a resident of Washington, D.C. Much honored, indeed idolized by many in NASA who had served under him, Webb was nevertheless frustrated. He believed the nation he loved and served had found a new frontier in Apollo, not only in space but in government management, but had stepped back from the opportunity and was the poorer for it.

Despite his leadership of one of the most extraordinary technological achievements in history, Webb is not well known. Avoiding publicity was a function of his personal style and administrative strategy. He understood the importance of sharing credit even in Washington, where credit is sought often for its own sake. A creator of the cult of the organization, not of the personality, Webb was more interested in NASA's aggrandizement than his own, although he certainly was intensely ambitious, conscious of his own personal power, and protective of his status. In many ways his career is a case study in what it takes to achieve administrative success in the United States—to be a master of the fourth branch of government.

THE MAKING OF A PUBLIC EXECUTIVE

James Webb owed his achievements in government considerably to his North Carolina roots and his stable family, from which he reaped strong values, a positive outlook, and the desire to succeed. Born on October 7, 1906, in Tally Ho, North Carolina, he had an older sister and would be joined later by another sister and two brothers. Their father, John Frederick (J.F.) Webb, and mother, Sarah Edwin Gorham Webb, were college graduates in an era when that was the exception for most Americans. Both native North Carolinians, Webb's parents were education oriented and instilled in Webb a love of learning.[1]

An educator, J.F. was appointed education superintendent for rural Granville County, North Carolina, one year after Webb's birth, and the family moved to Oxford, county seat of Granville, a town of four thousand.

Quiet and cerebral at home, J.F. liked to read and was fluent in Latin and Greek. Active and dedicated in his profession, he was zealous about raising the quality of schools.[2] The progressive spirit moved the nation then, its emphasis being that society could be improved and that government and education should be forces for change. In the south, North Carolina "led the way by generating public enthusiasm for education, pumping large additional funds into schools, lengthening the school term, and increasing enrollments."[3]

As a county school superintendent, J.F. was caught up in this progressive mood. Having attended and later taught at a private school of considerable note in Bell Buckle, Tennessee, run by kinsmen W. R. "Sawney" Webb and John Webb, he wanted to bring the high standards he saw there to the system of one-, two-, and three-room schools strung across Granville County, whose teachers were poorly prepared and sometimes not even college educated.[4] To upgrade personnel and consolidate the many small schools into a few larger, better-equipped ones, J.F. had to find community leaders who shared his vision—individuals "who would stand up and speak out for better schools—to serve on district committees and on the Granville Board of Education."[5]

For twenty-eight years, from 1907 to 1935, J. F. Webb tenaciously implemented a program to consolidate schools and upgrade personnel. He had reduced the number of schools from 150 to 7 by the time he left, and students were being transported to them by school buses. Closing schools in small towns met resistance. As the environment of the Progressive Era gave way to more conservative times and eventually to the Depression, the accumulated opposition forced J.F. out of his post at sixty-two.[6]

Not only the model of a dedicated public servant, deeply interested in improving society through education, J. F. Webb also passed on to James and his other children values he had gleaned from his Uncle Sawney, considered the most notable member of the Webb family. Sawney not only had founded a school with a national reputation but also, at age seventy, in 1913 had been elected to fill the unexpired term of a deceased U.S. senator.[7]

Sawney's philosophy was a major influence in the Webb household. Himself deeply affected by Sawney, J.F. repeated his uncle's words to his children, encouraging them to seek the "large life," to look for "somebody or something" to which to devote themselves, "never to do anything you've got to hide." They were told that "the will power is the man" but also warned that "to come in contact with human wills is not pleasant."[8] Above all, they should be self-disciplined, have integrity, and always do their best. Second best was not good enough. A grade of B was unacceptable for a Webb. The children were expected to achieve, and all did. Four of the five made Phi Beta Kappa in college. Two became lawyers and a third earned a Ph.D. degree.

Although James Webb respected his father, they were not close. His mother provided the nurturing, especially for James. Almost compulsively hardworking, she was a practical person, while J.F. seemed sometimes far removed from mundane realities, such as financial matters. That J.F. never made much money bothered his wife, who had to find ways to make the most of what they had.

Although J.F. and Sarah were demanding, and money was always in short supply, the Webb household provided a stability within which the children could have fun and develop. On weekends, the family took their horse and buggy, and later their car, to Grandmother's farm, to picnics in the country, to other relatives' homes along roads not yet paved. The values Webb learned were mostly traditional ones: neighborliness, hard work, and self-reliance. The Webbs were Presbyterians, and Sarah made sure the family went to church every Sunday, although religion did not dominate their lives. In spite of the prejudice in their Oxford environment, Webb's sister Olive recalled that "'nigger' was a forbidden word" in the Webb house.[9]

Education

Webb excelled in the public schools in Oxford. Active, serious about doing his share, to make money he cut grain, delivered papers, sold magazines, worked as a cashier and clerk in stores, and took odd jobs. In summers, he worked on the family farm. A positive youngster, he enjoyed interactions with people, and when he delivered newspapers, he took time to speak with his customers.[10]

When he was about ten years old, while at his grandmother's house, he fell and broke his right shoulder. With Oxford ten miles away, it took awhile for a doctor to get there and set it. As a result, it did not knit properly, and Webb had a weakness in his right arm and shoulder for years.[11] In consequence, he could not participate actively in athletics and channeled his competitive drive into his schooling. He learned to read carefully and retentively. With his unusually keen memory, he found no problem getting good grades. In his spare time, he worked, developed hobbies, and honed his mechanical abilities, proving unusually adept in organizing his time so that he could engage in a multitude of activities. As long as she can remember, Olive Webb Wharton recalls her brother having "this gift" for organization. Within the social unit of the Webb children, James seemed to feel a special responsibility and was the leader.[12]

In 1923, he went off to the University of North Carolina at Chapel Hill, following in his father's path. After a year of taking general courses, he had to drop out; there was simply not enough money for the family to finance him. He would have to make his way on his own.

He contacted R. G. Lassiter, successful owner of a large construction firm, for whom he had worked briefly as a driver between high school and college. A fellow Oxford resident, Lassiter lived in a big white-columned house not far from the modest Webb home. He knew and liked James Webb and asked him to serve as his chauffeur, secretary, and all-around aide.

Webb saw Lassiter as his best hope for getting back to college.

Lassiter's contracts stretched from North Carolina to Florida, and Webb went with him on most trips, driving all day and in the evenings helping Lassiter write letters and take care of other business. Over the course of the year he worked for Lassiter, Webb learned shorthand and typing and how to maintain and service the car he drove. A personable young man anxious to please, Webb became increasingly close to the Lassiters, who had no children. He and Lassiter would drive to Florida, where Lassiter had not only work but also a summer home. When Webb left to return to Chapel Hill in 1924, the two were friends.[13]

Webb now had clerical and business skills he could use to obtain further employment at UNC. With his father's help, he met the dean of the School of Education, N. W. Walker, a friend and schoolmate of J.F., who arranged for Webb to work in the school's Bureau of Educational Research, led by M. R. Trabue. The ferment for improvement influencing the state made this an exciting period at UNC. The School of Education went beyond instruction and research to service. The dean, like Webb's father an evangelist for education, emphasized its critical importance to social betterment. To this end, his bureau devised and ran tests to assess educational attainments of students in secondary schools. Having observed his father, the thoughtful practitioner, Webb now watched Walker and Trabue, the practical theorists. All were in the progressive tradition of what were called "reforming professionals."[14]

An education major, Webb took a range of courses in business, economics, and science. Living in dorms, going to classes, working with the Bureau of Educational Research, he not only enjoyed a vigorous intellectual life at UNC but found time for extracurricular activities, friendships, and social life. Many women found his broad shoulders, vigorous manner, and square, compact frame attractive. While he did not lack for social life, he kept it within bounds. Indeed, letters from his college years reveal an intensely hard-working young man. This industry, plus what one of his classmates regarded as a "photographic" memory, led to his election to Phi Beta Kappa before his graduation in 1928.[15]

Webb prepared himself to follow his father into education, possibly even educational administration. He applied for various teaching positions emphasizing science education, but before a position materialized, Trabue prevailed upon him to remain at the bureau as its full-time secretary, managing its business affairs. For the next eighteen months, Webb not only ran the business side of the operation but became involved in many of its sub-stantive projects.[16]

Still, Webb knew he could not stay at the bureau forever, and Lassiter pressed him to consider law as a career, offering to link him with his brother's law firm in Oxford. Lassiter was putting a lot of business into that firm, and he wanted it looked after properly. Webb could run the law office while studying law with Lassiter's brother or his brother's partner at night. In spite of his interest in education, Webb had witnessed (and wished to al-leviate) his mother's complaints about money. He admired his father's pub-lic service motives, but he also reflected his mother's practical bent. The Lassiter alternative was too enticing to refuse, and he moved back to Oxford.

While serving as law clerk for the Parham and Lassiter firm, Webb read law two or three nights a week, performed a variety of chores for his friend Lassiter, and formed and became first president of the Oxford Young Men's Business Club.[17] It looked as though he might remain in Oxford as a successful small-town lawyer and civic leader.

But in October 1929, the stock market crashed, and the economy col-lapsed. Webb's small-town world grew bleak; Oxford was devastated, and the law firm declined. Webb found that when he tried to collect fees, clients could not pay. Even Lassiter's business suffered, as no one built and no one sold. Farms and businesses collapsed. Unemployment was rampant. Al-though Webb encouraged others in his family, saying times would get better, he became increasingly frustrated and restless. He saw no future in Oxford.

One Sunday in the summer of 1930, while thumbing through the *New York Times*, he spotted an article reporting that the Marine Corps needed a group of men with college degrees to start a reserve force of marine avia-tors. The training would be at Valley Stream, Long Island.[18] Webb knew nothing about either the marines or aviation, but he had to escape from Oxford, even though he had not completed his legal training. If he did not qualify, he would still wind up in New York, which surely would offer more opportunity than did Oxford, North Carolina.

With a sense of desperation, Webb applied to join this initial group of marine aviators. To his amazement, he was invited to try out. Hence, like so many others during the Depression, Webb moved on, leaving a grim known for the hope of a better life elsewhere. Bidding a sad good-bye to family and friends, he left North Carolina a few months short of his twenty-fourth birthday.

Washington and Aviation

The first month's training in Long Island proved a difficult time of testing and elimination.[19] Surrounded by an elite group of young men, most of them Ivy League graduates and good athletes, Webb felt inadequate. After a poor start, however, he managed to make the grade and reported to Pensacola, Florida, for a year of further training at the regular navy school, where all naval aviators were trained. Under pressure to perform well, these men had to demonstrate judgment, courage, and poise. Aviation was still a new and risky technology—during his tour, Webb managed to cope with four engine failures. Having started near the bottom of the original group, Webb gained pride and self-confidence as he steadily improved. He liked the marines, the esprit, the sense of common purpose. Unlike most of its readers, he found the marine organizational manual interesting and studied how various units of the corps related. He also received leadership training.

Following the Florida tour, Webb was commissioned a second lieutenant and assigned to the East Coast Expeditionary Force at Quantico, Virginia, outside Washington, as a pilot on active duty. He loved airplanes, flew to Oxford to visit his family, and kept in touch with Lassiter, who gave him an old car to drive.

At Quantico, in 1931, Webb learned that another young man who had worked for Lassiter when he had was now in Washington as a secretary to Democratic representative Edward W. Pou of North Carolina. Webb renewed the acquaintance and glimpsed the excitement of working on Capitol Hill. Since his active duty tour was drawing to a close, he had begun worrying about what he would do next, with the country mired in depression.

When Pou's secretary was killed in a traffic accident, Lassiter immediately intervened to help Webb. As a friend of the Pou family, he called Pou's son and recommended Webb as a replacement. Informed of Lassiter's effort on his behalf, Webb moved quickly, drawn not just by the prospect of a job but by the chance to work in Washington and for Congress. For someone from rural North Carolina, this spelled action and possibility. Webb went after the position with an almost unseemly haste. He learned from his sister Olive that the funeral for Lassiter's secretary was to be in North Carolina. "Send flowers to that funeral," he told her. "Opportunity only knocks once."[20]

When Webb left active duty in May 1932, he went directly to work for Congressman Pou, one of the most influential members of Congress. As chair of the House Rules Committee, Pou saw virtually all important legislation. The power of the Rules Committee was based on the fact that it influenced procedure. Unlike the Senate, where the rules of debate were relatively fixed, in the House the rules changed for each major bill. Pou's committee wrote a specific "rule" governing procedure on every bill of significance. The Rules Committee played traffic cop for the House, letting some bills go forward under some procedures, others under different procedures, and holding still others up for lack of rules. It could determine how a debate was conducted and what amendments could be offered. Hence, as chair of the committee, in an era in which senior committee chairs received considerable deference from junior members, Pou was in a position to help or hurt other members of Congress—and also presidents.[21]

Pou had chaired the Rules Committee under President Woodrow Wilson, survived the succeeding Republican-dominated years, and become chair again in 1930, when the Democrats regained control and organized the House. For all his power, Pou was by now elderly and in poor health, in need of the help of able and loyal assistants. In that time of small congressional staffs, only two other people worked in Pou's Washington office. Once Webb took over, he soon had the office humming with unaccustomed efficiency. He took care of all correspondence, screened visitors, paid the bills, attended committee meetings and congressional sessions, and briefed Pou on all relevant matters. Pou eventually let Webb sit in on the critical meetings attended every morning by the House Speaker, party whip, and Pou. As Webb recalled, these three men essentially set the agenda for the House as a whole. The House would meet at noon, proceed more or less as Pou and the other House leaders had planned, and adjourn.

The congressional education Webb received at Pou's side was enhanced by the monumental events of the Great Depression. When he began working in Washington, the Democrats controlled the House, Republicans the Senate, and Herbert C. Hoover was president. The young man saw how deals were struck to enable the president to get legislation he wanted, and how the House Democrats, when they had the upper hand, employed their power against the Republicans in the upper chamber, sometimes quite ruthlessly.[22]

Webb observed with fascination the presidential campaign of 1932 and stood in the crowd watching Franklin D. Roosevelt's inauguration in 1933. Before the election, Pou had told Roosevelt he would assist him, and Roosevelt had responded with thanks, remarking how much he needed Pou's help to "put into effect the progressive policies advocated in our [Democratic Party] platform."[23] Just five days after his inauguration,

Roosevelt called the Seventy-third Congress into special session. Wherever necessary during the president's historic first "Hundred Days," Pou and his Rules Committee expedited the enactment of "measure after measure to bring relief and recovery to the depressed nation."[24] Roosevelt later thanked Pou for his help. As Pou's assistant, Webb ran errands, made calls, facilitated legislation, and eased the physical discomforts of a man who was often debilitated.

Friends who knew Webb in Washington during this period recalled how he seemed to be absorbing everything going on around him. Not an intellectual in the sense of one who enjoyed concepts for their own sake, he thrived on action but believed that actions could be guided by knowledge. An outstanding student, he was motivated to learn, apply, and improve. In this case what he was learning about, his friends remembered, was government. He was totally fascinated with government and the process by which it made policy.[25]

And no wonder! A peaceful revolution was under way in Washington. As Arthur Schlesinger wrote, what Roosevelt brought to Washington was "a government determined to govern," which unlocked "new energies" and affected everyone in and out of the capital. New hope accompanied the feeling that government was going to "do something" about the emergency facing the nation, the unemployment, bread lines, and gloom.[26]

Under Roosevelt Washington was transformed "from a placid, leisurely southern town" into a "gay, breezy, sophisticated and metropolitan center." A wave of new faces appeared, all talking about the big problems of the country and the ways they could be tackled.[27] Although the New Deal renewed many of the reformist ideals of progressivism Webb had absorbed from his father and mentors at the University of North Carolina, instead of progressivism's diffuse national effort, the New Deal was a presidential initiative, and its nationwide effects spread from Washington.[28] As the city and nation were transformed, so was Webb. He became a Roosevelt Democrat, one who saw the federal government as having a responsibility to lead and change the nation.

Both on Capitol Hill and at home, Webb was around people who discussed government and the politics that drove it. He lived at the Racquet Club (later called the University Club) at Sixteenth and L Streets, a men's club in the 1930s as well as a hotel used by legislators and others as their home away from home. Perhaps a dozen legislators lived there when Webb took up residence, including Joseph Martin, a Republican from Massachusetts, who would later be Speaker of the House.[29]

Pou had asked Webb to live at the Racquet Club so Webb could help him during and after the club's poker games, in which Pou was an avid player. One of Webb's jobs was to bring Pou to the club virtually every day for the four o'clock game, during which a lot of congressional business was conducted—and Webb was there to remember what was decided and by whom. One of his fellow Racquet Club residents recollected that Webb's job seemed to be "the care and feeding of Congressman Pou."[30]

The congressman not only provided Webb the opportunity to meet influential people but also passed on valuable advice about how to survive in Washington. He pressed home the need for a "line" of integrity. Inevitably, one would have to compromise, but under pressure, a person had to know where to draw the line, for adversaries would be watching for any missteps.[31]

Power attracted pressures, Webb could see. Like other legislative staff, he was perceived as being in a position to help those with special interests, a heady experience. Another ambitious congressional secretary, Lyndon Johnson, was Webb's contemporary in Washington and, like him, attracted by the city's excitement and fascinated by the machinations of policymaking on Capitol Hill. Both men were interested in power and its uses, and both made it a point to get to know important people and serve them well.[32]

Webb and Johnson had little contact at this point.[33] Both were extremely busy working for their bosses and pursuing their own agendas. Perhaps a notable difference between the two lay in their policy orientations. Although both favored the social policies of Roosevelt, Webb was far more interested in aviation and government's role in promoting this emerging technology. He maintained his flying status on weekends and met naval reservist Lloyd Berkner, another weekend flier, who was a young scientist with the Carnegie Institution of Washington, a research organization. With Berkner, who was destined for prominence not only in science but in space policy, Webb became good friends and enthusiastically discussed the future of aviation.[34] Another friend was Harris Hull, a fellow resident of the Racquet Club and reporter for the *Washington Post*. Also a flier, Hull recalled Webb as fervent about the prospect of aviation.[35] Government and aviation—these were Webb's passions.

One of Webb's many tasks for Congressman Pou was to escort important constituents from North Carolina around town. He picked them up at Union Station, took them to their hotels, introduced them to people Pou thought they should meet, and in other ways facilitated their stay in the capital. In January 1934, Pou asked Webb to help the former governor of

North Carolina, O. Max Gardner, get settled in the city.[36] A friend of President Roosevelt, Gardner was moving to Washington to set up a law practice. Although he had resigned his Democratic Party committee membership as a way of saying he would not trade on his associations, an action for which Roosevelt praised him, everyone knew that Gardner would not be just another Washington lawyer. Attractive, wealthy, smooth, and connected with the White House, the fifty-two-year-old Gardner was reputed to have helped coin the phrase "New Deal."[37]

The former governor was impressed and grateful for the alacrity and skill displayed by Webb, who "speedily organized Gardner's personal finances and even set up an accounting system."[38] As they met over time, the two men found they had an unusual rapport. When Gardner asked Webb what he wanted to do in the future, he confessed he felt stymied in his career by not having finished the law training he had begun five years before. Gardner warned that if he continued working for Pou, he would never have time to earn a law degree, and offered a way out: "Come and join me in my firm and I will make it possible for you to get through law school and make some money."[39]

Once again, Webb jumped at the opportunity, and Pou agreed to let him go if Webb would find him an adequate replacement. Webb already had a man in mind and made arrangements to everyone's satisfaction within twenty-four hours of his conversation with the congressman. The move was fortuitous for him, as Pou died within months of his departure.

Thus, at the beginning of 1934, Webb exchanged his office in the Capitol for one in the Woodward Building, at Fifteenth and H Streets. Here Gardner presided, and here Webb served as his all-purpose aide. He trained Gardner's secretary in bookkeeping, performed legal research, and, most importantly, served Gardner in the latter's role as representative for various private interests to the Washington establishment. As promised, Gardner provided Webb time to pursue his legal studies at George Washington Law School.

Not long after Webb had begun working for Gardner, a major national controversy erupted that had an impact on the careers of both men. In late 1933, Roosevelt's postmaster general, James Farley, had uncovered what he regarded as illegal (or at least unethical) behavior in the awarding of government airmail contracts to certain companies. In February 1934, Roosevelt summarily canceled all existing contracts and called on the military to fly the mail while an investigation was mounted. This action not only threw the private airlines into turmoil, since many of them depended on the steady business of the airmail contracts, but also put enormous pressure on the military. The Army Air Corps, which was assigned the task, had not responded efficiently, and several pilots died in accidents.[40]

The crisis affected all concerned. Charles A. Lindbergh, a national hero since his pioneering 1927 flight across the Atlantic, sent a "condemnatory telegram to the President that was released to the press before its receipt at the White House." He then continued to snipe, publicly embarrassing the administration. Meanwhile, aviation companies were losing millions of dollars every week.[41]

In the midst of the dispute, the Aeronautical Chamber of Commerce was born, led by Thomas A. Morgan, president of the Sperry Gyroscope Company, an equipment supplier to airlines. In late February or early March, Morgan and some seventeen association members convened in Washington to discuss their problems. It was clear they needed a Washington lawyer-lobbyist to help them, and the group approved the idea of hiring Gardner, with his connections an obvious choice. Although Morgan knew Gardner only by reputation, he had met Webb when the latter worked for Pou and had found him helpful in getting access to Congress. He concluded that the industry people should discuss Gardner's availability with Webb first. As an advocate of aviation, Webb undoubtedly looked to Morgan like a friendly route to Gardner.[42]

Morgan and Thomas Doe, who was a vice president of Sperry and president of Eastern Airlines, asked Webb to come over to the Shoreham Hotel, where members of the association were meeting, to listen to their case. He found an agitated group of businessmen eager for him to persuade Gardner to represent them. Noncommittal, Webb said he would convey the message. He also passed on to Gardner word that the association was willing to pay well for his services.[43] Gardner told both Webb and Morgan he would not sign on unless he could serve government as well as private interests. Then he called Roosevelt, who agreed to see him at once, whereupon Gardner caught a cab to the White House, where the president gave him the go-ahead.[44]

Gardner "was ideally situated to bring order to the chaotic aviation situation, for as a Roosevelt Democrat he felt that the Administration had made a colossal blunder and that the President's public position had been undermined. As a lawyer he found his clients disqualified and demoralized, some of them guilty as charged, others needing expert guidance in defending legal and property rights to the extent of many millions." The governor's first step in his new assignment was to tell Morgan to call off Lindbergh, "who had a vested interest in private aviation," but whose status with the American people made him a good weapon the industry could use against the government. Furthermore, he told Morgan, "the Aeronautical Chamber of Commerce must engage in no political agitation." With the president's blessing, he also started the wheels moving for compromise on the government's side.[45]

Near the end of March—by which time twelve military aviators had died flying the mails—Postmaster General Farley announced that airmail would be delivered again by the private airlines, as soon as new contracts could be let. In addition, he said, legislation would be written to place government-industry relations in this field on a permanent and sound basis.[46] The price industry paid was that thirty-one executives directly implicated in the earlier arrangement eventually had to step aside, and various companies went through reorganizations. Although most of the airlines that had carried the mails before the interruption carried them again, other carriers now had greater opportunity to get business. In June Roosevelt signed the Air Mail Act of 1934, which provided a new regulatory regime to protect the public's interest in the award of airmail routes and prevent collusion among airlines in dividing up the "spoils," as had been alleged was the case earlier.[47]

Most of what Gardner had done was invisible to the public. But in government and industry, those involved gave him high marks. As Gardner recalled, the resolution of the dispute immensely boosted his standing. "From that day on I had it made as a Washington lawyer."[48] He was now tied into civil aviation, and as his star rose, so did that of Webb, his right-hand man, who now saw Morgan frequently. Morgan sensed in Webb an intelligent, unusually hard-working individual close to Gardner and versed in Washington strategy. In spring 1936, he asked Webb to come to work for him. Webb said he would consider it, but he first wanted to finish law school and pass the bar. When he asked the governor's advice, Gardner said that he did not want to lose him but that he had "to learn how business is done in New York some time. You might as well go now."[49] Within months, his education and bar exam successfully behind him, Webb left to become personnel director and assistant to the president at Sperry Gyroscope Company. He was thirty years old.

Leadership at Sperry

Sperry attracted Webb for a number of reasons, among them the chance to make a substantial income in hard times and the challenge of executive power. He liked organizing people and offices and felt ready to help direct a large business. At Sperry he would also be an advocate for aviation. Webb's New Deal experience had given him a thirst "to make things happen," and aviation was his cause; the job seemed ideal.

Sperry's president, Tom Morgan, born in 1887, was a down-to-earth, self-made man who had grown up in a rural North Carolina county neighboring the one in which Webb was born. After graduating from high school in North Carolina, he served four years in the U.S. Navy, during which time he met Elmer Sperry, developer and promoter of the gyroscope, a device enabling ships and planes to be steered accurately.[50] Sperry hired Morgan in 1912, and Morgan eventually became president and then chair of the board. His philosophy was simple: "A lot of people want to take all and give nothing. They know all the facts before they see them. They're worse than breaking a mule. Not many of them are on my payroll." Morgan wanted people like Webb around him who looked ahead and were willing to "tackle the jobs others can't do or don't want to do."[51]

Webb moved into the St. George Hotel in Brooklyn, a sprawling structure that was one of the biggest hotels in the world at the time and just a short walk from Sperry's main plant, on Manhattan Bridge Plaza. When he earned a bonus, he shared his gains with his family. In 1937, he took time out to help his father, now sixty-four, start a community-supported savings and loan agency.[52]

In 1938, James Webb married Patsy Aiken Douglas, to whom he had been introduced five years previously by Lassiter's sister, who lived in Washington. Patsy was the youngest of five children. Her father was a noted Washington lawyer affiliated with Georgetown Law School who often represented foreign governments and frequently pled cases before the Supreme Court. Although Patsy had been born in Washington, her parents were South Carolinians, now socially prominent in the capital. Her father was a member of the Chevy Chase and Metropolitan Clubs. She had attended the Cathedral School in Washington and then studied for a year in Paris.

The newlyweds settled in a small townhouse in Brooklyn, where Patsy added substantially to Webb's aura of a man on the rise. She was at ease socially, came from a family with status, and was comfortable in the hostess role. Their relationship was typical of their era: he focused on work and career, she on the home. Patsy was a definite plus for Webb, and her appreciation of him was matched by her father's. "I don't know of anyone who can hold a candle to Jim," he told her.[53]

While an assistant to Tom Morgan, Webb doubled at Sperry as personnel director, his first major management responsibility. Because a market the company served—military airplanes and ships—was beginning to grow with the onset of World War II, Webb recalled that from 1936, when he came aboard, to 1941, Sperry expanded from eight hundred to thirty-three thousand employees. He hired and fired employees, managed training programs, and dealt with management-labor disputes and security issues, sharpening his skills in identifying talent and placing people. When it came to executive talent, he liked to place particularly promising young people under his own wing, train them, and then send them to divisions where they were most needed. Webb had once studied to become an educator, and he was now teaching in the context of a rapidly growing technical company.

If Webb was a teacher, he was also a student. He prepared himself for executive advancement by reading, taking courses on management, and attending technical orientations given the scientists and engineers Sperry hired. His quest to marry management theory and action became a trademark in his executive life. Management thinking during the period he was at Sperry underwent a transition from Taylorism to a focus on human relations. Frederick Taylor, an engineer, had favored "scientific management," which sought to apply rationalistic principles to human work. Jobs could be scientifically designed and engineered, in his view, and workers objectively classified, placed, and measured as to performance. Economic incentives held sway over people, who along with business could be "engineered."[54]

The new "human-relations" school of management thought coming into fashion dealt with interpersonal relations, motivation, spirit, and leadership.[55] Webb recalled being particularly influenced by the writings of Mary Parker Follett, an organizational social scientist ahead of her time who wrote and lectured early in the twentieth century. Increasingly popular as the human relations approach to management gained momentum, her writings encompassed business administration, government, and a host of other areas and emphasized human beings and their interactions as the bedrock of all organization. Rather than Taylorism's "one best way" to manage, this flexible iconoclast wrote of the "law of the situation." She discussed individuals and executives, but her real interest was group relations.

What struck Webb in her writings was how groups could be made to produce at an optimal level. Many committees at Sperry, he had noted, wound up compromising at a lowest common denominator. Follett argued that such groups could instead yield decisions based on their highest common denominator. As much a political as administrative theorist, for her the answer seemed to lie with power. But power was exercised not through bureaucratic controls, as in classic administrative theory. Executives had to consider power in a different way: "Whereas power usually means power-over, the power of some person or group over some other person or group, it is possible to develop the conception of power-with, a jointly developed power, a co-active, not a coercive power." This view of power led directly to Follett's concept of executive leadership in which the leader combined the "different wills" in an organization to create "a driving force," a "group power" that joined disparate, often conflicting, parts into a "team."[56]

Webb confirmed at Sperry what he had no doubt sensed before—that he liked to lead, and had both taste and talent for managing power of the kind about which Follett wrote, "power with" rather than "power over." "My forte," he said he discovered at Sperry, "was putting things together and getting a team that could play the ball game." He recalled that his attitude was to help Sperry "be the best company that it could be," and he was "going to also help broaden people" so that they could better contribute to the overall organizational goal. As an assistant to Morgan as well as personnel director, Webb had vantage points that helped him combine these macro- and microperspectives. Blessed with exceptional interpersonal skills, he saw leading as persuading. For all parts of Sperry to march to a common drummer meant coordination and integration with an eye to group performance. His pilot training helped him grasp some of the technical detail with which he was confronted at Sperry, but most of his management problems came down to people. "What I could do," he recalled, "was listen to a man in, say, production control who told me of the problems he was having getting his work done. He couldn't place the orders the moment they were coming in and feed them to the factories because of certain difficulties, like lack of cooperation of some one person who wanted to have all the power in his area, or something. We were able to listen to him and understand and figure out a way to get around the obstacle."[57]

In another instance, he noted that a number of new Sperry policies had been meeting resistance from "many of the older men who had been accustomed to fly by the seat of their pants," an inertia exacerbated by the activity of several unions. "In this situation," Webb recalled, he "made it a practice to go to the Council Room every Thursday afternoon at five o'clock and stated that any foreman or department head who wanted to come was free to do so, that I would explain the important decisions and action papers issued by top management during the week, and then would answer any questions that anyone wanted to ask. Out of the 75 or so people eligible to come, the group started with about 15 and slowly grew to about 40 to 50.

This turned out to be one of the most important ways we got the group feeling a central core of interest in the development of the company as an institution capable of doing the work that was required and of recognizing the management tools that were available to them. I constantly preached the doctrine that the Personnel Department didn't do the personnel work, but was an assistance to the foreman and he was expected to handle his personnel as well as the substance of his operation. This idea of marrying substance and administration for effective leadership is essential."[58]

Webb thus dealt with a range of organizational problems at various levels of the company. Because he was not the top man, he had to exercise power in concert with others. Personnel and then Treasury provided staff perspectives relative to the production side of the organization. His problem-solving technique for dealing with people became working together with individuals and groups. Once a person found he could help him, Webb realized, he would see Webb as more than just another administrator. Part of his approach to power, persuasion, and leadership at Sperry was to create in others a sense of obligation to him, even dependence. It was a matter of exchange, quid pro quo. Although he "was willing to use" his hierarchical power through Morgan when necessary, he much preferred indirect techniques.[59] His executive leadership style was thus a political one that combined or neutralized interests for the benefit of the larger organizational goal, a style particularly helpful in management-labor disputes. Given that Webb came into his first top management experience from a Washington background, it is not surprising that he adapted a political style to his organizational role, or that he found most compatible with his own thinking and skills the writings of an organizational theorist who thought in group dynamics terms.

Webb's role expanded in his years at Sperry as he moved from personnel director in 1936 to treasurer and secretary in 1941 and then to vice president. He dealt with external organizations such as subcontractors and government, as well as with issues strictly internal to Sperry. He helped make decisions about where to site new plants, participated in major research and development and other investment decisions, hired outside experts, and enlisted major consultants, many from universities—brainpower capable of dealing with the new technology. One specialist he came to appreciate particularly was Charles Stark Draper, a professor from the Massachusetts Institute of Technology (MIT) who would someday become famous for developing advanced guidance systems for military and space vehicles, including Apollo. Also, Webb kept in touch with Lloyd Berkner, his old flying friend from Washington. Berkner had moved up the ranks of the Carnegie Institution of Washington and then joined the navy's Bureau of Aeronautics during the war, to manage its radar program. Webb, who had once considered being a science teacher, liked technical people and was not awed by experts.[60]

At Sperry Webb thus found that he had the temperament to lead, exercise executive power, and manage a technical organization. One of his assistants during this period was David Riesman, later a renowned Harvard sociologist, who recalled that Webb "seemed to have his finger on everything." A "very impressive man, he was youthful, confident, vigorous. He imbued others with confidence. He was not dismayed with the disorder in the company" and seemed "quite comfortable" in his job. What perhaps distinguished Webb most for Riesman, who had to endure an executive less capable when Webb left, was his unusual ability to see and deal with interrelationships.[61]

This capacity was enhanced by the multiple roles Webb played. From the outset at Sperry, his administrative style was shaped by his close relation to Morgan. More than a personnel director, treasurer, or even vice president, he took a presidential perspective toward Sperry; given Morgan's orientation, this meant Webb was much more than an inside executive.

As Webb worked to build Sperry, he also played a role on the larger stage of civil aviation policy, in part because Morgan continued to work with the Aeronautic Chamber of Commerce. But, increasingly, Webb acted on his own, with Morgan's approval, propelled by his own desire to make a difference. Thus, he energetically worked to enlarge the National Aeronautical Association, an organization of weekend fliers and aviation enthusiasts, of which he was an active member. He helped form chapters in cities around the country, serving as president of the Greater New York Chapter and as a director of the national association, which actively promoted the interests of aviation. It held races, kept official records on achievements within the industry, and published a journal, the *National Aeronautic Magazine,* for which Webb wrote an occasional editorial.[62]

Because he believed government should do more to promote aviation, Webb went to Washington to lobby for changes in procurement policy and incentives to industry to invest in research and development that would improve equipment for government and nongovernmental users. He also served on a State Department advisory committee concerned with foreign airlines and in 1939 became treasurer of the aviation exhibit at the New York World's Fair. In these prewar years, he participated in conversations between Sperry and the military about industry's ability to mobilize for war and was a member of the group that selected an official song for the Army Air Corps, "The Wild Blue Yonder." Such efforts took him to Washington regularly and kept him in close touch with Gardner. In the process, he joined a group of men, centering around Gardner, who met once a month at the Mayflower or some other Washington hotel to dine and discuss major issues of the day. Among those who gathered around those linen-draped tables sharing after-dinner coffee and cigars were Robert Woodruff, president of Coca Cola, from Atlanta; Baxter Jackson, president of Chemical Bank of New York; Representative Fred Vinson (later chief justice of the U.S. Supreme Court); Senator Walter George; Representative Lindsay Warren. As the "junior man," Webb mixed drinks and made himself useful, widely viewed as Gardner's protégé, there to broaden his policy interests and get to know influential people.[63]

Webb had wanted to enlist when World War II began, but Morgan felt he needed him at Sperry, and the government needed Sperry to operate as a resource for the war effort. He received a deferment based on his war work in a critical industry. His desire to go to war increased when his youngest brother, Gorham, was captured by the Japanese early in the conflict. With his mother and father depressed and all family members deeply worried, Webb went to North Carolina and started some reconstruction projects on the house as a way to distract his mother.[64]

By 1944, Webb felt his time at last had come, even though Patsy was expecting their first child. Sperry's equipment orders had peaked, and a major layoff loomed. Although Webb wanted to do his duty by signing up, he may also have considered the effect of active service on his career aspirations, including political possibilities. Some at Sperry suspected this as another motive for his insistence on leaving the company.[65] Whatever the case, Webb convinced Sperry and the marines to let him serve. He went to St. Simons Island Radar School, in Georgia, for a month and then moved to Cherry Point, North Carolina, where he became commanding officer, First Marine Air Warning Group, Ninth Marine Aircraft Wing, first as a captain, later as a major.

The large numbers of troops getting ready in various training sites for the final assault on the Japanese-occupied Pacific islands would need air fighter support, but providing air traffic control from aircraft carriers might reveal their positions. The military's plan was to get radar equipment on the islands and control the night fighter activity from there. Webb was put in charge of this radar program, including the certification of technical readiness and transport of the equipment to a single embarkation point in the

United States. For a time, he had authority over all marine transport planes in the United States to expedite the gathering of the radar components at that site. (Existing radar equipment, too cumbersome for soldiers to carry, had to be modified so that it could be disassembled, carried on a man's back in water, and then easily integrated on shore.) He was also involved with the program to train fighter pilots and controllers to operate effectively at night using radar, working closely with marine headquarters and contractors in all these efforts.[66]

Webb's orders were held up a few days before he was to leave August 14, 1945, for the invasion of Japan. The atomic bombs dropped on Hiroshima on August 6 and on Nagasaki August 9 brought the war's official end on September 2, when Japan surrendered. Webb never saw combat. His brother Gorham survived internment in Japan as a prisoner of war, and Webb now had a six-month-old daughter—Sarah, called Sally—and could have returned to Sperry and a lucrative business career. But he was anxious to make a change.

DIRECTING THE
U.S. BUDGET

It was September 1945. The war behind him, Webb was at a decision point. He did not wish to go back to Sperry. Having played a major role in the corporation during the war, he did not see its fortunes as particularly hopeful in the postwar demobilization era.[1] Also, while Webb liked to make money, he was interested in public policy and how it was developed. When he sought O. Max Gardner's advice, Gardner said, "I wouldn't feel comfortable if you didn't come with my firm." When Webb countered that he wanted to do more than law, Gardner suggested he consider a political career.

In the end, they struck a bargain: Webb would return to Washington and work half-time in Gardner's firm, pursuing whatever other objectives he might develop. This agreement lasted only a few months, for when President Truman asked Gardner in 1946 to be his under secretary of treasury, Gardner immediately prevailed upon Webb to join him as his executive assistant. Only for six months, Webb said.[2] He became Gardner's bureaucratic troubleshooter, proving adept, in the many intra- and interagency conflicts that arose, at getting diverse parties to work together.

Taking over Budget

The director of the Bureau of the Budget (BOB), Harold D. Smith, resigned in June to become vice president of the International Bank for Reconstruction and Development (World Bank). John Snyder, secretary of the treasury and one of the first people Truman had asked to join him when he became president, was pushing Truman to appoint a budget director with whom he could work. Snyder and his under secretary agreed that Webb would be a good choice, and Snyder took Webb to the White House, introducing him to the president as "the young man about whom I have been telling you." President Truman began by discussing Webb's service in the Marine Corps. After what seemed to Webb like an interminable amount of small talk, he spoke up. "Mr. President, I am very happy in my work at the Treasury with Secretary Snyder and Governor Gardner, and I am not in any sense looking for a job. However, if you decide that I can be of service to you in the Budget, I will be very happy to serve you in any way I can . . ." The president interrupted. "Well, I have heard very fine reports about you and your work, and from all I can hear, you will have a chance to stay on at the Treasury."[3]

At a July 25 press conference, Truman was asked if he was ready to name Smith's successor. His reply—"Yes, I forgot that"—brought laughter. "That is," Truman went on, "I had so many things a while ago that some of my papers got lost. I will tell you who the new Budget Director is going to be, if I can find the papers down in here." The name was James Webb. It was not an auspicious beginning, for, as Webb recalled, "this meant that I was not known to President Truman, and I wasn't part of his White House coterie. I was really an unknown, as people said at the time." His appointment was widely interpreted in Washington "as a successful Treasury Department gambit in subordinating BOB to Treasury's control." Within BOB, the staff was concerned that such a subordination would mean that a staff agency created during the war, the Office of War Mobilization and Reconversion (OWMR), not BOB, "would emerge as the President's central staff agency." After the war, OWMR was headed first by Snyder, then by John Steelman when Snyder went to Treasury. It had "moved into traditional Budget Bureau turf of manpower policy, surplus property disposal, contract settlement, stock-piling, civilian control of atomic energy, and even legislative clearance responsibilities."[4]

OWMR had handled the Atomic Energy Act of 1946 on behalf of the White House, and Snyder, as OWMR director, had then commented that he "simply [did] not see why [legislative] policy is any business of the Budget Bureau." It was suspected that Smith's departure was the result, in part, of his loss of influence. Richard E. Neustadt, then a staff member of BOB, later a Harvard political scientist, said that "by mid-summer, 1946, the Budget Bureau's status in the presidential orbit had reached its lowest point.

OWMR seemed superficially to be assured a strong, perhaps a permanent position."⁵ Webb's appointment reinforced the negative view of BOB's future.

The bureau Webb was to lead had enjoyed a rebirth under Franklin D. Roosevelt. Created in 1921 and placed in the Treasury Department, in a major restructuring in 1939, BOB was moved out of Treasury and made the core of the new executive office. The man reputed to be the most competent state budget director in the country, Harold Smith of Michigan, organized BOB into five divisions. The largest was Estimates, with responsibility for formulating and presenting the president's budget to Congress. Staffed with some of the country's leading economists, Fiscal advised Estimates on matters of budget detail and assisted the director on matters of general fiscal policy. Legislative reference, which "assisted in the coordination and clearance of proposed legislation, enrolled bills, executive orders, and proclamations," while Administrative Management "was responsible for studies in organization and management improvement in government departments and agencies." Finally, Statistical Standards "assisted in the promotion of improving statistical information and standardizing report collecting." In the process of building a strong agency capable of providing high quality and "politically neutral" staff work for the president, Smith carved out a substantial niche within the executive office. Students of public administration at the time saw BOB as a prototype for "an American equivalent to the British civil service cadre at Whitehall."⁶

When Roosevelt died and Truman became president, however, the close personal relationship Smith had enjoyed with the chief executive disappeared. Others had Truman's ear, and Smith felt threatened. It was not so much that Truman was against Smith's vision of BOB; it was simply that Truman and the White House staff he hired did not understand this vision, or how BOB could help them accomplish their tasks. Moreover, once Snyder became secretary of treasury, Truman told Smith he wanted to make a change in the way presidential budgets were made, "to make this a tripod with the Secretary of the Treasury assisting you and me in building up the budget."⁷ The growing distance between Truman and Smith allowed others in the executive office and cabinet to chip away at BOB's influence.

Given the nature of his meeting with Truman, Webb was surprised when his appointment was announced. According to a later press report, Snyder had sold Truman on Webb's personality. BOB had a tendency to be somewhat stodgy, but Webb would energize the agency. "The President was sold on Webb as a high speed, high-tension individual who thinks fast and acts fast. . . . No matter how onerous or painstaking his day's work . . . Webb always appears to be a ball of fire ready to blaze forth with new energy."[8] Webb recognized the potential importance of the position even though he was aware of BOB's deteriorating situation. When he took office July 31, 1946, his management style, formed over years, called first for learning the new job. Ever the good student, he wanted to master the institutional memory embodied in BOB before making any changes. He spoke with Smith and then visited other former budget directors, including the first, Charles Dawes, appointed in 1921.

Confident and anxious to lead, Webb introduced himself to his top associates on his first day by emphasizing his activistic personality. "Boys, I'm the new boss! Let's get to work." But he showed he wanted to listen and learn, conferring with his staff and spending considerable time with Paul H. Appleby, the deputy director who had been his rival for the position. Despite some tension, Webb (as well as Truman) asked Appleby to stay, emphasizing to him and others his intention to provide continuity with Smith's policies and use the senior officials already there.[9]

Webb brought one young man aboard from outside as his assistant—Elmer B. Staats, who he asked to observe BOB with an eye to possible changes needed.[10] But he did not emphasize internal change, for he wanted to reassure the bureau. He knew he was being watched and measured, an unknown quantity not only to his own staff, but to almost every key official in government, including the president. Winning the confidence of BOB was important, but Webb knew that BOB, as a staff organization, would rise or fall in terms of its relation with Truman. The president was his primary constituent, and the relation between Truman and BOB was greatly in need of strengthening.

Early conversations between Webb and Truman were stiffly formal, and yet the two men shared small-town origins and an interest in organizational matters. A neat and tidy man frustrated by the disorder in his own presidency, Truman regarded the Roosevelt approach to executive management as too unstructured. He had been thrust into the White House unprepared. As Roosevelt men gave way to Truman appointees, disarray reigned. Webb sensed that Truman needed help in making his White House more efficient.[11]

At the same time, Truman was genuinely interested in the executive budget. He had inherited a large deficit from the war, and he asked Webb to balance the budgets over which he presided and if possible to bring in a surplus to help reduce it. "You know, I understand facts and figures," he told

Webb, "and I regard this economic picture as the very lifeblood of our country and our government. You and I must work this out together, and I will work with you."[12] Webb did not need a second invitation and made it a point to involve Truman as much as possible in the budget process. To be sure, Truman talked about a three-party arrangement involving Treasury, but whereas Smith had viewed this as a threat, Webb did not. He had worked in Treasury and knew how busy Snyder was. A powerful man who would have to be given deference, Snyder might sit with Truman and Webb at press conferences on the budget, but he did not have the time to absorb budget detail. For this he relied on Webb.

As Webb pointed out to his BOB staff, he had an advantage over rivals and potential rivals in that BOB was in the "flow of paper" to Truman. Other staff agencies, such as the Council of Economic Advisers (CEA) and OWMR, and even many White House staff members had to wait to be given presidential assignments and invent reasons to see the president.[13] BOB had ongoing assignments, like the budget or legislative clearance, that required conversations between Truman and Webb. This direct and routine access, combined with Truman's own personal predilections, represented assets that Webb could use to BOB's advantage. Webb knew that for the leader of a staff organization, winning the president's confidence was all-important.

Being in the "flow of paper," as Webb put it, also meant being in the flow of presidential battles. There were plenty, and these provided occasions on which Webb could win or lose presidential confidence. One that came almost as soon as Webb arrived at BOB involved a State Department foreign service bill in line for presidential signature. BOB, as the institutional staff arm, was to recommend to the president either approval or veto. This bill had never been cleared with BOB by State but had been negotiated between the department and Congress. Webb understood an end run when he saw one.[14]

He thought the bill was flawed on administrative grounds, insulating the foreign service from direct control by the secretary of state, James F. Byrnes. Moreover, he felt he had to show the bureaucracy and Congress that BOB would not be left out of the loop. A weaker BOB meant a weaker president. To counter a widespread perception at the time that Truman was a "little man in big shoes," the president's position had to be strengthened, and legislative clearance was critical toward that end.

Webb and Truman concluded that a veto might be in order. Webb's BOB associates tried to dissuade him from such a course, because Byrnes had testified in favor of the legislation. A veto at this stage would embarrass

Byrnes and hurt the Byrnes-Truman relationship. Webb saw the point. He recommended that Truman sign, but the file that went to the president contained Webb's substantive arguments against the bill. Truman told a member of his personal staff that he was still inclined to veto, and to let State know this fact. As Byrnes was out of the country, department officials mounted an intensive campaign on the bill's behalf when informed of Truman's intent. Schedules at State were rearranged, weekend plans canceled, and Byrnes himself caused to communicate with Truman from Paris. Along the way, Webb received a visit from a State Department official who castigated him for sabotaging the legislation. Ultimately, Truman signed the Foreign Service Act of 1946 into law. But Webb had made his point. The signal sent was that BOB (and the president) took legislative clearance seriously. Bureaucratic end runs would meet a prepared defense.

The contest with State Department won points for Webb with Truman. Two days after he signed the bill, in their first substantial private discussion, the president told Webb he had "a hard job, but next to members of the Cabinet and the President, the most important job in government." He said he was counting on Webb to give him the facts as he saw them, regardless of pressures; that he would make any decisions to deviate from the facts but did not expect Webb to try to anticipate him or color facts to suit him. Webb promised to follow this policy and told Truman that he was telling critics "the only way I could do this job was to call the shots as I saw them." "You just keep on doing that," Truman responded, "and we'll be all right," adding, "I will not make decisions about you behind your back—you can count on that."[15]

Increasingly secure in his relation with the president, telling everyone he took orders from Truman alone but would work with anyone he designated, Webb began rebuilding BOB's niche within the executive office. The potential rival BOB staffers had most feared, OWMR, was abolished in November, just three months after Webb became director. Its head, John Steelman, was reassigned to the White House staff. As compensation for losing OWMR, he was called *the* assistant to the president, a title that meant little in practice. Truman was his own chief of staff.

Speculation in Washington had Webb engineering the change, although he maintained it was Snyder who regarded OWMR as unnecessary and Steelman as a problem and who influenced Truman to terminate the agency.[16] But who influenced Snyder? It was a fact that Webb kept in close touch with Gardner and Snyder. He said little.

Meanwhile, with Truman anxious to make a record, the small White

House staff was overwhelmed. Without OWMR, only BOB had significant personnel resources, an opportunity Webb grasped at once. As Roger Jones, who worked at BOB, recalled, "Webb saw immediately the need to make himself and his organization indispensable to the President and he proceeded to do so with great dispatch, great vigor, and with tremendous intelligence. He made the bureau staff available to the White House staff to work with them. He volunteered to take some of the difficult problems the President faced back to the Bureau for further analysis."[17]

Webb's foray into the White House began cautiously in late 1946, as the White House staff was preparing the president's 1947 State of the Union message. He made an overture to Special Counsel Clark M. Clifford, the staff's rising star. Both were the same age, lawyers, able, ambitious, and loyal to Truman. Whereas Webb liked to run a large group, Clifford, by choice, had only one assistant. Webb pointed out to Clifford that some very bright individuals in the bureau—for instance, David Stowe, Ross Shearer, and David Bell—might be of help to him. Clifford accepted the offer, requesting that the group provide him with a draft of their ideas on possible labor legislation and that it keep track of the Taft-Hartley bill coming out of Congress; they assisted him in drafting the veto message after the bill had been enacted. Clifford thanked Webb for his help in correspondence addressed to "My dear Jim."

Early in 1947, Charles Murphy, a new member of the White House staff, was given an assignment to draft a bill on military unification, something Truman wanted badly. Anticipating opposition, the president asked Murphy to keep what he was doing quiet. After three weeks on this assignment, Murphy asked two BOB staffers on a confidential basis for their thoughts on costs; when these individuals passed on to Webb the nature of their contact, he was angry BOB had not been involved, for he had anticipated Truman's interest in unification and had some people working on the problem. It happened that Murphy was in Clifford's office when Webb's call of complaint came through. Furious over what he regarded as a breach of confidentiality, Murphy went over to Webb's office and expressed his displeasure. Webb apologized and said it would not happen again.

Shortly thereafter, he called Murphy to ask if he needed any help. When pressed, Murphy admitted that he did. When Webb offered anyone he wanted from BOB, anyone at all, Murphy asked for one of Webb's brightest young men, David Bell. Thereafter, all communication problems between Webb and Murphy ceased, and Webb and BOB became fully involved in the unification process without Webb's having to force his way via Truman.

By making BOB resources available to the White House, Webb co-opted even those staffers who had reason not to cooperate with him, such as Steelman, who found David Stowe, the BOB staffer Webb had loaned him, so valuable that he wanted to make him his deputy. Another North Carolinian, Stowe had known Webb through family friendships before the two became professionally associated at BOB. He discussed the situation with Webb, who suggested that Stowe's joining Steelman "might not be a bad idea, because John Steelman's getting into some of my business." Stowe took the job and helped ease tensions.[18] Webb thus got credit for providing help at the same time he kept track of possible rivals.

Enlarging BOB's Role

By 1947, it was clear that Webb was more than an institution maintainer, although he had taken over from Harold Smith in 1946 promising continuity. He was an institution builder intent on innovating and making his organization more influential. The new relations he established with the White House staff fit into a pattern of changes that extended his reach. While he understood Smith's concern for the line between institutional and personal presidential staff, between administration and politics, the reality was that the president and his White House staff needed help, and Webb had the people with the knowledge. He did not want his people involved in presidential politics but viewed as important their active part in the analysis behind presidential policy.

Webb later said that the "fundamental difference between himself and Harold Smith was his predecessor's protectiveness of the Bureau, whereas Webb thought that the Bureau was strong enough to stand on its own feet and swim in perilous waters." Smith did not want staffers directly involved in his meetings with Roosevelt; Webb began bringing staff members with him to the White House. These were not casual occasions. Webb held dry runs to prepare himself and his associates for meetings with Truman. If the president had questions, Webb wanted BOB to have answers. At the same time, by including staff with him in his meetings with Truman, he "did not have to try to master every single detail on every complex subject." Nor did those actually doing the detail work in BOB "have to rely on memoranda from me," Webb said, "as to what the President wanted done. This made for a very effective working relationship."[19]

As for the "politicization" of BOB that Smith had feared, Webb took responsibility for buffering his agency from that problem. When he brought staff to talk with Truman, they discussed policy, administrative matters, or both. If sensitive political matters arose, the staffers left, and Webb continued the discussion with Truman. He would later explain to BOB some of the political concerns that might make a "rational" course the agency favored unworkable.

Webb was walking a thin line, moving BOB closer to policy but not politics, but the process seemed to work to everyone's advantage. BOB staffers, concerned at first that Webb might not be up to the job, were impressed. If Smith had taken the agency to a higher level, Webb was elevating it still further, establishing both the perception and reality of an organization critical to the operation of the Truman presidency. As he reached out to the White House staff and president in new ways, Webb also sought stronger links with the cabinet and Congress. Smith, as the president's man, had not gone out of his way to accommodate agency and department heads. His constituents were the president and his peers in the public administration community. To be an institution builder, Webb had also to be a constituency builder, and his constituency was as broad as he could make it.

Webb saw how the Budget Bureau could be more useful to both the president and Congress, meeting Truman's need, as an ex-legislator, for a more systematic method of dealing with Congress than Roosevelt's unpredictable approach. Many of the bills Truman wanted to forward as he shifted to a peacetime America fell under his concept of the "Fair Deal." At Webb's instigation, the president's State of the Union address in 1947 was accompanied, for the first time, by his budget message. Tying what the president wanted to do with resources to achieve his goals was new, and only a short step away from pulling together in one place his entire legislative program. This concept of a comprehensive "presidential program," presented at the beginning of the year, was also novel.

The attempt to forge a presidential program obviously had legislative implications. Here, Webb saw ways he could innovate through BOB. He had inherited an Office of Legislative Reference, essentially a research entity, headed by Fred Bailey, who was close to retirement. With the intent to make this a more proactive unit, Webb moved in his own assistant, Elmer Staats, as Bailey's deputy and ultimately his successor. He spoke with Truman about using Legislative Reference as an "institutional channel of communications" between the president and Congress, a way BOB's professional staff could talk with congressional professional staff.[20]

Webb suggested that one person have primary responsibility for legislative liaison, and that he be a Republican, since Republicans controlled Congress. When the President agreed, Webb appointed Roger Jones, who at first worked directly under Webb. When Bailey retired and Staats took over as assistant director, Jones moved over to work for Staats. Within a year, this was a rather substantial institutional channel. As Jones recalled, Webb and Truman believed that it was essential for Congress to have a grasp of what the president wanted to do and for the president to be aware of what bills were being proposed by Congress. It was an effort to make "divided government" work better, in spite of partisan wrangling. In 1947, Webb initiated a system of "direct referrals" by which Republican congressional chairmen could inquire what Democrats intended on various legislation. Jones, who was the prime contact, later noted that "we were expositors, explanatory people. We were not peddlers of doctrine."[21]

Besides linking his own staff with legislative staff, Webb began communicating with elected legislators personally. Over lunches with small groups of congressmen, he discussed governmental affairs, treading carefully, since he was not supposed to be political.[22] But he wanted government to work smoothly—and Truman to be helped legislatively.

This growing legislative role meant, of course, that BOB and White House staff needed to work even more closely in formulating a presidential program. From a beginning in 1946 with the Webb-Clifford contacts, in 1947, "and becoming more systematic and comprehensive in each year thereafter, the Bureau worked out a partnership with the Special Counsel to the President in developing affirmative legislative proposals, covering all aspects of foreign and domestic policy," thereby transforming both the Office of Legislative Reference and the concept of legislative clearance. From a policing tool, a negative mechanism to keep departments in line when Webb came in (as in the case of the State Department's Foreign Service Act of 1946), legislative clearance had become a "prime means of focusing staff efforts to help meet the President's needs." What the agencies wanted to do could now be screened and directed in accord with a preexisting road map of presidential intent. The process started with a concept of presidential leadership based on a program of legislative proposals devised at the beginning of the year. To devise such a program required good staff work, and that meant BOB's involvement at the inception of policy.[23]

Webb used the Administrative Management Division to help BOB become involved with many of the largest issues of the Truman administration, for example, the Marshall Plan. In the 1947 commencement address at Harvard, Secretary of State George C. Marshall called for an unprecedented

program of economic assistance to a Europe in danger of collapse and Soviet subjugation. The substantial but piecemeal assistance of the past was
no longer good enough. A large-scale comprehensive program had to be
put into place as soon as possible. With vast economic implications for the
next year's budget, the Marshall Plan also entailed significant organizational issues.

The responsibility for studies and reports contributing to the plan's
legislative presentation gave Webb substantial influence over both its budgetary and administrative aspects. He commissioned studies of wartime
agencies and how they operated to achieve huge, urgent tasks, of institutional models that might serve to help organize the Marshall Plan. The
"draft legislation was finalized at a meeting . . . of the principal agencies involved" at the office of Donald C. Stone, assistant director of BOB for administrative management. "Until that time," Stone recalled, "the title for
the implementing agency had been left blank. We agreed on Economic Cooperation Administration (ECA)."[24]

On December 19, 1947, President Truman sent a message to Congress
on the U.S. role in what would be a comprehensive plan for the recovery of
Europe. The ECA was designed as an independent agency in part to symbolize the importance of the enterprise—its director would report to the
president. The original cost was estimated at $20 billion over four years, a
huge expense in that era.[25]

To help assure the critical bipartisanship, Republican senator Arthur
Vandenberg and Republican representative Charles Eaton, chairs respec-
tively of the Senate Committee on Foreign Relations and the House Committee on Foreign Affairs, were kept fully informed on aspects of the program design along the way. The establishment of ECA as an agency
independent of the State Department (in spite of initial BOB staff misgivings) also reflected congressional desires. To assuage Congress and especially the Republicans, Paul Hoffman, a Republican with an outstanding
managerial reputation, was chosen as administrator. Hoffman, however,
had no experience in government. To ensure that he would be joining an
ongoing effort, Webb hired a management consulting firm to survey the
country for recruits to help run the program. He had studies done of the
economic problems of the various countries with which Hoffman would
work. And he fought through opposition for Hoffman's right to pay a select
number of top executives and specialists a higher salary than ordinarily
paid government personnel in similar positions.[26] Hoffman held his initial
meetings about ECA at BOB. After the ECA legislation was passed in early

1948 and Hoffman was officially appointed, Webb lent him Don Stone as a righthand man (after two months, Stone decided to stay with ECA). For his assistance, Webb received the warm and sincere thanks of both Hoffman and the president. He had helped a totally new agency, with an unprecedented mission, get off to the fastest possible start.[27]

Webb was using his organization in new ways, making it a fuller part of White House decision making. He had by this time found that some of the BOB innovations were of special interest to Truman and provided a way he could keep close to his boss. As Richard Neustadt recalled, Webb

> invented, among other things, "Economic Indicators," a set of charts updated monthly, which he later handed on to the then infant Council of Economic Advisers, which has produced them since. It was wonderful to watch Webb's use of his indicators. He would carry them around in a leather folder tucked up under his arm, whipping them out at the slightest provocation to help vivify a point: "You see what I mean, Mr. President. . . . Look at what's happened to unemployment, here . . . and to industrial production. See that . . . and notice farm production . . . and oh, see the demand for home mortgages? Here. Now what it all adds up to, sir, is this: "we'd better. . . ." Webb talked with those charts the way some people talk with their hands. Truman ate it up.[28]

In building a broad constituency, Webb never forgot who his chief constituent was.

Participating in debates over postwar organization of the executive branch, Webb recognized presidential power as the primary issue at stake.[29] He developed a consistent vision of its importance in government and applied that vision of a strong presidency to the 1947 struggle over military unification. The bureaucratic and legislative politics surrounding the unification act were intense, involving the creation of an air force as a separate service co-equal with the army and navy. The most influential opponent of unification was Secretary of the Navy James Forrestal, who feared that the navy would lose autonomy and resources. His alternative designs revealed a theory of presidential submersion that both Truman and Webb opposed.

Forrestal had come to Washington from Wall Street in 1940, at forty-eight, as an aide to Roosevelt; he moved to Navy, becoming secretary in 1944. Princeton educated and public service oriented, Forrestal was combative and known as a Washington infighter. Like many who had served under Roosevelt, he did not think highly of Truman, although his overt behavior remained always correct. As intense and hard-working as Webb, where Webb was upbeat, Forrestal was often moody and carried his burdens visibly.[30]

Webb crossed swords with Forrestal over budget issues, and he personally disliked the navy secretary's patrician air and lack of respect for the president. In 1946 Forrestal and a few other members of the cabinet had begun having informal lunches together and discussing matters of policy, independent of the president. When Dean Acheson, then under secretary of state, mentioned his misgivings about this practice to Webb, the two went to see Truman. At the next cabinet meeting, the president stated he wanted no more cabinet meetings without his presence, nipping the practice in the bud with no recriminations.[31]

But Webb was now aware that Forrestal, like himself a student of administration, harbored a concept of cabinet government that Truman regarded as a threat to a strong presidency. When the two met to discuss unification, their different intellectual assumptions exacerbated their disagreements. Forrestal argued *against* a strong defense secretary and *for* a strong National Security Council (NSC)—an advisory committee to the president consisting of the secretaries of defense and state, and other agency officials concerned with national security. Such a body might be an alternative to unification or a step on the road to a cabinet secretariat that would provide guidance to the president and make him a captive of collective agency decision. When Webb accused Forrestal of trying to create a body with power over the president, rather than power with or under him, Forrestal denied any such intent but admitted to a philosophical liking for the British cabinet model of government. No, said Webb, you are "thinking in terms of power to push the President in one direction or another."[32] At one meeting, after listening to Forrestal discourse on the virtues of a cabinet secretariat, an exasperated Webb finally exclaimed, "We are not interested in having you organize the President. The President will organize you."[33]

In August 1947, the National Security Act was passed, pulling the services together in a Department of Defense (initially the National Military Establishment), and creating a National Security Council. Though he had fought the unification bill, Forrestal was Truman's choice to be the first secretary of defense. Now Forrestal would not only have to administer the law he had helped weaken but do so with no deputy secretary or assistant secretaries. The army, navy, and air force had the status of executive departments, entitling them to cabinet representation; their secretaries served along with Forrestal on the National Security Council.[34] Webb, ever the organization man, sent a memo to Forrestal suggesting how he might operate as secretary of defense, in spite of the law's deficiencies, gratuitous advice to which Forrestal did not take kindly. As Webb recalled, "He threw it in the waste basket; that was the beginning of his major trouble."[35]

Budget Wars

The election of 1948 preoccupied Truman, Clifford, and many others on the White House staff. For Webb, government had to go on, and the critical issue in 1948, the defense budget, became a major contest that would last virtually the entire year, serve as a dramatic climax to Webb's Budget Bureau tenure, and bring Webb and Forrestal into direct conflict.[36]

Presented in January 1948, the fiscal year (FY) 1949 budget was handicapped by the need to provide new billions for the Marshall Plan to Europe. Webb had followed through on Truman's desire to balance the budget and if possible bring in a surplus so as to reduce the World War II debt. But a substantial gap between revenues and expenditures loomed unless Webb could control spending, especially by the military. His task became more difficult when, under pressure because of the world situation, Truman agreed in March to a FY 1949 supplemental appropriation enhancing military spending.

One of the reasons Truman had sought unification was his feeling that the services were "heavy spenders and blatant lobbyists for ever-larger appropriations." He wanted Forrestal, as secretary of defense, to hold them in check. But this did not seem to be happening, and Truman was increasingly frustrated. Webb told David Lilienthal, chair of the Atomic Energy Commission (AEC), that "the President is his own Secretary of Defense right now; he has to be because Forrestal won't take hold."[37] He expressed to friends his dismay that Forrestal had "lost control" of the military and was being continually "bulldozed" by the services; as a result the rearmament program might now "run away." In Webb's view, a stand had to be made on the FY 1950 budget, a firm ceiling established that Forrestal and the military would have to respect. When he and Forrestal met to discuss both the FY 1949 supplemental and FY 1950 budgets, Webb proposed that the supplemental be set at $2.5 billion, and that the budget for the next year be limited to $15 billion, an increase over FY 1949. Forrestal reacted negatively. "Is the world situation such," he asked, "as to warrant appropriations of this order at the present time?" He told Webb that in his judgment as secretary of defense it was not. A larger program was "essential" because the next two years would be "a critical period in our relations with Russia."

Webb countered with his own question. "Can we carry out such a military program, support ERP [European Recovery Program, i.e., the Marshall Plan], provide a merchant marine program, and implement the atomic energy plans without having available the controls and sanctions [over the civilian economy] which it seems very doubtful that we will get this election year?"[38] Forrestal said he wanted to take his case to Truman.

Present at that requested meeting were General George C. Marshall, secretary of state; Snyder; Steelman; and Sidney Souers, Truman's assistant for the National Security Council; along with Webb, Forrestal, and Truman. Webb had apprised the others of his views and had been authorized by the president to be especially attentive to Marshall, whom both Truman and Webb respected enormously. After Forrestal explained the need for larger increases in military spending, he said he could appreciate domestic economic considerations; then he stressed the threat abroad. Truman asked Marshall what he thought. Marshall said that State's foreign policy was based on the "assumption that there would be no war," adding that it would be unwise to "plunge into war preparations which would bring about the very thing we were taking steps to prevent." Truman followed this up, saying that in agreeing to a supplement for the FY 1949 budget, he had not meant to signal any preparation for war. He wrote in his diary after the meeting that "Marshall is a tower of strength and common sense. So are Snyder and Webb. Forrestal can't take it. He wants to compromise with the opposition."[39]

Forrestal subsequently asked that the president meet with the service secretaries, Joint Chiefs, and himself to explain his intentions, not just for the supplement but also for fiscal year 1950. Ever conscious of presidential power, Webb advised Truman not to do so, saying that the president did not have to explain anything. But Truman agreed to a meeting at which he read from a prepared statement. He set the supplemental at $3.2 billion (higher than Webb wanted), but agreed to Webb's limit in FY 1950 of $15 billion. Truman said that the increase in the FY 1949 budget was "for the purpose of demonstrating a continuing firmness in world affairs, with the thought that we were preparing for peace and not for war." He said he would adhere to the $15 billion ceiling "unless world conditions deteriorate much further" and that he expected his decision to be supported "fully, both in public and private."[40]

The struggle did not end there. A lot could happen in the world between May 1948 and January 1949, when the budget would have to go to Congress, and Truman was expected to lose the November election. Forrestal would spend the next seven months in a sustained effort to reverse the president's decision. Along the way, he tried to use the National Security Council to provide "guidance" in formulating a FY 1950 budget that would be higher than the Truman-Webb figure; he spoke to Secretary of State Marshall again and again; he reached out to friends in the press and influenced the writing of editorials supporting his position on a stronger defense.[41]

Forrestal was being pressed hard by the services, who said they needed $23.6 billion, and $18.6 billion just to stay even. Webb's leverage was hurt when Truman seemed to weaken in his resolve, in the fall allowing Forrestal to prepare an $18.5 billion budget as a contingency against a worsening international situation. For Truman, "contingency" meant contingency. For Forrestal, the larger budget became his budget, or at least a point of departure for a budget not much lower.[42] Webb continued to hold the line at $15 billion.

As the election approached, rumors were rife "in Washington that Forrestal, assuming a Republican victory in 1948, had been in secret contact with Dewey in the hope of staying on as Secretary of Defense," and thus winning the budget battle he appeared now to be losing with Truman. Truman had told Webb directly that if he ever saw anything going on in Washington that he needed to know about while he was campaigning, he should contact him, wherever he was, using a "personal code" to privately alert him. Webb recalled having had to do so only once. The likelihood is that this was in connection with Forrestal. But whether he heard it from Webb or not, Truman did hear of "the Forrestal problem."[43]

In the November election, Truman defeated Dewey in one of the greatest upsets in U.S political history, strengthening his determination to hold the defense budget in check and enhancing both his power and his budget director's authority. To deal with this unanticipated state of affairs, Forrestal wrote the president citing three budgets: one for $23 billion, representing the Joint Chiefs' demands; Webb's budget of $14.4 billion ($15 billion minus funds for stockpiling critical and strategic materials), which Forrestal regarded as inadequate; and a third, for $16.9 billion, which would allow "a maximum benefit from funds provided for military activities." He advised the president to accept the intermediate figure, noting that Marshall had authorized him to say $16.9 billion would be most helpful. The letter arrived early in the morning and Truman read it shortly after he awoke. He apparently saw the $23 billion budget as the Joint Chiefs of Staff budget, not that of the secretary of defense. Hence, only two "counted" in Truman's view. He immediately dictated a response to Forrestal: "Received your recommendation at the two levels of the budget; the $14.4 is approved." "I don't know why he sent" the second budget, said his cover note to Webb on the memo. "The $14.4 billion budget is the one we will adopt."[44]

Webb quickly contacted the president, indicating there might be a better way to handle the matter than by this somewhat abrupt memo. Truman agreed. He met with Forrestal, the service secretaries, Joint Chiefs, Souers, and Webb and asked for a briefing on what the two budgets would mean. As soon as Forrestal and the other defense representatives had finished their presentation, he thanked them and announced that the May ceiling still stood. After a few minutes of informal conversation, the meeting was concluded, having lasted less than an hour.[45]

Further battles over the defense budget would, of course, be forthcoming. But Webb and Forrestal soon ceased to be the leading antagonists. As the first Truman administration gave way to the second, Truman made it known that Webb would be retained, not as budget director but as under secretary of state. As for Forrestal, Truman hedged for a while and then asked for his resignation.

As a tragic aftermath, Forrestal's emotional health, already poor, deteriorated rapidly. In May 1949, late at night, in the midst of severe depression, the nation's first secretary of defense leapt to his death from a sixteenth-floor window of the Naval Hospital in Bethesda, Maryland.[46]

MANAGING THE
DEPARTMENT OF STATE

Webb's 1949 appointment as under secretary of state, as the United States was forging a new world, showed Truman's regard for him and seemed at first a chance at an even larger stage. Over the next three years, however, Webb's reputation as an effective administrator would suffer, his achievements at the Budget Bureau offset by disappointments at the State Department.

In December 1948, the end of Truman's first term, Webb thought seriously about leaving government. While he had lucrative offers from several corporations, the opportunity that most intrigued him was dean of the School of Commerce at the University of North Carolina, an opportunity that might lead to the university's presidency. He was now the father of two; a son, James Jr. (Jimmy), had been born in 1947. The idea of settling down and contributing to his native state sounded appealing.[1]

Clark Clifford abruptly brought him back to Washington reality. The Secretary of State, George C. Marshall, and his under secretary, Robert A. Lovett, were leaving the administration, Clifford told him. "The President is going to appoint [Dean] Acheson as Secretary of State and he would like you to come over as Under Secretary." Surprised and flattered, Webb reminded Clifford he knew nothing about foreign policy. No problem, said Clifford. Acheson and other officials at State had the expertise. "A certain amount of [bureaucratic] orderliness is necessary in our foreign relations, and the President feels that you could provide that and provide it in a way that he would feel happy with." Truman believed Webb's managerial abilities would prove an asset to Acheson and a means to enforce what Truman wanted. When Webb asked Clifford what Acheson thought about that, Clifford said he approved.[2] Webb could not say no to Truman. The president announced the appointment in January 1949, and within weeks Webb was under secretary of state.

Reorganizing the State Department

He and Acheson had worked together before, in 1946, when Acheson was under secretary, allied in defeating James Forrestal's incipient rebellion in Truman's cabinet. Still, their basic respect for each other could not hide their differences. Webb was painted by the Washington media of the day in Horatio Alger–like terms. Acheson had nothing of Horatio Alger in him. Fifty-six to Webb's forty-two, he was "the very model of the Eastern establishmentarian."[3] The son of a distinguished Connecticut Episcopal bishop, he grew up financially secure, with patrician values. Educated at Groton, Yale, and Harvard, he became a partner in one of Washington's most successful and influential law firms. In and out of government since 1933, he had helped formulate the Truman Doctrine for bolstering Greece and Turkey against the Soviet Union. He had also helped prepare the conceptual groundwork for the Marshall Plan.

Acheson's intellect and experience made him self-confident to the point of arrogance. "Brutal and condescending" to almost anyone, with the president "he was unfailingly polite, patient, and deferential."[4] If Truman wanted Webb, his secretary of state would agree. But this did not mean Acheson personally wanted him.

Acheson wrote in his memoirs that Webb "knew more about administration than foreign policy," not necessarily a compliment. He nevertheless recognized that the department needed someone with Webb's managerial flair, and, perhaps even more significant, he knew Webb was close to Truman. "It was of utmost importance to strengthen the President's confidence in the department," he wrote. "To Truman," David McCullough has written, "the State Department was 'a peculiar organization, made up principally of extremely bright people who made tremendous college marks but who have had very little association with actual people down to the ground.' They were 'clannish and snooty,' he thought, and he often felt like firing 'the whole bunch.'"[5] Some in the department thought that one reason Truman had made Webb the under secretary was that he needed someone in State with whom he felt completely comfortable. The rapport between Truman and Acheson would evolve only after Truman overcame his initial uneasiness.

Knowing his drawbacks and Acheson's reputation, Webb surely had mixed feelings about the assignment. Not all the problems stemmed from Acheson's personality; the State Department was known to be notoriously difficult to "manage." The culture of the Budget Bureau was ideal for someone with an administrative bent. But the basic work of State was diplomacy, and those who set the tone for the department—the foreign service—saw diplomacy as an art, practiced by individuals who needed freedom from management. By any criteria, State's task and methods, and the extreme diffuseness in measuring short-run success and failure in foreign policy, rank the department among the most complex of all government organizations to "run."[6] Some believe no one can do so; at best it is a burden. Moreover, since Webb, unlike other under secretaries, had no foreign policy credentials, he was perceived as being a "pure administrator," a lesser form of humanity to many State Department careerists. Like Acheson, however, Webb was loyal to Truman. An unlikely match from the outset—Webb and State—it was one Truman had arranged to suit *his* needs. For Acheson and Webb, that was that, and they would make their own association work. Whether it would work well enough for Webb to manage State remained to be seen.

Webb did not see himself as the "brilliant administrator" or "miracle man" he was being painted as in some quarters. He saw as his "first need . . . to get the people already on the job working close together and create topside leadership which will generate their maximum effort and effectiveness. That must be based on confidence and will take time."[7]

In BOB, that time had been there. Webb was able to get the lay of the land and become familiar with his personnel before making major changes. Not so in State. His first assignment from Acheson was to bring about a major reorganization as soon as possible, always a disruptive process. Webb thus began his tour in State as someone who caused pain for the officials who saw themselves affected adversely.

The decision to reorganize State was Acheson's own. As under secretary at the outset of the Truman administration, he had seen State crowded out by other agencies seeking to give Truman foreign policy advice. To be influential, State had to be better organized, "capable of providing the President with the most accurate information and soundest advice available." The key was to better unite State and its knowledge with the power of the presidency, through the secretary of state.[8]

Webb was also Truman's instrument. On January 11, just four days after announcing the Webb appointment, Truman showed Webb a report a personal consultant had prepared for him that had found the State Department "inefficiently organized," "badly manned in most of the top policy-making positions," and suffering a "breakdown of morale." "The gravest danger to be seen in the conditions now obtaining in the Department is the deplorable trend, which is increasing with every month that passes, toward the subordination of the State Department to the Department of Defense." Truman did not know how many of these points to take seriously, he said, but Webb should know what he was getting into.[9]

Whatever its other problems, State was definitely losing influence to the military. The *Foreign Policy Bulletin*, a publication of the Foreign Policy Association, commented at this time that the "post-war rise in the influence of the armed forces in United States foreign policy is due partly to the weakness of the State Department as an institution."[10] The department simply had not adapted to post–World War II realities. As it grew to 22,000 people during and after the war, incorporating a number of activities in ad hoc fashion, it had become a collection of fiefdoms with little coordination at the top.[11] It lacked coherence in part because legislative authority often was vested in officials below the secretary. Although Secretary of State Marshall had been so highly regarded by virtually everyone that he could function in spite of these drawbacks, even he had imposed on the department a new coordinating mechanism—a secretariat that reported to him and assembled information and funneled it upward or elsewhere as needed.

But this was not enough. The State Department's increasing responsibilities throughout the world meant new operational roles, such as presiding over a broadcasting network bigger than any private network and communicating the U.S. version of the truth in a multitude of languages to people under communism. As other agencies enlarged their own foreign policy activities, State had to coordinate foreign policy across the government. The perception that State needed change was as critical to its influence as the reality.

Acheson told Webb to act immediately, so he did.[12] Before January was over, he had legislation introduced in Congress authorizing, in addition to the secretary and under secretary, two deputy under secretaries (one for policy, one for administration), eight assistant secretaries (based on geography and functional specialty, such as economic affairs), a counselor with the rank of assistant secretary (to head the Policy Planning Staff), and a legal adviser. All would be presidential appointees, requiring senatorial confirmation. All laws granting authority to subordinate officers were repealed, and all authority to direct personnel, including the Foreign Service, was vested in the secretary.[13] This reorganization not only created a much tighter agency and a stronger secretary of state but carried congressional legitimacy and elevated State, through the multiple White House appointments, to a clearly "presidential agency." When it became law in June 1949, Webb again made headlines as the "wunderkind" of the Truman administration.[14]

He did not stop with legislation; he also began to improve internal and external communications, using the existing secretariat to facilitate the flow of information. He saw the secretariat not just as a "communications and switching center" but as a means by which "substantive judgment would be applied to guide and expedite the business of the department."[15] The secretariat grew into a 150-person organization directly under his control, its staff the executive officers for all the intra- and interagency bodies concerned with foreign policy. They provided these entities with up-to-date information of all types, and that information was shared. The State Department would in this way coordinate and lead by controlling the flow of information underlying policy. Knowledge was power.

The prime constituent of State, of course, was the president. For him and for the secretary of state, the secretariat would assemble a top-secret report on world developments, drawing on Central Intelligence Agency, military, and State's own intelligence sources, as well as specialized reports on economic affairs, public opinion, and so on. Webb instructed the secretariat to store information for easy retrieval, as an aid to future decision making. While less sanguine than Webb about what administrative tinkering could accomplish, Acheson let him develop his communication system and other reforms. The secretary could only benefit from a system designed to arm him with the best information his department and the government generally could provide when he went to advise Truman. Also, if Webb could relieve the secretary of a mass of minor decisions by streamlining the machine of State, that was all to the good.[16] The stronger State was and appeared as an organization, the stronger Acheson would be in Truman's eyes as its secretary.

Inevitably, Webb ran into resistance from forces within State. In his early days, he frequently began a conversation with disarmingly modest words: "You understand, of course, that I speak out of a wealth of ignorance."[17] Some of his State Department colleagues agreed. Charles "Chip" Bohlen, a top career foreign service official, told Webb that he might think he was creating a great communication system with his secretariat, but in reality he was "building a sewer system." "What you don't know," Bohlen told him, "is that what flows through that system is shit!"[18]

Richard Neustadt recalled that shortly after Webb arrived at the department, he tried to apply the notion of economic indicators he had innovated successfully at BOB to foreign policy, asking his career staff to prepare some foreign policy indicators:

> A senior career diplomat explained to one of Webb's own aides (brought over from BOB): "He won't get these things. We'll see to it he doesn't. Can you imagine the Under Secretary bounding around the building (not to mention the White House) brandishing his charts and saying, Ok, why's Cold War production down? Yugoslavia came over last month; why not Albania this month? Preposterous! It can't be allowed to happen."[19]

Webb never did get his foreign policy indicators.

Paul H. Nitze, then deputy director of the Policy Planning Staff, recalled that the reaction to Webb's reforms was extremely negative among many senior officials at the department. As he recollected, at one of the first meetings with high level officials under Webb's command, the under secretary explained his ideas and how he wanted State to work more closely with other agencies having a foreign policy interest, accusing State of having its "nose in the air" in dealing with others in government. Nitze and other senior officials determined not to let Webb "become a focus of policy," lest he "turn over power to some incompetents in . . . other agencies." They would surround him with knowledgeable staff to keep him and the department out of trouble and "protect Webb" from his own "ignorance." He could get credit for decisions, but others would do his thinking for him. In the process, a number of his naive reformist schemes could be reigned in.[20]

The most significant early contest came between Webb and George F. Kennan, easily the most famous official in the department apart from Acheson, and the architect of the "containment policy" that governed U.S. foreign relations with the Soviet Union. The Policy Planning Staff he headed, a small unit of the department's top conceptual thinkers, had been created around Kennan by Marshall and located adjacent to his own office. Kennan was a close policy adviser to Marshall; he was brilliant, influential, and sometimes inscrutable. In Webb's view, he was also impulsive, proposing ideas on the spur of the moment. Webb complained that Kennan liked to get hold of incoming telegrams, walk through the door between his office and Acheson's, and announce, "I don't think we ought to answer this telegram," or "We ought to answer it this way." Under the Webb management system, however, that telegram had already been communicated by the secretariat to the assistant secretary most deeply involved with the part of the world or problem associated with it. "It was premature for the head of the Policy Planning Staff to come in and recommend a course of action when he wasn't in on the play, and a hundred and one other things were going on in that part of the world," said Webb. He and Acheson were trying "to involve the department as a department, so that you could count on a matter being handled systematically and properly, no matter what it was [and so] that there was a routine for handling things."[21]

The open debate over this clash began in September 1949, when Kennan sent a paper to Acheson. It went first to Webb, who routed it to certain assistant secretaries and other specialists for comment. When some of these officials disagreed with the paper, and Webb asked Kennan to try to reconcile the disagreements and revise the paper before sending it to Acheson, Kennan took strong offense. He did not want Policy Planning Staff papers "subject to the veto of any of the chiefs of the operational divisions of the department." The whole purpose of his staff, he argued, was "to render an independent judgment on the problems coming before the Secretary or the Under Secretary."[22]

Acheson backed Webb, in part because his own relationship with Kennan had been deteriorating. According to Lucius D. Battle, Acheson's personal assistant, "They admired each other enormously but there was just not a meshing either of goals or of thought processes." "George Kennan had a sense of being the philosopher king," recalled Dorothy Fosdick, a staff member who was close to him. "He felt he had special insights . . . he felt he should make policy."[23]

No philosopher king would challenge Acheson's judgments. Webb's interest for organizational purposes meshed with Acheson's for maintaining his own role as the dominant policymaker within the department. On September 29 Kennan told Webb he would leave as director of policy planning as soon as possible, and get out of government altogether by June 1950. Paul Nitze, Kennan's deputy director, succeeded him as head of policy planning.

Webb's contemporary in age, Nitze came to Washington during the war from a successful career on Wall Street. He was a New England Brahmin, his great assets his sharp mind and incredible persistence. (Nitze would serve under six presidents, from Roosevelt to Reagan, in more than a dozen national security–related posts.) Like Webb, he was an "in-and-outer" rather than a career civil servant, and he loved being at the center of large policy issues. Upon his appointment as head of policy planning, he saw it essential for his office to win back its privileged position within the department.[24]

Unlike Kennan, however, Nitze was willing to abide superficially by the formal rules set by Webb. What could not be challenged formally might be combatted informally, if not now, then later. Nitze, like Webb, was calculating. Where Kennan had erred in leaving the arena of battle, Nitze determined on a more patient strategy that he had no doubt would prevail. The key to victory was Acheson, not Webb. He would bide his time.

In his quest to improve interagency coordination, Webb could give only so much energy to internal management. He was not trying to abdicate State's leadership role, as Nitze and some others in the department feared, but attempting to strengthen it. In addition to informal meetings, he convened what was known as the "Little Cabinet" monthly for dinner—all the departmental under secretaries, assistant secretaries, and other key federal executives of comparable rank concerned with foreign policy—so they could get to know one another better and exchange information more easily.[25] But here he would soon be undercut by the new secretary of defense.

In March 1949, Truman had appointed Louis Johnson to the position previously held by Forrestal. Johnson was a lawyer and prominent Democrat, principal fund-raiser for Truman's 1948 election. Described as "two hundred pounds of power, competence, acerbity, wit, and bumptiousness," he savored confrontation and made it clear he did not intend to follow the State Department's lead in any way. He ordered that all major political-military communications involving State and the Department of Defense (DOD) go through an individual reporting directly to him, Major General James Burns, a highly centralized liaison procedure that obstructed smooth working relations between the departments and stymied Webb's vision of coordination led by State.[26]

As he took command of the Pentagon, Johnson gave every indication of wanting to be Truman's principal adviser in national security—a concept that in his mind subordinated foreign policy, and thus State. To rise in relation to Truman he felt he had to pull down Acheson, which he tried to do by ridiculing Acheson behind his back. Acheson gritted his teeth, continuing to work with the defense secretary in spite of his growing aversion.

By fall 1949, Truman had learned of these tensions and, on a cruise on the presidential yacht, drew Webb aside. "Acheson is a gentleman," he said. "He won't descend to a row. Johnson is a rough customer, gets his way by rowing. When he takes out after you, give it right back to him." Clearly, Truman saw Webb as a rough-and-tumble fighter, and Webb interpreted this presidential advice as a directive to protect Acheson from Johnson. Back at the department, he, his assistant and head of the executive secretariat, Carlisle Humelsine, and Lucius Battle, Acheson's personal assistant, formed a cabal to deal with "the Johnson problem."[27]

The Louis Johnson Problem

Webb viewed the Acheson-Johnson feud as a personal and institutional power struggle. He understood that Truman did not want to decide between the two men, to be forced to weigh Acheson's foreign policy expertise against his own intense loyalty to Johnson, who had helped him in the campaign of 1948 when practically nobody else had given him a chance. Webb also knew that, in terms of the institutional struggle, the president thought more of DOD than of State. All of Webb's reform efforts were aimed at changing Truman's perception of State. Finally, Webb saw a congressional dimension to the power fight. DOD had influential support on Capitol Hill, and State was something of an orphan, lacking a domestic-political constituency. Defending Acheson was complicated and multifaceted at best, and Acheson had created lots of ill will with Congress. As Clark Clifford remembered, he "had a certain contempt for the political process, which caused him difficulty. . . . Many of his appearances as a witness before Congress left behind bruised and offended congressmen who would not soon forget the sarcasm and scorn with which he answered their questions."[28]

Webb thus spent much time mending congressional fences. Adept with legislators, he was the primary force at State in getting funds for various programs the department supported. Even he, however, could do little to offset the gathering storm in Congress over loyalty-security issues in the State Department. The McCarthy era was beginning, and Acheson and the department were targets of congressional Red-baiters. Secretary of Defense Johnson was not above using this mood to build support within Congress for himself and against Acheson.

Aware of all these nuances, Webb cautioned Acheson to be more cognizant of Congress, and of impressions generally. What worried him especially was how Acheson would deal with the Alger Hiss affair. A high-ranking State Department official until 1947, Hiss had served with Acheson, and the two were said to be close. In 1948, a young Republican representative from California, Richard M. Nixon, had gained national prominence as a member of the House Un-American Activities Committee through his in-

vestigation of Hiss, who was accused of having passed government information to a Russian spy ring during the 1930s. In 1949, Hiss was brought to
trial and charged with perjury for denying his role in the transfer of information. On January 25, 1950, he was convicted and sentenced to five years in
prison. Scheduled for a press conference that very day, Acheson was sure to
be asked about his former colleague.

Webb advised Acheson to speak with care. In the context of the Acheson-Johnson, State-DOD contest, Acheson did not need to weaken his
cause. But Acheson was adamant about doing what was "right," regardless
of the consequences. In response to a reporter's question, he said that, although it would be improper to discuss the "legal aspects of the case,"
"whatever the outcome of any appeal which Mr. Hiss or his lawyer may take
in this case, I do not intend to turn my back on Alger Hiss." At that moment
on the Senate floor, Republican representative Karl Mundt of Indiana, who
had used his membership on the House Un-American Activities Committee during the 1948 investigation to launch his Senate career, accused Hiss of
espionage. It was wholly probable, said Mundt, that Hiss, with his "effective
Harvard accent," had influenced the policy "which has helped bring about
the entire subjugation of China by Communist forces directly from
Moscow." Senator Bourke B. Hickenlooper of Iowa accused the Truman administration of taking the country "down the road in shaping policies fa-
vorable to the Communist Party."[29] Republican senator Joseph McCarthy of
Wisconsin called for the removal of Acheson and charged that "the balance
of the Hiss ring is still in the State Department . . . [and] several extremely
dangerous men are still occupying high State Department posts . . . it does
not matter whether Acheson knowingly keeps Communists in the State Department—the point is, he's doing it!"[30]

What Webb had feared had come to pass. The damage was done.
From now until he left the State Department, Webb would cope with a fever
of congressional and public anxiety about Communists at State, dealing
with the repercussions of Acheson's remarks and redoubling his efforts with
legislators. Acheson, aware that he had hurt himself, his department, and
the president, went to the White House after his defense of Hiss and offered
to resign. The president refused.[31] But Acheson's enemies nevertheless re-
joiced, including the secretary of defense, who seized the opportunity to
step up his attacks.

That Truman had supported Acheson instead of accepting his resignation gave Webb hope for State. Another source of hope that Acheson and
State would yet prevail was Johnson himself, who was staking out a budget-

cutting policy position on defense spending that was extreme, in Webb's view, and left him vulnerable. Johnson was trying to hold DOD to a budget of $13 billion, $2 billion below the ceiling Webb had set as budget director, in spite of the escalating Cold War. In August 1949, the Soviet Union had exploded an atomic bomb, which had led Truman, in January 1950, to approve development of the hydrogen bomb. With the USSR sure to counter the U.S. action, a nuclear arms race was under way. While Truman appreciated Johnson's budget consciousness, his policy was questionable under the circumstances. Webb saw that the defense secretary could not "win" against Acheson or State if his judgment on so vital a matter as the defense budget was flawed. The issue for State was to persuade the president that this was the case.

Truman was already leaning toward change. In deciding to go ahead with the H-bomb, he had authorized the National Security Council to review U.S. security policy. Within the State Department, the Policy Planning Staff was already engaged in such a study. Under Nitze, the staff was taking a decidedly more "hawkish" stance than under Kennan. A joint group established with DOD performed the NSC analysis.

Johnson suspected any State Department involvement in "his business," especially with State working toward *more* military expenditures, at odds with Johnson's recommendations. He and Acheson disagreed on a range of policy matters, and even when they concurred, as on Truman's H-bomb decision, the two saw each other as seldom as possible. Johnson wanted Acheson out as much as Acheson now hoped Johnson would go.[32]

In March 1950, State and Defense officials, including Acheson and Johnson, arranged a briefing on the results of the policy review, called the NSC-68 report. As Nitze presented it, NSC-68 provided "an alarming view of the international scene," anticipating that the Soviets would command a "great coercive power for use in time of peace" and that war could yet occur through miscalculations or misinterpretation. NSC-68 recommended that the United States contain the Soviet system "by all means short of war." Without sufficient military power, the United States would not make the containment policy credible—it would be a "policy of bluff." A "strategy of the cold war" must include "building up our military strength in order that it may not have to be used." Rather than the $13 billion Johnson defense budget, something on the order of $40 billion would most likely be needed. Johnson exploded, complaining vociferously that he had not had sufficient time prior to the meeting to read and digest the draft report. "Banging down his chair, shouting objections, hammering his fist on the table," asserting that at the moment he would agree to nothing in the study draft, he stomped out of the meeting.[33]

Acheson was appalled. The acrimony between him and Johnson continued to fester. Both publicly denied "problems," but within government it was well known that they barely spoke. Acheson, who made no secret of his disdain, felt Johnson's conduct was "too outrageous to be explained by mere cussedness." In his view, Johnson was mentally ill.[34]

Although getting rid of Johnson had entered the realm of the possible, as his style bothered many others in Truman's administration, Webb did not think this was the time to press for his dismissal. The State Department was anxious that the military alliance established in 1949, the North Atlantic Treaty Organization (NATO), get off to a strong start. NATO was critical for the overall military buildup NSC-68 proclaimed as needed. With Johnson scheduled to represent the United States at an important upcoming NATO meeting in Europe, firing him at this point would be highly disruptive. Webb's immediate concern was to persuade Johnson to say what State wanted him to say at the meeting, without his knowing who was calling the tune.[35]

Also, as Webb saw it, "the Johnson problem" was one with "the Acheson problem." The bipartisan coalition in Congress that had been so instrumental to many of the Truman administration's foreign policy achievements was in danger of unraveling, thanks in part to the Hiss controversy and Acheson's weakening support in Congress. Johnson had allies in Congress partly because he was an adversary of Acheson.

Over dinner on March 25, Webb and Acheson discussed Johnson and the need to shore up Republican support in Congress, among other matters. The next day Webb flew to Key West, where the president was vacationing. Apart from the substantive foreign policy issues Webb wanted to talk over with Truman, he intended also to deal with the Johnson issue. He first gave the president a copy of the NSC-68 report, so he could see for himself the focus of the latest dispute between Johnson and Acheson, then turned to the question of what to do about Johnson. Truman had heard a number of complaints about his defense secretary and was himself dueling with him over a particular appointment in the Pentagon. "By God, I'm going to fire him," he told Webb, who responded, "You can't do that. We need him for the meeting in Europe."[36]

Johnson had to go to Europe and make the "right" statements at the NATO meeting, Webb explained. He asked the president to call the defense secretary down to Key West and give him certain careful instructions before he took off for Europe. Johnson would never listen to Acheson or Webb, but maybe he would listen to the president. To put under Johnson a competent individual with whom Webb could deal, Webb further recommended bringing his own former deputy and successor at BOB, Frank Pace, over to DOD as secretary of the army and moving the incumbent to a special assistant role in the White House.

Finally, to woo back Republican legislators who were retreating from Acheson and thus from Truman's foreign policy, they needed to bring someone the Republicans trusted into the State Department at a high level. Webb recommended John Foster Dulles, a former New York senator and a Republican spokesman on foreign policy (later Eisenhower's appointee as secretary of state). Truman disagreed. "By God, I won't have Dulles in my administration," he told Webb. "He was in with us, he knew what was going on, and he lied about it to the people in New York, and I'll be damned if I'll have him in my administration."[37]

"All right," responded Webb, "what about John Sherman Cooper, another Republican?" Cooper had been associated with Governor Gardner's law firm, and Webb knew him well. Truman agreed. He later called Johnson to Key West, got him to agree to Pace as secretary of the army, and gave him specific instructions on the U.S. position to present at the NATO Defense Ministers' Conference.

Meanwhile, Webb was arranging for Cooper to join State as a special assistant to Acheson, at least temporarily, when he got a call from Truman. He didn't want to be "small" about the Dulles matter, the president said. If Webb and others thought it was important to bring Dulles in, "bring him in." "But go talk to [Senator] Vandenberg about it first." The senator, the Republican symbol of bipartisanship, gave his blessing, and Dulles agreed to join State, leaving Webb with the embarrassing task of extricating himself from the understanding with Cooper.[38]

All of these machinations strengthened the support base for NSC-68 —the basic reappraisal of U.S. national security policy—which State was attempting to lead. In early April, Acheson, the Joint Chiefs of Staff, and the service secretaries all signed off on the plan. Johnson reluctantly went along, and the document went officially to Truman, who had, of course, already seen it. The same day, Webb accelerated work on the congressional front in behalf of NSC-68, arranging special briefings for key legislators to prepare the way for acceptance. On April 20, Johnson stated privately after a meeting with Truman that his austerity program at DOD was dead, and that he had shaken hands with the president on it.[39]

At 10:00 P.M., Saturday, June 25, Dean Rusk, deputy under secretary, called Webb at home to inform him that the North Koreans had moved across the border with South Korea. Their tanks were making rapid progress. "Do you want me to come right down?" Webb asked. "No," said Rusk, "but we're going to have to work all night and we'll be involved tomorrow, and we talked to the president [who was away from Washington at the time]. He didn't want to alarm the country by flying right back immediately, but he's coming back tomorrow afternoon. You get a good night's sleep and come down tomorrow afternoon and prepare to take over from us some of these things that we're doing."[40]

The next day, Webb, together with Acheson and others at State, worked out three possible U.S. responses: to go to the United Nations, to send the navy Pacific fleet into the China Sea, or to authorize the air force to knock out North Korea's tanks under the pretext of providing cover to evacuate Americans. The State Department preference was to hold off on using the air force until it had a better sense of the situation in Korea. Also, State was unsure whether this was an isolated event or the first of a series of attacks by Communist nations. Johnson, however, speaking for DOD, saw no reason to hesitate and argued strongly for sending in the air force. Although Webb knew that it would be in the national interest for State and DOD to speak with one voice, he believed that this was unlikely as long as Johnson was in power at the Pentagon.

Who would have the president's ear? Webb, Acheson, and Johnson went to the airport to meet Truman. When they got in the car, Acheson sat in back with Truman, with Webb and Johnson in front of them on the jump seats. With the window rolled up between the four of them and the driver, Truman exclaimed combatively that he did not believe the North Koreans could support the military action, given the limitations of the Trans-Siberian Railroad, and "by God, I'm going to let them have it."[41]

Johnson turned around, stuck out his hand, and shook hands with him, declaring: "I'm with you Mr. President." Webb wanted to head off Acheson, in view of the tensions between him and Johnson and aware that Johnson would leak anything Acheson said to the *New York Times*, whose report would suggest that the secretary of state was "soft on the Communists." Before Acheson could respond, he interjected, "Mr. President, we have done a great deal of work with all concerned during the last two days. We have distilled our recommendations into three specific ones, and I think you should hear these carefully worked out recommendations before making up your mind as to any action to be taken."[42]

The Joint Chiefs of Staff and several others met them at Blair House, where Truman was staying while repairs were made to the White House. Johnson and Acheson went into the large reception room, while the president went to put his hat in the coatroom. Webb followed him in, closed the door, and outlined the three recommendations. He told Truman that Acheson and he felt strongly that only two of the recommendations should be approved that night and that the third, calling for use of force, should be held over another day or two, particularly since the United States was presenting the situation to the United Nations in New York. The president thanked him and left the coatroom.

Truman decided not to open discussions until after dinner. After the thirteen officials present had all had their say, he chose to do what the State Department had proposed, taking the less aggressive stance first, postponing air force action until more was known.[43] The next day, Webb had been scheduled to give a speech and then take his family on a three-week vacation to Nags Head, North Carolina. Acheson told Webb not to change his plans but to get some rest so that he could take over for some of the other officials later on, who would surely need a respite. Webb went on vacation. The president, meanwhile, decided to use force in Korea.

Secretary of Defense Johnson, soon the target of a great deal of criticism from the media and Congress for the lack of U.S. preparedness for war, blamed Acheson. When Webb returned from a vacation cut short by events, he defended Acheson in informal meetings on Capitol Hill. Senators were being attacked by rivals at home for having supported the secretary of state. Rather than bringing Acheson and Johnson together, Korea drove them even further apart. With Webb's maneuvering, W. Averell Harriman became a White House presidential assistant charged with conciliating the feud. In July, Harriman suggested that Acheson, Johnson, and he dine together once a week. The dinners were a failure. To get Harriman on his side, Johnson hinted privately that if Harriman could help him remove Acheson, he would help Harriman become secretary of state. By September, relations between Acheson and Johnson had sunk so low that the situation seemed beyond repair.[44]

Webb now believed the time was ripe for Johnson's dismissal. He had been keeping close tabs on the defense secretary through contacts in government and the media and knew that his reputation had been badly damaged by the Korean War.[45] Former allies were distancing themselves from him. He had many enemies in Truman's administration besides Acheson because of his personal abrasiveness. Webb's style was to work behind the scenes, wherever possible, but his assistant, Carlisle Humelsine, watched him go into action.

> This was a very messy business. Jim Webb got Johnson and Johnson did not even know it. Jim had strong ties to the Hill. He especially had strong ties to the southern bloc. His performance in respect to Johnson was one of the most sophisticated power plays I have ever witnessed. He went to the Hill. He worked within the Executive Office of the President and with the agencies. The State Department won the battle [with DOD]. This was because of Jim. It was his greatest accomplishment at the State Department.[46]

And it was accomplished in secret. Truman certainly heard from a number of advisers, including Harriman, the peacemaker turned Johnson adversary. Webb's contribution, as Humelsine noted, was strategic and carefully timed. Webb later described his role this way: "I was a participant in the process—I carried the message that the time had come."[47] Most important, according to Humelsine, was Webb's bringing legislators into a coalition against Johnson to speak to Truman at this moment. Involving Congress and others in the ouster was critical. Webb did not want it to appear the doing of Acheson, for whom many on Capitol Hill had little sympathy. That was one reason Webb made it a point to stay in the shadows.

When the time came, Truman found it hard to act. He said he felt "as if I had just whipped my daughter, Margaret." But when he made the decision, he did so at a point when he clearly gained from the choice and lost little. Johnson's leaving was announced September 12, coupled with news that George Marshall would come out of retirement to serve in his place. A hero to Truman, Webb, and many others in the United States, Marshall was the perfect choice.[48] Whether Webb had any influence on the decision to bring Marshall back is unknown, but he surely would have considered the question of Johnson's replacement and would have favored Marshall as the ideal secretary of defense under the circumstances.

The impact of the change was immediate. Overnight, State-Defense relations shifted from extremely guarded to extraordinarily open. As his principal deputy, Marshall brought in Robert Lovett, who had held Webb's job at State and with whom Webb could work easily. The crisis in relations between State and Defense was over, a crisis that might have had seriously negative implications for the conduct of the Korean War along with other important aspects of national policy. Truman had told Webb to protect Acheson against Johnson, and he had done so.

Losing Influence at State

Because Webb was the State Department's prime domestic-political strategist, his involvement with major policy issues of the day came primarily in this context. While he participated in foreign policy discussions, represented the department at ceremonial and social functions, and made certain decisions when Acheson was out of town, he was for the most part a supporting player. After his prominence and influence as budget director, Webb found the under secretary's job constraining.

As "number two," he had only the pieces of the action Acheson let him have. One that most fascinated him was science and technology. Early at State, he had brought his friend Lloyd Berkner on as a consultant. Webb noticed that while DOD had strong relations with scientists and the universities, State did not, partly because State felt it had all the expertise it needed to chart the U.S. course. That was an attitude Webb did not share, as he made clear to department insiders. In October 1949, he asked Berkner to study State-science relations. He also worked out an arrangement whereby the National Academy of Sciences could assist Berkner as necessary.

In April 1950, Berkner submitted a report, "Science and Foreign Relations," describing the nature and significance of basic problems in international relations raised by scientific and technical developments.[49] Berkner had examined the principal activities of the department affected by these problems and set out recommendations that, put into effect, would enable the department to meet its responsibilities in the scientific and technical aspects of foreign relations. Webb found the Berkner report stimulating and, with Acheson's concurrence, he began to implement its recommendations. Within relatively short order, a science office was created under Webb and a system of science attachés established at various embassies abroad. Although these moves represented the potential for significant change for State, Webb wanted more. He set out to move the department into a closer relation with universities, adapting a DOD mechanism called "summer study." If DOD could use talent at universities through summer studies, why couldn't State? With an eye to broadening the number of able people observing department problems, Webb launched Project Troy.

Managed by MIT, Troy entailed an interdisciplinary effort to study problems surrounding radio propaganda communications behind the iron curtain, as well as psychological warfare. The psychological aspect was important to Webb. NSC-68 had pointed up the psychological dimension of the Cold War, and Webb wanted State to give the propaganda component of the U.S.-USSR conflict more attention. Outsiders could help. He believed the interdisciplinary approach would provide a comprehensive look at the problem. Hence, Project Troy included natural scientists plus social science experts in such fields as psychology, anthropology, economics, and foreign relations.[50] Among the experts involved was an MIT engineer named Jerome B. Wiesner, who later became President John F. Kennedy's science adviser.

An activity quite innovative for State, Project Troy was "the first academic 'summer study' supported directly by a nominally civilian agency of the federal government. As such, it illustrates both the marked expansion of the nature and scope of what was considered essential to national security and the formal extension of an already extensive network of associations between civilian experts and the military to the areas of diplomacy and foreign relations."[51]

But many of Webb's dreams for creating a more perfect State Department were thwarted, put on hold, or derailed by events and individuals over which he had little control. Korea proved a watershed for Webb. Before the war, he had been an outsider in the department, but at least he had felt he had an important supporting role to perform. After the war began, and once Johnson was gone, he became an increasingly peripheral figure. His ability to push for change at State in the latter half of 1950 and in 1951 was weakened by the steady diversion of departmental energy to the war.

As Acheson's leverage over U.S. foreign policy increased, he continued to exclude his under secretary from important decisions, although he praised Webb publicly in 1950 as an administrator:

> I do not know any man in the entire United States, in the government or out of the government, who has a greater genius for organization, a genius for understanding how to take a great mass of people and bring them together; so that he pulls out of them all the knowledge and all the competence that they have; so that each person is doing what he ought to be doing; so that the whole effort of this vast group are pulled together to get a tremendously powerful result.[52]

But Acheson did not believe Webb had much to contribute to foreign policy, an attitude that diminished Webb's influence not only with Acheson but with those below Webb. Foreign policy expertise, not administrative ability, was what mattered in State. Moreover, Webb's personal style began to grate on Acheson. In a better time, the voluble Webb was "sunny Jim." In wartime, he was a nuisance for the overburdened secretary, who liked discussions short and to the point. Some of Webb's expressions, such as "I want to get the flavor of your thinking," bothered Acheson, who could be fastidious in language as well as appearance. The secretary was absorbed with Korea, pilloried by his critics in Congress and the media every day, and under stress. Always short fused within State, now Acheson was even more prone to lash out at Webb with some biting remark, such as "I do not have time for such trivia!" when Webb tried to discuss an administrative matter.

"It wasn't that these men were at each other's throats or wouldn't speak to each other," recalled Burton Marshall, a former State Department official, "but there was not close collaboration between them."[53]

In addition, Webb was losing the struggle to guide and coordinate policy advice that he had waged from the time he arrived. Paul Nitze, head of the Policy Planning Staff, succeeded in escaping Webb's control where Kennan had failed. Working quietly and persistently to restore the special influence of his office, from the moment he took command, Nitze cultivated Acheson. His star rose swiftly. As main author of NSC-68, he gained particular prominence as architect of a new order. The Korean War and Cold War buildup greatly strengthened his hand, along with those of all who had taken a hard line toward the Soviets. As Nitze gained greater access to Acheson, he refashioned his office into an entity capable of performing as Acheson's personal crisis staff rather than as a long-range planning unit. The staff conference room, located next to Acheson's office, "pulsed with excitement," and Acheson frequently would "slip through the side door to sit in on the staff's contentious sessions." David Callahan wrote that "by 1951 the Policy Planning Staff's standing in the State Department could not have been better. Acheson relied heavily on the staff and made an effort to keep Nitze's people in the loop."[54]

Nitze viewed coordination as fine for the rest of the department—but not for policy planning. As Webb saw the tide moving against him, his health worsened and prevented his fighting back. The occasional migraines of the past became more frequent and intense. The constant string of meetings and tensions, the heavy demands of evening social activities for a senior State Department official, the absence of positive reinforcement within the department—all began to take their toll. A friend remembers seeing Webb going to the State Department one day, his head pressed against the side of the vehicle in which he rode, his face contorted in pain. Webb began to think seriously about leaving the department.

In May 1951, McWilliam Pauly, a high-ranking official whom Webb had helped bring into the department, told Webb he wanted to resign because he did not feel he was "on the team." Also, Pauly said, "there are all kinds of rumors that I am after your job, and I want to set that straight." "Don't worry about the rumors," said Webb, assuring Pauly he was on the team. Besides, he admitted, he himself might not be around much longer. His "most urgent personal desire" was to go as soon as possible.[55]

A confrontation with Nitze in the latter part of 1951 triggered Webb's departure. Nitze was out of work for a period with a serious infection. When he returned, nerves frayed, still feeling poorly, he found a memo from Humelsine in his In box, prepared at Webb's request. At issue was how the policy planning function might best be reorganized. The role of the Policy Planning Staff was mentioned, as was that of other units, on the apparent assumption that as Nitze had moved his office closer to immediate policy issues, he was giving less attention to long-range policy planning; this problem had to be addressed. Nitze read the memo as a plan to convert his office into "a think-tank with no current policy connections at all. It would be a group that would look five to ten years down the line, but it would have no impact on today's policies." He was furious. Not having been consulted about this idea, he saw Webb as attempting a fait accompli. He stormed into Webb's office, absolutely livid, and told Webb "exactly what I thought," charging that Webb's handling of his office had been a destructive influence in the department, that from their first conversation in 1949, Webb had revealed little "understanding of the problems facing the department, that on a number of occasions running back over two years or more he had been 'very angry' over decisions" Webb had made. He claimed that he respected the position Webb held, but not the man in the position, and he ended by recommending that Webb resign. Stunned, Webb replied he had had no idea Nitze had felt that way, and he would think over how he would respond. Nitze recalls that Webb appeared "shattered" and canceled the reorganization order on the spot. After the meeting, Webb reflected that the memo and its handling were "very bad" and felt a measure of responsibility for what had transpired.[56]

He was shaken by the experience. He regarded Nitze highly for his ability, if not for his manner of operation, knew he was valuable to Acheson and to the country, and understood that he—unlike Kennan—was now personally close to Acheson. Webb could not distance Nitze and Acheson through organizational devices if Acheson wanted proximity. At the same time, officials aware of the blowup were extremely agitated. Although Acheson and Nitze operated on the same wavelength, both "policy intellectuals," the secretary had a strong regard for the chain of command. He would be incredibly cross-pressured if the Nitze-Webb situation continued. As word spread, men and women in State took sides. Lucius Battle worried that Truman himself might get involved if the conflict got out of hand.[57]

The matter was quelled quickly, however, by Webb, who wrote a message to Acheson, who was away, informing him of the blowup. Whether Webb ever sent that note is unknown. What he did send Acheson was word of his decision to resign as soon as possible because of poor health.[58] When Acheson returned, he asked his secretary what had transpired, especially in regard to Webb. She told him about the Webb-Nitze dispute. Acheson had Nitze come in and give his version of the altercation. When Nitze admitted that he had recommended that Webb resign, Acheson responded, "If you are not careful who you fire when I am away, you may be next!" Acheson also spoke with Webb. He knew about the migraines, and that it was in Webb's best interest to step down as soon as a replacement could be found. Remarkably, Webb went about his business, including that with Nitze, revealing no outward sign of recrimination.[59]

Acheson did not try very hard to dissuade Webb from leaving, and some felt he secretly welcomed the opportunity to choose his own under secretary. Acheson's son, David, recalled that "Webb's leaving was no great tragedy" for his father, who chose as his next under secretary a man with foreign policy expertise, David Bruce, then ambassador to France.[60]

On January 19, Webb wrote the president a letter of resignation. Aware of Webb's health problems and need for rest, Truman accepted Webb's decision with "most profound regret" and asked Webb to please be available in the future, writing, "I truly feel that it would not only be a personal loss to me, but also a loss to the country as a whole if the experience you have gained in your outstanding career were not further to be used in the public service."[61]

By the end of February 1952, Webb was out of government for the first time in six years. His years with the Truman administration had brought both great success and deep disappointment. There is a sense of rise and fall to the period 1946–52, with Webb heralded as budget director and contributing notably to the shaping of the institutional presidency, then, in

4

The Oklahoma Years

After leaving State, Webb underwent medical tests to determine the cause of his migraines, which were found to stem from his allergies to alcohol and tobacco. He now refrained from both and rested at home, following doctor's orders. With his health improved, at Truman's behest Webb served on an advisory committee on management to the president. He was appointed to the board of directors of McDonnell Aircraft, a position that garnered him needed income and allowed him to resume his longstanding association with aviation, and did some legal work for his old firm of O. Max Gardner, now run by Gardner's associate, Fred W. Morrison. A number of friends and associates contacted him, offering to help him get resettled.[1] He said no, he would gradually ease into a new job, although he was not sure what it would be.

A powerful man in Washington who had observed Webb while he was in the Budget Bureau and at State was Robert S. Kerr, senator from Oklahoma, president of Kerr-McGee Oil Industries, and reputedly the wealthiest individual in the Senate. Governor of Oklahoma from 1943 to 1947, Kerr came to Washington in 1948 and moved to high visibility in the Senate with remarkable speed.[2] With Lyndon Johnson of Texas and Hubert Humphrey of Minnesota, he was one of a number of members of the Senate "class of 1948" with whom Webb became acquainted. Kerr stood six feet three and weighed 220 pounds, a self-confident, overbearing, and influential senator with a thunderous voice.[3] When he walked down the Capitol's corridors, he resembled a "Sherman tank in search of a target."[4] Exceptionally intelligent, an excellent debater, he was a devout Baptist who taught Sunday school, neither drank nor smoked, but was ruthless at achieving his interests. When he looked a man in the eye from across the desk, that man paid attention.

In Webb's State Department years, he had gotten to know Kerr well, working with him on the congressional front to solidify backing for the administration's military policies once the Korean War started.[5] The senator had wanted to run for president in 1952, assuming Truman was not running, and in 1951 had begun to try to recast his image from that of parochial wheeler-dealer, oil-state senator. One way he did this was by speaking out on foreign policy issues, over which he conferred with Webb; Webb in turn used their meetings to cement Kerr's support for the State Department. The two men frequently had breakfasted together at State when it was Webb's turn for Sunday morning duty.[6]

During this time, Webb had called W. J. "Jamie" McWilliams, a close assistant, into his State Department office. "I don't want to see Kerr make a lot of dumb statements about foreign policy and get us into trouble," he said. "I'm going to call him. I know he is going to make speeches. I'm going to tell him when I talk with him that when he wants to talk about foreign policy, he should call you and you should tell him what he needs to know. Write him briefing papers. These will be a basis for statements. I do not want Kerr to go around with a loose lip."[7]

McWilliams had become Webb's liaison with Senator Kerr and his staff. Soon, Kerr was speaking out about trouble spots around the globe, and what he said harmonized with the State Department position. While Kerr served his own purposes by beginning to sound "presidential," the interaction served Webb by keeping the ambitious senator under a measure of control and helping State in the process. In early 1952, as Webb left State, Kerr moved his campaign into a higher gear, his close adviser Clark Clifford.[8] Truman indicated he was not going to run again but wanted to influence the choice of his successor. He gave his blessing to Kerr to enter the February 6 Nebraska primary against Senator Estes Kefauver of Tennessee, whom Truman did not want to see in the White House. Kerr lost. Although he continued to campaign until Governor Adlai Stevenson of Illinois was nominated as the Democratic standard-bearer in the summer of 1952, he never recovered from that defeat. He had desperately needed credibility as a viable national candidate and had staked a great deal on winning Nebraska. Kerr was too intelligent and realistic not to know by February 7 that his winning the nomination was a long shot.[9]

Hence, it is not surprising that in March 1952 Kerr was thinking not only about the White House but also about Kerr-McGee Oil Industries and its problems. Webb could do his company some good, he decided; he also lived by the code of exchange—friends were rewarded and enemies punished. Webb was a friend. Kerr asked him to come over for a visit. Looking Webb in the eye, Kerr said, "Mr. Webb, you're the kind of man we could use in Oklahoma." Webb, seldom at a loss for words, said nothing. Kerr waited, then slowly continued, "You're not listening to me. I know you are not listening to me because you haven't asked me *how much* you are needed in Oklahoma." Before Webb could say anything, Kerr went on. "One million dollars."[10]

Kerr explained that he, his partner Dean A. McGee, and an associate had purchased Republic Supply Company from Republic Steel. A supplier of pipes and valves and other oil rig equipment that oil drilling companies like Kerr-McGee needed to dig for oil wells, the run-down company was losing money, its management inept. Kerr wanted Webb to use his managerial talent to turn Republic Supply around and to be the principal adviser to Dean McGee and himself in terms of Kerr-McGee Oil Industries as a whole. He did not expect Webb to be a Washington lobbyist; he had employed Clifford for that. He wanted a professional manager who could think on a scale big enough to suit him.[11] His salary, stock options, and other arrangements, Kerr promised, would make Webb a millionaire. The initial commitment between them would cover five years.

Kerr could be extremely persuasive one on one, much like Lyndon Johnson, with whom he was friendly, one of those larger-than-life men who exuded power and could move others with their presence. The characteristics so persuasive in a small group came across poorly on a wider stage. Too much the rough-hewn Oklahoman, Kerr could not advance his career to the presidency he coveted, but he continued to build influence in Washington, where he would be called the "uncrowned King of the Senate," once Johnson had left Congress for the vice presidency.[12] Like Johnson, Kerr found that his senatorial role helped build his business wealth. One of his damaging weaknesses was his deserved reputation for using pork-barrel politics to benefit his home state. He saw Webb in this light: another Kerr gift from Washington to Oklahoma.

Webb knew he had to be careful, for Kerr liked to dominate. One of the friends from whom he sought advice after the meeting was McWilliams, who had become head of the State Department's executive secretariat with the advance of Carlisle Humelsine to assistant secretary of state for administration. "I've just talked to Bob Kerr," Webb told him, "and Bob said that if I come to Oklahoma for five years, he'll make me one million dollars.

What do I do?" McWilliams didn't have to think twice. "Go! You have no money. You have two kids. Why don't you go and get your million and then come back here?" Webb agreed. "I guess that makes sense."[13]

He nevertheless mulled Kerr's offer over further, discussing it with his wife and others. Patsy loved Washington, and the thought of moving far away did not appeal to her. Not until the day after Eisenhower's inauguration as president and ten months after his meeting with Kerr did Webb write Truman that he had decided to move his family to Oklahoma and work for Kerr-McGee. He explained his new position, noting that he would remain on the board of directors of McDonnell Aircraft in St. Louis and hoped to see the former president when he returned to his home in Independence.[14]

In February 1953, Webb and his family left Washington.

Prospering with Republic and Kerr-McGee

To a man seeking renewal after six battle-filled years of government service, Oklahoma offered change and respite. When Webb arrived, the state economy was booming, in large measure because of the oil business. Such public officials as Kerr helped by directing federal money to the state. The feeling prevailed that Oklahoma City, in particular, stood on the threshold of great prosperity and expansion. To Webb, everything seemed new; scarcely a major building in the city had been constructed prior to World War II.[15]

At the same time, the Webbs perceived some negatives in Oklahoma. First was its marked provincialism. Even the people of the largest city and capital, Oklahoma City, masked a sense of inferiority with western swagger. Out of the mainstream of national power and world affairs, most business and political leaders were naive in terms of the larger issues of the day. Athletics—particularly the University of Oklahoma football team—was the primary source of pride. Many cared more about how the football team fared against Nebraska and Texas than how the state progressed in other respects. Washington, D.C., and its political concerns were far away. Second, the Webbs had mixed feelings about the general level of education their children received in Oklahoma City schools, Sally in a private school, Jimmy in a public school. That education was less highly valued in Oklahoma than elsewhere was reflected in school funding, typical of a state dominated by a conservative rural legislature that took a minimalist view toward government services. While Webb met wealthy Oklahoma oilmen who felt they could do almost anything as individuals, they were stymied as how best to act collectively in regard to public goals.[16] The dichotomy between individual drive and public neglect was reflected symbolically in the thousands of oil and natural gas wells that marred the landscape of Oklahoma, even the front lawn of the state capitol.

Webb's primary responsibility was as president of Republic Supply, a company losing $40,000 a month when he arrived. A relatively uncomplicated organization, most of its three hundred employees were blue-collar workers, along with a sales force, a financial group, and a set of district managers who had supply stores under them. In contrast to Webb's earlier business assignment with Sperry, Republic Supply was a low-technology, simply structured organization.[17]

The problems started with the existing management, products of a "good ole boy" network and many incompetents—only one top official he inherited was still with Republic Supply when Webb left. He brought in a more professional set of managers, starting with a new chief financial officer, Arthur McLawton. The two initiated a budget system. He held budget hearings, forcing the various divisions to justify what they wanted and what they were doing with their money. He instituted a personnel system that called for merit-based evaluation of company officials, including sales people and managers, and a promotional system based on performance.[18]

An organizational culture primarily rooted in personal relations gradually became one that took a professional approach. Webb found that people in the field thought only in terms of personal contacts, relating not to Republic Supply headquarters but to particular people. To create a sense of the organization as a whole, he prepared organization charts so that everyone involved could "see" Republic Supply and how its parts related to each other. Changes in these charts reflected the actual shifts Webb was making, trying to bring everyone along with him as he did so. He wanted employees of the company to comprehend his perspective of Republic Supply as an organization with offices and roles, rather than as a collection of individuals.[19]

Gradually, Republic Supply began to reflect the more professional, coordinated approach Webb sought. Kerr's son, Breene, who was on the board of directors of Kerr-McGee at the time, recalls that "Webb did a superb job of recasting the entire organization." The result, very soon, was a new efficiency at Republic Supply, which led gradually to visible results in profits. (After Webb's departure from Oklahoma, Kerr-McGee was able to sell Republic Supply back to Republic Steel at a substantial gain.)[20]

At Republic, Webb kept Senator Kerr fully informed but at arm's length. When Kerr called Webb every week to say "I'd like to have money switched from this bank to the other bank or to this account," Webb had to tell him firmly, "I am running this company. You can't manage this money. I have to do it." Webb knew he had to be tough.[21] As Kerr's biographer wrote: "For Robert Kerr other men were either equals or subordinates. He saw everyone in terms of political power and responded to them after determining how they could help him."[22] As long as he was getting positive results, Kerr would respect Webb's judgment. The end for him was money. Webb wanted to control the means. Although he chose executives with experience in the oil business, he also wanted an alter ego, an able individual who understood his style and mode of operation. He thought about Jamie McWilliams, still at State, who had supported his move to Oklahoma, and by the end of 1953, he had McWilliams aboard.

In addition to being president of Republic Supply, Webb was also assistant to the president of Kerr-McGee Oil Industries and a member of the Kerr-McGee board. When he moved to Oklahoma, Kerr held the title of president, but Dean McGee, a geologist, ran the organization. He had joined Kerr when the company was relatively young and had literally grown up with the enterprise. In 1941, the company had become Kerr-McGee. Webb was, in form, assistant to Kerr; in reality he advised McGee, the executive vice president.

Webb got along with both men—the bombastic Kerr and the more modest, reticent McGee, a "provincial-minded geologist, who likes big structures, big lease blocks and big gambles, with resulting big stakes if successful." Webb characterized McGee as an elephant hunter. "I mean," said Webb, "he would never go out looking for small game and he would not take his eyes off of a big possibility in a way of new discovery." Kerr was also a big-game hunter, Webb noted, who was always thinking, "Gee, we've got to find that herd of elephants and think what a great thing we could do with all that ivory." But McGee, while looking for the herd, was thinking, "We've got to be very careful that we don't stampede them and get trampled in the process."[23]

A midsized oil company moving toward diversification and growth, Kerr-McGee ranked forty-first on the basis of capital structures among ninety-eight petroleum companies. At the time Webb came to Oklahoma, it had mapped out its largest oil drilling program ever and had become the first oil company to move into uranium mining. Successful in various states in the Southwest, Kerr-McGee was drilling in Israel and Alaska and had set its sights on offshore drilling in a substantial way.

Like Republic Supply, Kerr-McGee had been managed personally; the difference was McGee's competence. But by 1953 the company had become too large and widespread for the old ways to continue. Also, there was the anomaly of Kerr's having the title of president. As assistant to the president and a member of the board, Webb had a right to speak up about Kerr-McGee's management structure. Not an oilman, Webb was nevertheless perceived as extremely knowledgeable about management, and his first year at Republic was proving that Senator Kerr had made a wise decision in bringing him aboard.

Defining Webb's exact role in Kerr-McGee's development is difficult. He was part of a group decision-making process for which documentation is not available. Nevertheless, in 1954, some extremely important changes took place at the company. The bylaws were amended to create for the first time the position of chairman of the board, and Senator Kerr assumed that position, allowing McGee to move up from executive vice president to president. The change also helped Kerr in his campaign for a second term in the Senate, for his opponent had charged that as president of Kerr-McGee he was not spending enough time on his Senate job. But the senator still participated "actively in all policy decisions" involving Kerr-McGee.[24]

This shift at the top was followed in June by a major reorganization that created a much more formally structured approach to management. Kerr-McGee "established a layer of middle management by the creation of four new vice presidencies to go along with those that already existed": exploration, Gulf Coast operations, manufacturing, and general engineering. Managers were appointed for two departments: drilling and manufacturing. "The result," Kerr-McGee's historian has written, "was a streamlining and coordinating of function, with better channels of communication from the top to the bottom of the organization and vice versa. Furthermore, it assured greater stability for the company in case of unanticipated loss of a member of top management."[25] The likelihood is that Webb significantly influenced these decisions, including the move of Kerr from president to chairman. While Kerr had hired Webb as a "professional manager," he knew Webb's political sophistication.

Kerr-McGee flourished under the new organization. Total assets rose from $38.6 million with 1,210 employees in 1953 to $43.2 million and 1,245 employees in 1954 and $67.5 million and 1,325 employees in 1955.[26] As Kerr-

McGee prospered, so did Republic Supply. If Kerr-McGee, its principal customer, bought equipment from Republic, Republic could make money—if it were run efficiently. The interconnectedness of the companies was not lost on Webb.

Founding Frontiers of Science

By fall 1954, Webb felt less need for intense, day-to-day involvement in the details of running Republic Supply, which by then functioned well under his management system. He began setting goals and letting Mc-Williams (whose initial job was vice president without portfolio) and his other senior associates implement them, meeting with them once a week to check on progress. McWilliams gravitated toward sales, where he began making a positive difference. Improvement was steady.

Meanwhile, Kerr-McGee prospered. McGee, who considered himself a good manager, remained considerate and attentive to Webb in spite of his wariness toward him. McGee's secretary recalled that Webb would have run the whole corporation if McGee had let him.[27] Instead McGee encouraged this restless man to reach out beyond the company, once the larger organizational changes in Republic Supply and Kerr-McGee were behind him, happy to let Webb play a public relations role. Fully recovered from his health problems, Webb was anxious to find a channel for his excess energy, and the public arena offered the real opportunity he had sensed when he arrived in Oklahoma.

A newcomer, Webb was viewed with some suspicion by conservative Oklahoma businessmen with whom Truman was unpopular. But Kerr-McGee was a strong and credible base from which to operate, and he soon gained the confidence of several members of the financial elite of Oklahoma City. A neighbor and oilman, John Kirkpatrick, became a close friend of Webb and helped him meet other powerful Oklahomans. Another friend in town was banker Morrison Tucker, who had lived at the Racquet Club when Webb did. In 1954, Webb became a member of the board of directors of the city's Chamber of Commerce. In dealing with Kirkpatrick, McGee, Tucker, and other Oklahomans, he found a great deal of latent public spirit. These men wanted to do something positive with their money. The question was, what?

In 1955, a number of Oklahoma business leaders began discussing how the state would celebrate its fiftieth anniversary, scheduled for 1957. The major proposal on their agenda was to ride the Chisholm Trail, which had been traveled by early settlers. There could be a huge chuck-wagon breakfast. This "cowboy show" had support, and it was felt the event would bring the media to Oklahoma and give the state exposure on national television. But Webb argued against it. "Instead of riding the Chisholm Trail," he said, "why don't you look to the future?" He pointed out that Oklahoma was rightly proud of its frontier tradition but that it needed to emphasize a new frontier. He told them about *Science: The Endless Frontier,* the report by World War II science leader Vannevar Bush that had led to the establishment of the National Science Foundation (NSF) in 1950. As budget director, Webb had dealt with Bush and believed that investing in science would have long-run societal benefits. He urged them to think about the frontier of science as it applied to Oklahoma.

Webb's words had a striking effect on business leaders. "You've had a different experience than we've had," they said. "Let's talk."[28] Webb encouraged them to think not only "big" (which they tended to do) but in new ways. In 1955, a Frontiers of Science Foundation was established, with Webb as president; Dean McGee as chairman of the board; E. K. Gaylord, another wealthy Oklahoman, as vice chairman; and as executive director, Robert MacVicar, a former vice president of Oklahoma State University. To join the foundation's board, a member had to invest $25,000, at the rate of $5,000 per year.

While looking to 1957 and the Oklahoma anniversary, Webb argued that the foundation should have a broader, longer-lasting focus and proposed that this be science education. Those associated with him agreed. Before the year was out, the new Oklahoma foundation had joined with NSF to sponsor a year-long training institute for high school science teachers and had embarked on a statewide project to improve not only Oklahoma's public schools but also the teaching of science in Oklahoma's universities.[29] Webb, meanwhile, had been appointed to advisory boards of the state's two major universities, the University of Oklahoma and Oklahoma State.

In a January 1956 letter to Truman, Webb mentioned the Frontiers of Science Foundation as "an outside activity" that he hoped would "really do some good in this state" and serve as a model for other areas of the country. "I wish it were possible to expand this to some kind of regional development in the Arkansas, White and Red River Basin and also in the Missouri River basin."[30] This extracurricular activity became his driving interest and the platform from which he communicated his vision for the future of the state with enthusiasm and infectious energy. Oklahoma was going to become a science center, and science and technology could lead to new industry.

Meanwhile, Webb accepted appointments to national advisory committees and boards, some of which also had science and technology emphases, including the National Advisory Council to the U.S. Public Health Service and the board of directors of Oak Ridge Institute for Nuclear Studies, an entity connected with the Oak Ridge National Laboratory. He also maintained contact with Bush and Berkner. Berkner, in particular, proved a frequent source of ideas and encouragement. He was now president of Associated Universities, Inc., based in New York, a consortium set up to govern the Atomic Energy Commission's Brookhaven National Laboratory on Long Island.[31]

Webb drew on his outside connections for a constant flow of fresh ideas to his Oklahoma associates. He used the Kerr-McGee plane to transport a group of top state business leaders to Oak Ridge; then on to MIT, where they met Vannevar Bush; to Brookhaven and a visit with Berkner; and to Bell Labs, in New Jersey, where he also had contacts. Impressed with the men they met, the Oklahomans went home raring to make Oklahoma part of the *new* frontier that science and technology were creating. Although the Frontiers of Science Foundation was Webb's concept, he worked hard to transfer a sense of ownership to others, to make it truly a product of Oklahomans.[32]

Gradually, the nature of the fiftieth-anniversary celebration of Oklahoma's statehood took shape. It would be held June 17, 1957, when top high school students from all over the state would converge on Oklahoma City's largest auditorium. They would hear about science and technology from some of the nation's leading scientist-statesmen and -stateswomen in a meeting that would symbolize the future of Oklahoma—the next fifty years—and illustrate how science and technology and Oklahoma could benefit one another. Webb personally took charge of getting top people to come: Vannevar Bush; Mervin Kelly, president of AT&T's Bell Labs; William Baker, also of Bell Labs; Fred Seitz, a leading scientist and later president of the National Academy of Sciences; Lee A. DuBridge, president of Caltech. He found Kelly particularly helpful in getting some of his friends and associates to come. June 17 came, with three thousand at a day-long symposium and a capacity six hundred at a special dinner that evening. It contributed substantially to the feeling of a number of Oklahomans that their state was getting on the map and looking to the future.

In October, when the Soviet Union placed the first satellite in orbit and science and technology became a larger national priority, the impetus behind the Frontiers of Science Foundation, already great, accelerated. The main thrust of the foundation was to improve scientific and technical education in Oklahoma at all levels. Webb and the Oklahoma business leaders pushed the political leaders of the state to invest more money in the educational system, including higher teachers' salaries. The foundation gained a number of new members and sponsored various additional projects, including the preparation of innovative educational materials.

At the same time, Webb was able to demonstrate that science and technology could pay economic dividends. A few days after the state anniversary celebration, Kelly was back in his corporate office when a committee from Western Electric and the Bell System came in to discuss the location of a new multimillion-dollar manufacturing plant. Kelly looked over the options. "Say, I have been down in Oklahoma recently," he said. That's "an enthusiastic place. Have you thought about Oklahoma City?" No, they had not, but that was where the plant was eventually built.[33] Kelly told Webb that what Oklahoma needed were stronger research universities that would help draw companies like his. Oklahoma business leaders had not done much for the academic prowess of their universities, and Webb hoped the Frontiers of Science Foundation would galvanize not only them but even the state government into doing its part.

Meanwhile, President Dwight D. Eisenhower decided to take advantage of Oklahoma's activity for his own purposes. Although he had been unable to attend the June 17 celebration, after Sputnik, he was anxious to display an interest in science and technology and to recognize state initiative. He announced he would be visiting the Sooner State to see for himself what was going on, and to use Oklahoma as an example of grassroots enterprise other states could emulate. His November address in Oklahoma City, "Our Future Security," was broadcast and televised. In his remarks, the president emphasized that the U.S. response to Sputnik had to include science education. He specifically commended Oklahoma. "Right here in Oklahoma City you have established a superb mechanism for the mobilization of needed resources to strengthen our pursuit of scientific knowledge. It is the Frontiers of Science Foundation."[34]

Reentering the National Scene

By 1958, Webb was ready to phase out of Kerr-McGee/Republic Supply and even the Frontiers of Science Foundation in favor of other activities, particularly at the national level. As much as he liked Oklahoma and enjoyed his work there, he missed the larger stage. His five-year commitment to Kerr was up. If he was not already a millionaire, he was surely moving in that direction; Kerr had lived up to his part of the deal. Webb asked Kerr if he was satisfied with his work, adding, "Have you made money on me?" Kerr-McGee Oil Industries had made the *Fortune* 500 list for the first time in 1958, and Republic Supply was in the black. Kerr replied, "Yes, I have, and I'd like to have another five-year contract." "No," Webb told him, "I've got a good man to be president. I'll be chairman of the board, and I'll work for you half time, and do a good job." He sensed that Kerr wanted to get a collar around his neck, and he was "determined" not to have his "life completely controlled by him or anyone else."[35]

Webb's desire to disengage from Kerr went beyond the matter of control. Although concerned about his independence, he was also bothered by the senator's free and easy ways in mixing politics and business, and what this might mean for his own reputation. Kerr cared not at all about complaints that decisions he made in Washington enhanced his wealth in Oklahoma. When critics questioned him on conflict of interest, he was defiant. "It happens that my personal interests coincide with those of Oklahoma. It's a happy union and I don't apologize for it." One Kerr venture that especially bothered Webb concerned a new uranium-mining activity developed during the period Webb served with Kerr-McGee. Critics charged that Kerr, in combination with Clinton Anderson, senator from New Mexico and a senior Democrat on the Joint Committee on Atomic Energy, had pressured the Atomic Energy Commission into buying practically all the uranium Kerr-McGee could produce. Webb could have become involved with the uranium-mining venture but had chosen to keep his distance.[36]

Kerr agreed that Webb should become chairman of the board of Republic Supply and go half-time overall. Jamie McWilliams, whom Webb had been grooming to take over for some time, would replace him as president. Republic Supply was now a financially profitable firm, and McWilliams was ready to take the helm.[37] At the same time, the Frontiers of Science Foundation had an excellent executive director, and the business community of Oklahoma remained engaged.

In the wake of Sputnik, Webb wanted to pursue the opportunities for national service that had come his way. One was to lead a new entity, Educational Services, Inc., which had been set up under MIT auspices. For Webb, it was a natural extension of the Frontiers of Science Foundation. Its aim was to enlist the efforts of university experts in improving educational materials and curricula in science at the high school level, a multimillion-dollar endeavor supported by foundations and government; Webb's administrative competence was needed, and he was asked to run the operation on a part-time basis. Among the professors with whom he worked was an engineer, Jerome Wiesner, whom Webb knew from his State Department days. Wiesner was also a consultant to Kerr-McGee and adviser to Senator John F. Kennedy of Massachusetts. Webb agreed to the assignment and soon was commuting back and forth to an office near MIT.[38]

As he became more involved with this venture, he served as a bridge between the work of Educational Services and that of the Frontiers of Science and other foundations. The sense of crisis due to Sputnik made everyone anxious to respond to a challenge to American science and engineering education. Through Educational Services, Webb began working closely with a number of the top scientists, engineers, and university presidents around the country. His orientation was to help the technical people with the business side of the operation, particularly distribution of materials they developed.[39]

Once it became widely known that Webb was open to national public service activities, requests and offers poured in. Able to pick and choose, he focused on domestic science education and public administration, although he went on one assignment for President Eisenhower that involved foreign travel. As a member of the Municipal Manpower Commission, established by the Ford and Sloan Foundations to study personnel and management needs in the nation's cities, Webb contacted leaders in local government, universities, and foundations. By 1960, Webb was chair of the commission, with an office in Washington along with his Educational Services office in Massachusetts. He now spent two-thirds of his time on public service activities, mostly in the East. He and his wife had grown quite fond of Oklahoma, but their hearts were really in Washington, and they decided to move back to the nation's capital in January 1960. Webb's friends were not surprised by the move; they knew he did not yet feel fulfilled.[40] He was seeking a new frontier of his own to conquer, they felt, and they hoped he would find it.

NASA:
FROM APPOINTMENT
TO APOLLO

While Webb hungered for a leadership opportunity in government, he neither sought nor particularly wanted to be administrator of the National Aeronautics and Space Administration (NASA). NASA nonetheless would turn out to be a perfect match of man and organization.

In January 1961, Webb was in Oklahoma City at a Friday Chamber of Commerce luncheon honoring Senator Robert S. Kerr, now head of the Space Committee. He was passed a note saying that Jerome Wiesner, President Kennedy's science adviser, was on the telephone. Wiesner asked if Webb would come to Washington and speak with Vice President Lyndon B. Johnson and then the president about the leadership of NASA. Completely surprised, Webb tried to back out of any meeting, but Wiesner pressured him into agreeing to be there the next Monday.[1]

Taking on NASA

Webb flew to Washington that evening and spent the weekend familiarizing himself with national space policy. Lloyd Berkner, as head of the National Academy of Sciences (NAS) Space Science Board, was in a particularly good position to brief his longtime friend on the problems any NASA administrator would face. Webb also talked to former associates in the Budget Bureau and on the Kennedy White House staff. He found that perhaps nineteen different people had been considered and rejected or had turned the offer down. Why was this job so hard to fill? Why was he now on the list?

A major problem, he discovered, was a fight between scientists (led by

Wiesner) and politicians (particularly Lyndon Johnson) over what kind of individual should head NASA, and, by extension, what direction the agency should take. Scientists wanted someone with strong technical credentials and an emphasis on space science, while Johnson preferred someone with experience in dealing with Congress and the executive branch with whom he would feel comfortable. Kennedy had tired of the squabble. He had made all other top appointments in his administration and had told Wiesner and Johnson that if they did not quickly come up with a viable candidate, he would find someone himself. When Johnson had asked Senator Kerr for suggestions, Kerr had pointed to Webb. Wiesner, independently of Johnson, had also thought of Webb, whom he knew to be comfortable with science and technology, although not a technical person himself. He broached Webb's name to Johnson, and they agreed that Webb was an able man. Johnson suggested Wiesner make the call, since the calls he himself had placed had not panned out.[2]

Another problem, Webb learned, was that NASA was in trouble with the Kennedy administration, or at least with its scientists. A task force headed by Wiesner had given Kennedy a report sharply criticizing NASA management and the Mercury space flight program; NASA was also putting too much emphasis on manned space, and not enough on space science. In addition, Webb discovered, the air force was out to make itself the nation's primary space agency, displacing NASA. Finally, he found that the president, rhetoric aside, had no space policy. Kennedy had many high priorities, particularly in foreign affairs, but NASA and space efforts were not among them. Indeed, the president had assigned space policy to Johnson not only to give the vice president something to do but to relieve himself of concerns about this area.[3]

Whoever took on NASA would be assuming a large number of conflicts and problems, with little likelihood of strong support from the White House. The NASA administrator might well have to report to Johnson. It was no wonder that many prominent individuals, including Berkner, had refused the job.[4]

By Monday morning, Webb was sure his would be another in the long line of refusals and was mainly concerned with how to turn down the president if he made the offer.

When Webb reached Johnson's office, he found the NASA deputy administrator from the Eisenhower administration, Hugh L. Dryden, waiting. A long-time government scientist and administrator, Dryden had offered his resignation but heard nothing, and was serving as acting administrator of NASA. Webb told him that he was supposed to talk with Johnson about the NASA job and said, "I don't think I'm the right person for this job because I'm not an engineer and I've never seen a rocket fly." Dryden agreed. "Well, can you tell the vice president?" Webb asked. "I don't believe he wants to listen to me on that," Dryden replied. In walked Frank Pace, who had succeeded Webb at BOB and whom Webb had helped bring to DOD while he was under secretary of state. He was scheduled to see Johnson first, so Webb asked him to tell the vice president that neither Webb nor Dryden believed Webb should be NASA administrator. Pace promised to do so, but after a short time with the vice president, he came out of his office in such a rush, it almost seemed as if he had been thrown out.[5]

Webb went in and listened to what Johnson had to say but made it clear that he would not accept the position except by direct invitation of the president. Johnson indicated that Kennedy would see him that afternoon. As Webb left, he noticed that Phil Graham, publisher of the *Washington Post,* was waiting. Webb explained his predicament and asked if Graham could extricate him from the NASA appointment. "No," said Graham, "there's just one man in town who can get you out of this, and that's Clark Clifford." As soon as he reached the privacy of another office, Webb called his former associate from the Truman years and asked him to use his influence to change the president's mind. Clifford laughed heartily and said that he was one of those who had recommended Webb. "I am not going to get you out of it."

In the early afternoon, Webb went to see the president, whom he had met casually once or twice. Kennedy immediately destroyed Webb's primary defense—namely, that NASA was a technical agency, and he was not a technical man. Kennedy said he did not want a technical man; he saw the NASA administrator as having a policy job. "There are great issues of national and international policy involved in this space program," said Kennedy. "I want you because you have been involved in policy at the White House level, State Department level."

With his reverence for the institution of the presidency, Webb could not refuse. He did have the presence of mind to ask if Kennedy had a preconceived space policy, and Kennedy said he did not—that it would be up to Webb to propose a plan. Webb also asked that Dryden continue as deputy at NASA. Kennedy agreed. Webb then said he would take the job.

The president escorted him through the White House corridors to the office of his press secretary, Pierre Salinger. He lit up a big cigar, told Salinger to "call in the press," and made a fast exit through a side door. Salinger announced to the press that James Webb, standing by his side, would be NASA's new administrator. Once Webb freed himself from the reporters, he called Patsy, who had just heard the news on the radio.[6]

In the two weeks between the Kennedy announcement and the confirmation hearings, Webb spoke with many people about NASA and U.S. space policy at an office in a small building he owned in downtown Washington. He deliberately did not go to NASA. Before subjecting himself to staff pressures, he wanted to be fully cognizant of the total NASA situation and key personnel. He did have lunch with Robert C. Seamans, Jr., associate administrator or "general manager" under T. Keith Glennan, previous NASA administrator. He quizzed him on his management views, delighting in the fact that Seamans was a Republican. This would make NASA a nonpartisan, or bipartisan, agency, he noted. He spent time with Dryden and discussed their working relationship. For the most part, however, he talked with non-NASA or ex-NASA people. For example, he invited Willis H. Shapley, the principal Budget Bureau examiner for NASA, to lunch at the University Club and got his perspective on NASA and the issues he would face.[7] He spoke by telephone with Glennan, who was out of the country, as well as with Johnson and people on Capitol Hill.

The NASA about which Webb learned was a relatively young agency, although its roots went back to 1915, when the National Advisory Committee for Aeronautics (NACA) was formed. In 1957, following Sputnik, President Eisenhower decided to make NACA, a civilian research agency, the core of the new NASA. Under Glennan, NASA had been organized from disparate research and development organizations throughout the federal government, and by February 1961 it consisted of 16,000 employees, more than 95 percent of whom worked in facilities (called centers) located in California, Ohio, Alabama, Florida, Virginia, and Maryland. Its budget stood at approximately $1 billion, 85 percent of which was spent by outside contractors. This approach of using industry and universities was a Glennan innovation and distinctly different from the NACA and military in-house laboratory tradition.[8]

A new headquarters apparatus had been formed, primarily to handle three major programs that had been organized: manned space flight, space science, and space applications. The manned space flight program was called Mercury, and the seven test pilots selected to be America's first astronauts had already been made into celebrities by having what writer Tom Wolfe called "the right stuff."[9] NASA had long-range plans for a successor program to Mercury, Project Apollo, an effort that could put an American on the moon. However, a moon landing was just one Apollo option, and Apollo itself was not an approved program. President Eisenhower had in fact scoffed at such "moon-shot" notions due to the expense and had rejected NASA proposals to include funds in its budget to start such a program.[10]

Webb pondered the institutional interests within and outside NASA. He understood NASA's Cold War origins and recognized that future opportunities rested with U.S.-USSR rivalry. Maintaining U.S. prestige among the nations necessitated matching and ultimately surpassing the Soviet Union's space successes. Webb quickly perceived that certain key political leaders were driving the U.S. space effort, a number of whom—such as Johnson and Kerr—he knew well. All seemed especially enamored of manned space flight and wanted to see an aggressive Mercury program beat the Soviets into space. With Kennedy in the White House, many members of Congress hoped the United States would expand its space program, although Kennedy's preinaugural statements on space were ambiguous.[11]

The media, including the increasingly active and influential television journalists, watched NASA carefully. Unlike the activities of other agencies in the dull, grey bureaucracy, what NASA did was highly visual—dramatic, even spectacular. Webb knew that at NASA he would be in a fishbowl and would have to deal with the media as never before. The trade press had already criticized his appointment as administrator. *Aviation Week & Space Technology*, for example, noted acidly that the Wiesner report had called for "technically competent top management." Webb failed this test, *Aviation Week* concluded, before the start.[12] *Science* magazine, a publication of the American Association for the Advancement of Science, was also disappointed.

Indeed, inside NASA various technical people questioned quietly whether Webb was up to the job. John Naugle, then a midranking scientist-administrator at NASA, recalled how many of his peers regarded Webb as "inappropriate" for a technical agency.[13] Seamans, an engineer, was less concerned about Webb's technical know-how than his administrative credentials. As one who would have to work directly with Webb, he had investigated Webb's previous tours in Washington, including the embattled stint at State. Seamans worried that Webb might want to foist upon NASA something like the secretariat he had used at that department, a device Seamans regarded as inappropriate at NASA.[14]

Whatever others thought or imagined, Webb was beginning to look forward to running the space agency. As a board member of McDonnell Aircraft, the firm building the Mercury capsule, Webb had become familiar with developments on the industry side of space. He understood Washington and the political context of NASA, having had more than his share of encounters with the Department of Defense, Congress, and the White House. Finally, he had been playing an ever larger role in scientific and technical education, and NASA would surely be involved on this front. His network of friends and contacts included many of the individuals with whom he would be dealing closely. The more he thought about it, the more he felt ready for the assignment.

Webb sailed easily through Senate confirmation hearings and on February 14, at NASA's temporary home in the Dolley Madison House on Lafayette Square, he was sworn in by Vice President Johnson. He then announced to the assembled officials that Dryden would remain as deputy administrator and Seamans would continue as associate administrator. Webb said his goal as administrator would be to work toward creating an environment within which NASA could be as innovative in the management of its programs as it was in aeronautics and space science. Management innovation would be his theme.[15]

While stressing innovation, Webb reassured NASA by the continuity of Dryden and Seamans. He immediately told both men that he wanted NASA policy leadership to be a triad. They would hammer out the big decisions together, but "each would undertake those segments of responsibility for which he was best qualified." "In effect," Webb later wrote, "we formed an informal partnership within which all major policies and programs became our joint responsibility, but with the execution of each policy and program undertaken by just one of us. This meant that everyone in and out of the agency knew all three of us would be involved in all major decisions; that with policy established, the orders for its execution could be issued by any one of us; and that, while NASA had an Administrator as a single point of final decision, to the fullest extent possible we would act together."[16] Webb took the lead as "Mr. Outside," with Seamans as "Mr. Inside" and Dryden as "Mr. Science," responsible for relationships with the national and international scientific community, but with few operating responsibilities.

The three men complemented one another. Webb was fifty-four, a hard-driving, politically adept top administrator. Dryden, at sixty-three, was an eminent scientist, a home secretary of the National Academy of Sciences, a long-term federal science administrator at NACA, then NASA, a science-statesman, wise and trustworthy. Seamans, forty-three, was a former MIT engineering professor and industrial research manager, an excellent detail man who had worked closely with Stark Draper at one point. Webb appreciated this connection, for he remembered Draper from his

Sperry days, admired him greatly, and wanted him to assist NASA.

At first skeptical of the triad concept, Dryden and Seamans went along with Webb. He customarily asked the most junior member, Seamans, what he thought of a particular issue; then he would query Dryden; finally he would give his own views. Webb believed the union of perspectives would yield better decisions. Certainly, the triad concept helped compensate for his lack of technical expertise and thus strengthened his credibility within NASA. But Dryden and Seamans would also gain from Webb's understanding of the political context; the triad concept would keep the powerful managers in the program offices and centers from making end runs or using statements by one senior official to undermine the position of another. Webb knew that NASA contained strong subcultures, one of which was NACA, whose people would rather deal with their old boss, Dryden, than with Seamans, a situation that would weaken Seamans's position as general manager. NASA leadership would speak on policy with one voice, Webb declared.

This approach also brought Webb close to Seamans's internal decisions. When Seamans spoke, he implicitly or explicitly carried the backing of the administrator and his deputy. To get that backing, Seamans was expected to bring important internal issues of general management to Webb and Dryden. For Webb, the triad concept was an article of faith—a tool for management leadership he raised to the utmost importance. It embodied Mary Parker Follett's notion of group power at the level of organizational leadership. Also, perhaps because he had seen how his own role as general manager at State had been weakened by Dean Acheson, Webb was especially determined not to let that happen with Seamans.

Nevertheless, for all his rhetoric and reliance on the triad, no one doubted—least of all Dryden or Seamans—that Webb held the cards. The way Webb immediately reached out to program managers and center directors also indicated that he did not intend to be separated from his organization by the triad concept. It was only one device for leadership he would use in managing NASA. What mattered to most NASA officials at this point was less Webb's organizational design than his policy direction. They wanted to know how the new man would deal with the big questions facing NASA and the nation.

Paving the Way for Apollo

Webb had hardly arrived at NASA when he was confronted with a major test of who was in charge of space policy. He of course was fully aware of the debate and controversy concerning manned space; his own view was that getting human beings into space was the primary means to advance the nation's capacity to operate in space in whatever way it might later choose, and that developing this capability was NASA's major mission. While he strongly supported such related activities as space science and applications such as weather and communication satellites, manned space was not only the centerpiece of the space program but the area where the U.S. position was likely to be most visibly and seriously challenged by the Soviet Union.

The situation when he arrived was this: America's only manned space program, Mercury, was seeking to place the first astronaut in space. To get to that point, NASA's technical leadership was convinced, a Mercury space capsule would have to be mated with an Atlas rocket. An initial Atlas test in mid-1960 had failed, but NASA's experts felt they were ready for another try. This course of action was opposed by both Wiesner, who had advised Kennedy prior to Webb's appointment, and by the air force, which supplied the rockets. Wiesner had felt so strongly that he had suggested to the president that he not allow "the present Mercury Program to continue unchanged for more than a very few months," and that he not "effectively endorse this program and take the blame for its possible failures." Next to Mercury, Wiesner was most critical of the nation's booster program, particularly of the inability of U.S. rockets to lift heavy payloads into space. The Russian program was way ahead, he concluded, and he criticized reliance on the Atlas rocket. Moreover, he had implied that NASA lacked "vigorous, imaginative, and technically competent top management." In effect, its judgment could not be trusted.[17]

On February 18, just four days after coming aboard, Webb was briefed by NASA officials on the Mercury dispute, and particularly the Atlas. NASA wanted Webb's okay for a test launch linking Mercury and Atlas as early as February 21. Soon after Webb gave the go ahead, he received a call from the air force asking him to reverse the decision. Atlas was a booster for missiles. If it failed in an open civilian test, the Russians might doubt the credibility of the U.S. deterrent. Webb questioned his NASA specialists about the viability of the Atlas and had Seamans check with knowledgeable individuals outside NASA and decided to go with his organization against the air force and against the views of Wiesner and the president's Science Advisory Committee (PSAC).[18]

The air force protested vehemently. Webb refused to budge. The air force argued that an improved "thick-skinned" Atlas would be ready in the not-too-distant future. The White House, aware of the controversy, chose not to intervene, making the issue a major test for Webb and NASA and their credibility with the president. Webb held that NASA had to take technical and political risks to get the U.S. space program moving forward. As he later noted, an administrator has to take account of all factors possible in making a decision. But "if you've got to take that island, you'd better get in there and take it and not wait for every last suggestion that could be made."[19]

When the Mercury-Atlas test succeeded, Webb breathed easier, as did those in NASA who had advised him. It proved an auspicious beginning for the new administrator. By backing NASA's technical judgment against that of powerful critics, not only did Webb immediately win the gratitude of NASA's professional cadre but both he and NASA won the grudging respect of the air force, which now knew Webb could not be intimidated. Finally, because NASA's technical judgment had proved correct, the air force would not be so quick next time to challenge Webb and those advising him.

In his first week of office, Webb had issued a statement to various key constituencies. Capitalizing on the Mercury-Atlas success, he pressed forward to get a new understanding with the Defense Department civilian leadership concerning respective NASA–air force roles. He had been talking with the deputy secretary of defense, Roswell L. Gilpatric, about who did what and how in space. Gilpatric had been a civilian official with the air force when Webb had been under secretary of state. Webb knew him well and had tried to get him to consider coming over to State as his replacement when he decided to leave. The trust between the two men smoothed the difficult negotiations that produced an agreement that NASA and DOD would not initiate development of space launch vehicles or boosters without mutual consent. NASA would develop the advanced technologies for space as an R&D organization, and the military services would perform necessary research as it related to the application and use of these technologies. This helped clarify roles, missions, and NASA's place as the dominant R&D agency for space. For the first time, NASA had a measure of control on air force ambitions.

Agreement was possible because Secretary of Defense Robert S. McNamara, himself trying to constrain the expansionist tendencies of the services, knew what it would cost the air force to compete with NASA in manned space development. Further, Webb and Air Force Secretary Eugene M. Zuckert had known each other for years and were friendly. A Webb-McNamara meeting confirmed a formal agreement on the basic division of labor and established the principle of continuing communication between

Webb and Gilpatric on NASA-DOD matters. McNamara thereby indicated his support for NASA's taking the lead in accelerating the nation's space program, in fact using NASA as a check on the air force. Also, both he and Webb recognized that if they failed to settle differences at the NASA-DOD level, Lyndon Johnson would have the opportunity to stake out a stronger claim for coordinating them through the National Aeronautics and Space Council.[20]

This agreement, coming on the heels of Webb's Atlas decision, blunted the air force (and to a lesser extent, DOD and Space Council) as rivals to NASA. As Webb had worked to establish State as lead agency for foreign policy over Defense and the NSC, he now established NASA over rivals in space policy.

As Webb reminisced, he saw this period as part of a ritual in which NASA and air force moved "like two strange animals . . . sparring around, smelling each other, seeing what could be done, testing each other out."[21] Regarding the Atlas decision, he explained that he "knew first of all that [the NASA specialists] were honest men and were giving [me] the very best advice they had as to what was the right thing to do. Secondly, I knew if I turned their advice down, and took advice from outside of NASA, I would have a very hard time building the confidence of the staff. Everything they said made me feel that it was safe to follow their advice." Webb said that not only was a rocket being tested, "I thought that I was being tested too."[22]

Also in his first week at NASA, Webb met with Kennedy's budget director, David Bell, his own former subordinate in the Truman administration. BOB was pressing all agencies to review their programs as quickly as possible so that Kennedy could send his requests for changes in the Eisenhower budget to Congress. The president had run on a platform of getting the country "moving again," which meant stepping up the pace of the space program. Although NASA had a ten-year plan for Apollo that could lead to a circumlunar or even moon-landing mission in the early 1970s, Webb was told that technically an earlier date was feasible. Dryden and Seamans wanted to go faster. Webb "endorsed an acceleration of NASA planning under which a lunar landing might be accomplished in the 1969–70 period, rather than 'after 1970' as specified in the NASA ten-year plan."[23] The problem was how to get funded for this goal.

NASA submitted to BOB a request for an addition of $308 million to its FY 1962 budget on March 17, a 30 percent increase over the $1.1 billion Eisenhower budget, providing funds for new technologies and facilities for manned lunar landing. Rather than propose a specific policy decision for such a move, however, Webb was "testing the waters" to see what BOB and Kennedy might accept.

BOB countered by okaying a minimal $50 million add-on, thereby deferring virtually all policy decisions until later in the year. When Webb, Dryden, and others from NASA met with Bell and his associates to discuss the BOB decision, Bell told NASA that he did not think Kennedy had enough time then to become involved in the space program to decide on NASA's request for budget changes. "You may not feel he has the time," Dryden told Bell, "but whether he likes it or not he is going to have to consider it. Events will force this."[24] Even more direct, Webb said that Bell should know better than to try to flimflam him as he would a newcomer to Washington, reminding him that he had once held Bell's job. The president made budget decisions, not the budget director, and he intended to take his case to Kennedy, as he had a right to do.[25]

Webb and Kennedy met at the White House with a number of other officials, including Bell, Wiesner, and Johnson. Webb reviewed President Eisenhower's decision to eliminate funds to proceed with manned space flight projects beyond Mercury, claiming that it "emasculated the ten-year plan before it was one year old, and unless reversed, guarantees that the Russians will, for the next ten years, beat us to every spectacular exploratory flight." He reviewed recent Russian accomplishments: they had orbited animals and lifted much heavier weights than had the United States. The present Soviet rocket had a 750,000-pound thrust, and the best the United States could do was 320,000, with Atlas. The additional funds he was requesting of BOB would allow NASA to accelerate development of "a cluster of eight Atlas engines, known as Saturn, which will have a thrust of 1,500,000 pounds" and to begin working on an even larger rocket, Nova. He argued that such booster capability would benefit DOD, as well as NASA. Finally, he requested funds to develop "a new space vehicle" that could be linked with the Saturn booster. Eisenhower had eliminated funds to begin the design studies for this effort. Such a vehicle (Apollo) was essential to go beyond Mercury "to make flights about the earth with multiple crews or trips to the vicinity of the moon."

Kennedy called another meeting in his office the next day, inviting Johnson, Edward Welsh (executive director of the National Aeronautics and Space Council), Wiesner, and Bell, but no NASA people. Bell held to the BOB position, which would have postponed decisions on Saturn and Apollo. Johnson and Welsh argued for the NASA position. Wiesner supported the start on increasing booster capacity. Kennedy decided to strike a balance between NASA and BOB, what Wiesner had suggested as a "compromise," approving add-ons for Saturn and other rocket developments and postponing decisions on the Apollo vehicle. The supplemental would be $125.7 million. The president's intent at this time was to assign the issue of developing options for manned space flight to Johnson once legislation passed, making the vice president the National Aeronautics and Space Council chair. A thorough study would be undertaken, and the president could take up the matter during the development of the FY 1963 budget in fall 1961.[26]

The mood of caution about space that prevailed among many members of the Kennedy administration changed soon after the April 12 flight of Soviet cosmonaut Yuri A. Gagarin. The Russians had once more beaten the United States to the punch and had capitalized on it. "Let the capitalist countries catch up with our country!" boasted the Soviet premier, Nikita S. Khrushchev. The Central Committee of the Communist Party claimed that in this achievement "are embodied the genius of the Soviet people and the powerful force of socialism." The USSR said that the flight showed, as had Sputnik, that the Soviet system could produce world leadership in science and technology.[27]

As head of NASA Webb issued his congratulations, but he was disappointed that Mercury had not progressed faster. He thought it obvious that the nations were competing in a race, and that the Russians were reaping enormous benefits in prestige from their performance. The "rationalistic" arguments of such critics of manned space as James R. Killian, Eisenhower's first science adviser, left him cold. "There is such a thing as national pride in accomplishment," Webb wrote him on March 28.[28]

The moon was clearly the great prize from the standpoint of a U.S.-USSR competition, and a NASA plan to reach the moon could be modified to make such a feat possible by 1969–70. But the recent Kennedy decision to give NASA half a loaf was not the kind that would win such a race. What Webb and NASA needed was a national decision to go to the moon. Because he sensed that Congress was ready for such a decision but was less sure about the president, when Webb spoke publicly, he defended the president's measured program. On the *Today Show* on April 13, he tried to reassure the country that the U.S. space program was sound and making progress. Afterward, he went to Capitol Hill to testify on NASA's budget before the House Space Committee, finding himself in the awkward position of defending a budget he did not regard as adequate. He knew the Republicans on the committee, especially Representative James Fulton of Pennsylvania, would have a field day criticizing NASA and Kennedy. On the way to the committee hearing, Webb rehearsed with his chief of legislative liaison, Paul G. Dembling, the way he would handle the attacks. He wanted to convey the message that this was a time of national decision without appearing to be forcing the president's hand, and he had to deal with Fulton, who could be nasty, without alienating him, at the same time winning sympathy for his situation from others on the committee.

Dembling remembered Webb's performance at the hearing as remarkable. Everything went as he predicted, with Fulton and Webb winding up in a shouting match in which Webb said that Fulton could try running NASA himself if he felt so sure about what was the right course to follow. During the Webb-Fulton exchange, Fulton had demanded that Webb stop holding NASA back. What are you waiting for? he asked. "I'm ready to go. Send me!" After the hearings, a reporter told Webb, "Send him [Fulton], and let me do the countdown. It'll be a fast one!"[29] Dembling saw that when Webb went to Congress, he prepared himself not just for the questions, but for the emotion and politics behind the questions, and that he seemed to anticipate and thrive on the interplay.

Kennedy scheduled a meeting in the Cabinet Room the following evening "to explore with his principal advisers the significance of the Gagarin flight and the alternatives for U.S. action." He also scheduled a not-for-attribution interview with *Time-Life* correspondent Hugh Sidey on the same evening. In preparation for the meeting, Ted Sorenson, Kennedy aide and speech writer, Bell, and Wiesner met with Webb and Dryden to discuss "the next steps in the space race." When Kennedy joined the meeting, which Sidey was allowed to attend, he was briefed on the discussions. The president asked about the possibilities of overcoming the Soviet lead, and Dryden pointed out that the Manhattan Project kind of effort required could cost as much as $40 billion. Kennedy was stunned. "The cost," he said, "that's what gets me." After further discussion, Sidey later reported, Kennedy looked at each of the men attending and said, "There's nothing more important." Webb left the meeting feeling Kennedy had been anxious to impress Sidey with his engagement in serious discussions on space policy, but that Kennedy had made no decisions.[30]

The U.S.-supported invasion of Fidel Castro's Cuba by Cuban exiles began the next day, ending almost at once in total failure. Known as the "Bay of Pigs," this foreign policy disaster left Kennedy visibly depressed and grim. Although no explicit evidence links the Bay of Pigs to Kennedy's action on space, the fiasco created an atmosphere at the White House in which the president felt he had to assert leadership right away. He talked with the vice president about space policy and the next day sent a memo asking Johnson to investigate options in space "in accordance with our conversation." "Do we have a chance of beating the Soviets by putting a laboratory in space, or by a trip around the moon, or by a rocket to land on the moon and back with a man? Is there any other space program which promises dramatic results in which we could win?" Kennedy wanted answers "at the earliest possible moment."[31] At a press conference on April 21, he said his administration was studying the options and costs of space. "If we can get to the moon before the Russians, then we should."

Webb felt he was on something of a "roller coaster." He had only recently been rebuffed by the White House on his budget request, then raked by Congress for defending the president's decision. Now Lyndon Johnson wanted to act on a new course at once. Webb was present at the crucial April 24 meeting where Johnson asked various experts and personal advisers for their views. As Wiesner recalled, "Johnson went around the room saying, 'We've got a terribly important decision to make. Shall we put a man on the moon?' And everybody said yes. And he said 'thank you' and reported to the president that the panel said we should put a man on the moon."[32]

To Webb, Johnson's approach seemed cavalier. "I'm a relatively cautious person," he recalled. "I think when you decide you're going to do something and put the prestige of the United States government behind it, you'd better doggone well be able to do it." He was not, of course, averse to a national decision to go to the moon, having himself pushed NASA toward a bolder stance in this respect. He simply wanted to contain and shape the decision to reflect favorably on NASA, the nation, and himself.

Influencing Kennedy

What Kennedy would be willing to approve depended less upon what Johnson said than upon the president's confidence in Webb and NASA, to which a key was the first Mercury flight, carrying Alan Shepard, which would take place May 5. Although short and suborbital, and not comparable to that of Gagarin, the Shepard flight was a first for the United States and must succeed, given the state of anxiety in the White House, if there was to be a presidential moon decision.

Meanwhile, during the first week of May, Webb met virtually every day with Johnson, who wanted him to commit to moving formal and official recommendations forward to Kennedy. For his part, Webb sought to maximize advantages from the decision process. After all, he was the one who would have to translate the president's decision into bricks, mortar, rockets, and astronauts. The issue for Webb was to match presidential problem with technological solution, and to use the present circumstances to make everyone look before they leaped. He wanted NASA to do some soul-searching in terms of its own technological capacity, the elected officials to examine their political will to back NASA over the long haul, and a technical and political consensus to which he as administrator could respond. Pretty sure of the outcome, he wanted the process to produce a context as well as a decision.

That there might be opposition down the road, Webb knew. Wiesner and the PSAC had little enthusiasm for the direction decision making was taking. While Wiesner would not oppose a Project Apollo to the moon, he would not want it justified on scientific grounds. Webb wrote him that he wanted to make sure that the program set in motion would have "real value and validity and [be one] from which solid additions to knowledge can be made."[33] On the same day, Webb set up a study team within NASA to investigate "on an urgent basis and in detail, the requirements for a program aimed at a 1967 manned lunar landing." He told Johnson he wanted to wait for this group, which was to draw on total NASA resources, to report to him. Exasperated, Johnson came "close to demanding" that Webb make a specific recommendation in a conclusive way rather than discuss options and hold back until yet another study was done, possibly thirty days distant. But, after a two-hour meeting with Johnson on May 3, Webb was still not convinced that NASA and the United States were ready to take steps of the dimensions the developing consensus seemed to indicate. Johnson was pushing NASA, saying that if the United States was capable of beating the Soviet Union to the moon, then NASA officials should advocate a lunar landing program.

All evidence, including classified intelligence, made Webb feel that a lunar landing was "the first project we could assure the president that we could do and do ahead of the Russians, or at least had a reasonable chance to do."[34] When he told Johnson this, the vice president came back with "Are you willing to undertake this? Are you ready to undertake it?" Webb said he was, "but there's got to be political support over a long period of time, like ten years, and you and the President have to recognize that we can't do this kind of thing without that continuing support." Johnson related what Webb had told him to Senator Kerr, who said that "if Jim Webb says we can land a man on the moon and bring him safely home, then it can be done."[35] Because Webb had not played the advocate role in the Johnson discussions, his "yes" was taken all the more seriously.

Thus, when Shepard made America's first manned flight, the decision process had moved to a critical point. The Shepard flight was a success. At an afternoon press conference, Kennedy announced that he was going to accelerate the space program and that he planned to undertake "a substantially larger effort in space."[36] Webb's stock with the president soared with the Shepard achievement, not only because of its technical success but because Webb had been right during a preflight debate over media coverage. Some advisers had urged Kennedy to close the flight to the media, lest the United States advertise another failure. Still reeling from the Bay of Pigs fiasco, Kennedy had worried about another blow to U.S. (and his own) prestige. But Webb had said that the flight would succeed and the country would gain from having an open space program, in contrast to the closed Soviet space effort. As he predicted, the technical success, openly observed by all, gave the country, NASA, and Kennedy a boost they needed.

Early Saturday morning, the day after the flight, Webb, Dryden, Seamans, and Abe Silverstein (head of NASA's Office of Space Flight) met at the Pentagon with McNamara, Gilpatric, the newly appointed director of defense research and engineering, Harold Brown, his deputy director, John Rubel, and BOB's Willis Shapley. Glenn Seaborg of the Atomic Energy Commission was also present for a portion of the meeting. The group agreed that prestige as measured by other nations was a factor in national undertakings and that large space projects "reflect the capacity and the will of the nation to harness its technological, economic, and managerial resources for a common goal." For this reason, they felt, "a successful space program validates your claim to other capacities." Webb argued that the overall industrial strength of the United States gave it a good chance to overcome the Soviet lead.[37]

At the end of the meeting, McNamara suggested that Seamans, Shapley, and Rubel meet over the remainder of the weekend to consolidate the decisions reached and to put them in the form of a memo of recommendations for Johnson to give to the president, working from a draft Rubel had been preparing for him. Webb agreed, adding that he personally wished to be involved in writing the memo. Seamans, Shapley, and Rubel went to work, while Webb coordinated plans with White House staff for appropriate ceremonies at the White House and State Department for Shepard. Seamans kept Webb informed of progress on the memo, which was taking the form of a thirty-page report, replete with background information. While Seamans concentrated on material regarding the lunar landing, Shapley focused on financial aspects, and Rubel on the DOD portions. The next day, after Webb met with members of the Shepard family to make sure all the accommodations were in order, he and Patsy Webb took them to dinner.

At 10:00 P.M., Webb joined the memo-writing group and spent the next few hours not only editing the text but also making substantive changes. Seamans recalled Rubel's draft, with which they had started, had been prepared from a Defense Department perspective and had to be adapted to NASA's civilian point of view as well as written for a presidential decision. Having prepared many documents for presidential consumption when with Truman, Webb knew how to craft such a memo—which was taking the length and form of a report—and was persuasive in arguing for necessary changes. "Webb was masterful in his discussions with John Rubel," Seamans recalled, "and by 2:00 A.M., there was agreement on the report." Webb signed off, his name going above that of McNamara, who would see the document and affix his signature later that morning.[38]

The four men were all exhausted from the events of the weekend. After Shapley and Rubel wished Seamans and Webb good night, Webb offered to take Seamans home, since he was without his car. He also asked the two secretaries who had labored conscientiously on the successive drafts of the report if they needed assistance in getting home. One said she did have a problem. "No problem at all," said Webb, "you come with Seamans and me." He drove her home through a hard rain, well beyond the District, and the three waited in the car until the downpour let up. Webb finally dropped Seamans off at 3:30 A.M. and went home to bed.[39]

A few hours later, Seamans hand-delivered the memo to McNamara, who signed off, then took it directly to Johnson. The vice president and his staff passed it on unchanged to Kennedy later in the day. In the memorandum, classified secret, Webb and McNamara argued that manned flights in space could enhance national prestige. "It is man, not merely machines, in space that captures the imagination of the world." "All large-scale projects require the mobilization of resources on a national scale. They require the development and successful application of the most advanced technologies. Dramatic achievements in space therefore symbolize the technological power and organizing capability of a nation. It is for reasons such as these that major achievements in space contribute to national prestige."[40]

The memorandum set forth guidelines for the program, "Project Apollo," which called for considerable rocket development. The major change from earlier discussions in this area was the provision for concurrent development of two types of boosters, one liquid fuel and the other solid fuel. The air force would develop the solid-fuel rocket to specifications set by NASA, and by 1964 NASA would choose which system to use for the moon voyage. The program also provided funds for developing as soon as possible: (1) the spacecraft for the lunar flight and for the unmanned flights to survey the moon prior to manned landings; (2) a nuclear rocket; (3) satellites for global communications; and (4) satellites for weather observations.

While emphasizing Apollo, manned space, and satellite applications, the memorandum indicated the need to augment space science activities, including support of universities and education. Webb had calculated that the more he put into the memo for presidential consideration, the more leeway he would have later, after the decision. Being involved in the document's writing had allowed him to maximize his advantages.

While the Webb-McNamara memorandum reflected group decision making, Apollo made NASA the dominant agency in America's drive for space supremacy. Although the air force had a role via solid-fuel rockets, it had to meet NASA requirements. Also, in going beyond a lunar program, the proposal reflected Webb's strong desire to run a balanced program with Apollo as its focus but including many other elements. Kennedy talked to a number of his advisers about the memorandum, but as National Security Adviser McGeorge Bundy recalled, "The president had pretty much made up his mind to go" and was not by then particularly interested in hearing arguments to the contrary. "Kennedy approved the program exactly as it had been set out in the Webb-McNamara memorandum."[41]

The Webb Agenda

No one understood or appreciated at the time that, while the decision to go to the moon was unfolding, a separate decision process—mainly in Webb's own mind—was going apace. This was the personal agenda Webb had brought to NASA—a mission to use science and technology, and now Apollo, to strengthen the United States educationally and economically, the Oklahoma Frontiers of Science effort writ large. It had been germinating in discussions with Berkner over the years, and Webb had a few aides in NASA designing it while the much larger planning exercise of Apollo moved ahead.

Much of what Webb had in mind, though still quite inchoate, would eventually be incorporated in an activity called the Sustaining University Program (SUP). At one level, it served to win support from the community of scientists and universities not favorably disposed toward Apollo.[42] But much more than that, it maximized the benefits of space for Earth in terms of research, education, and economic development. Walter McDougall has called the fully developed concept Webb's program for a "Space Age America."[43] Webb had made sure the recommendation memo to Kennedy provided room for him to launch this effort along with Apollo.

He then communicated his agenda, a grand mix of noble vision and pork-barrel politics, to Vice President Johnson in a way he would understand. He pointed out to Johnson that both Albert Thomas, chair of the House Appropriations subcommittee responsible for NASA's budget, and George Brown, friend of Johnson and Texas political ally, "were extremely interested in having Rice University make a real contribution" to the Apollo program. Noting that Rice had thirty-eight hundred acres of land available and that NASA needed to establish a new research facility for Apollo, Webb told Johnson that he believed it would serve the national interest to build up a strong science and engineering center in the Southwest, similar to those that had grown up around Harvard and MIT in New England and around the University of California on the West Coast. Noting the availability of easy water transportation of heavy rockets by barge to Florida, Webb saw the Houston location near Rice (which Thomas represented) as very attractive, adding that George Brown had been extremely helpful in bringing this possibility to his attention.[44]

Webb went on to point out that Berkner (who would be pressing the NAS–Space Science Board to endorse Apollo) was establishing a $100 million research center in Dallas, while "Senator Kerr and those interested with him in the Arkansas, White, and Red River System" were pushing to open the whole Arkansas/Oklahoma area and develop potential for Mississippi. The Dallas-Houston axis "would provide a great impetus to the intellectual and industrial base of this whole region." Webb's vision now enlarged to a national complex including high technology centers: "In California, running from San Francisco down through the new University of California installation at San Diego [LaJolla], another center around Chicago with the University of Chicago as a pivot, a strong Northeastern arrangement with Harvard, M.I.T. . . . some work in the Southeast perhaps revolving around the research triangle in North Carolina (in which Charlie Jonas as the ranking minority member on Thomas's Appropriations Subcommittee would have an interest), and with the Southwestern complex rounding out the situation."[45]

Webb's administrative ambition was racing. The memo reflected his wish to use NASA as a vehicle to move the whole nation to a "new frontier" of enhanced technology-based educational and economic development. Not only was this space policy meshed with industrial policy, it was a glimpse at the way Webb was moving to broaden the political support for his agency, using Apollo.

Two days later, on May 25, Kennedy spoke to the nation. In a speech titled "Urgent National Needs," billed as his second State of the Union message, Kennedy told Congress of his belief "that this nation should commit itself to achieving the goal, before this decade is out, of landing a man on the moon and returning him safely to the earth. No single space project in this period will be more impressive to mankind, or more important for the long-range exploration of space; and none will be so difficult or expensive to accomplish."[46]

Webb was one of a very few who knew about a last-minute change made to Kennedy's speech. An earlier draft had set 1967 as the date of arrival on the moon. As discussions between NASA and the White House concerning the speech proceeded, Webb saw the need for what he called an "administrative discount," a margin of flexibility weighted against what the technical experts thought was possible, just in case something went wrong. He did not want the prestige of the nation (much less his own reputation) resting on an overly optimistic deadline. The words had been changed. Webb's deadline and the goal for the nation became "before this decade is out."[47]

Webb also had raised the "final" estimated cost for the lunar landing that NASA projected privately for the president. After many studies had placed the costs at different levels, NASA's technologists came up with an estimate of from $8 billion to $12 billion, which looked much too low to Webb. Because no one could anticipate all contingencies, he enlarged the figure NASA sent Kennedy to $20 billion for the first lunar journey. As Seamans recalled, these changes were typical of the way Webb applied his "generalist" judgment to estimates given him by technical specialists, using administrative realism to counter technical optimism in setting Apollo's deadline and price.[48]

Now, having maneuvered and shaped the decision to go to the moon, all Webb had to do was implement it.

LAUNCHING A
STRONGER NASA

President Kennedy's decision to go to the moon changed a great deal for James Webb. It set a national goal with, upon the ensuing congressional endorsement, an initial political consensus. It was a national strategy within which Webb could perform as master tactician. But the NASA administrator was not sanguine about the honeymoon lasting the full decade. He knew his time was limited. While others used the word *commitment* in association with the president's decision, Webb did not. "I felt [Kennedy] had given us the authority to start," he recalled later. "It was up to [us] to go as far and as fast as we could, and bid for his support by doing a good job."[1]

Enlarging Apollo's Support

For Webb, the internal actions of the administrator were governed by the external circumstances, and vice versa. He had multiple constituencies, beginning with the president. The most important fact about Kennedy's decision, for Webb, was that it linked the president's prestige, possible political fate, and place in history with his own. Webb had wanted a direct relation with Kennedy from the outset but had found himself one of a group of officials dealing with him. Now, Webb was Kennedy's prime instrument for getting to the moon. He depended on Webb to make him look good, and that gave Webb power vis-à-vis Kennedy.

It also settled a matter important to both men—the role of Lyndon Johnson in space policy. Webb was perfectly willing to deal with Johnson and let him take credit and think he had power, but he did not want Johnson running NASA. When Webb talked with the president about Johnson and reporting relationships in general, Kennedy said he should deal directly with him and the budget director. Webb suggested a way the president could keep Johnson occupied on important matters, yet make sure he did not become a problem to them: make clear to the vice president that Kennedy would set the agenda of the Space Council. No one would lose face. Kennedy agreed, and Johnson and the Space Council were soon completely occupied with communication satellite policy.[2] Also, Senator Robert Kerr, chair of the Senate Space Committee, "performed a great service for me," Webb recalled. "He told Johnson this story about my independence [the Webb-Kerr relation in Oklahoma], how I wouldn't be kicked around, which meant Johnson never tried."[3]

Apollo also raised Webb's bargaining capacity with Congress. He felt he "had as much capability and power to make trouble for an individual member of Congress as he had to make trouble for me."[4] Armed with a national mission, Webb was now in charge of the most visible front of the technological Cold War with the USSR. Moreover, he would have lots of money to dispense. How and where that money was spent mattered to Congress. As Webb put it, the legislators "were interested in selling their influence with the space program for other kinds of benefits they could get in their districts and committees." Webb had to tell them that he was "going to get this job done." To do that he had to "hold enough power within [his] own right personally to make sure it would be done," which meant excluding other influential people from decisions.[5]

Above all, he had to succeed—and to appear successful.[6] He had to convince influential legislators (as well as others) that he "knew what [he] was doing and that [he] could be a winner. They would not support a loser." The most significant man in the Senate for Webb was Kerr, who was, said Webb, a "protector of NASA. But he was also a pressure point. His style was to cooperate with people who cooperated with him. You had to convince Kerr that you could help his image and you could help him with the White House. You had to offer him something. And, if you could not offer him what he wanted, you had to offer him something else instead."[7] Shortly after the May 25 presidential announcement, Webb made it a point to go to Oklahoma to help Kerr stage a meeting on space policy with various local and regional leaders so the folks back home could see that he was a major figure in Washington in this glamorous new field.

In the House, the most important person for Webb was Albert Thomas, chair of the Appropriations Subcommittee that set NASA's budget and a Texan who also expected an "exchange" for his political support. In dealing with Thomas and others in Congress, Webb studied the incentives that made them move this way or that on space. He also knew that he would be asking for huge sums and that he could help make his case that every penny was needed if he did not appear to be living luxuriously as administrator. Instead of using the limousine to which his position entitled him, he drove in an old Checker cab, painted black. "It's the little things that can get you into trouble in Washington," he told his friends. As he prepared to build a multibillion-dollar agency, he acted—at least around some in Congress—the frugal country boy.

Politicians were only one of Webb's constituencies. Although he had said he would march under the banner of management innovation, he also emphasized continuity in his first months at NASA so that he could absorb information from his organization. "To be innovative," he said, "you have to start somewhere. What I needed to know from NASA was what had worked in the past. I needed to know what NASA people knew. But I brought to NASA a whole bunch of theory and doctrine."[8] The emphasis on continuity shifted after the Apollo decision to one of financial and organizational change.

Webb's immediate staff was small. He began with his personal secretary and executive assistant and gradually expanded. His executive assistant, R. P. "Rip" Young, became Webb's extra eyes and ears; as the job enlarged, Young brought in other people to augment the flow of information. They became a secretariat, but a much smaller and less threatening version than Webb had created at the State Department, intended to keep track of information coming into the administrator's office and make sure it was channeled to those who could benefit from it. Webb wanted each member of the triad to be informed of whatever came in to any one of the three. He also wanted the secretariat to keep after the program heads to get them to make sure information came up to the policy leaders that should come up, in return for information that came down.[9]

Working closely with the leadership triad on all substantive decisions, Webb met regularly and as necessary with Hugh Dryden and Robert Seamans, each of whom had his own area of responsibility.[10] Webb's outside political role was reflected in those within headquarters with whom he worked most closely—Paul G. Dembling, who was in charge of the Office of Legislative Affairs, and Hiden T. Cox (later Julian Scheer), in charge of Public Information. These were Webb's prime points of contact between NASA and Congress, and NASA and the media.[11]

This topside emphasis on congressional and public relations was new to NASA, as was Webb's use of a succession of consultants. His predecessor, T. Keith Glennan, had used consultants in a formal way, for management decisions and organizational planning. Webb eschewed such uses. Perhaps arrogantly, he thought he knew more about management than any consultant. Those he used gave him ideas about program substance or helped him keep tabs on what was going on in his organization. The latter group he called "scouts."[12] His principal scout was Arthur Raymond, retired top executive from Douglas Aircraft, who joined NASA in 1961 and stayed throughout Webb's tenure, roaming the NASA system and providing him "early warnings" on developing problems.[13]

Webb's administrative style combined the formal and informal. At the apex of a pyramid, he respected the chain of command where appropriate but ignored it at other times. As well as part of the triad, informally he was at the center of a wheel whose spokes carried information both ways; he conversed on the phone with program directors and center directors, making it clear they could see him as needed. Webb proclaimed to all he encountered that he would "use the best administrative theory and doctrine we can get." He realized that neither Congress nor the scientists and engineers in NASA had any idea what he was talking about, but he said it anyway. What Congress wanted, said Webb, was "a man they could trust who could get the job done and would make them look good." "Management innovation" and "orderliness in administration" were his flags. He wanted those who observed NASA from outside to have confidence in the agency rather than to look "askance" at it.[14]

In dealing with both his internal and external constituents, Webb moved quickly but with forethought. Government involved separation of powers and checks and balances, and one of the powers was bureaucracy. It provided administrative competence, organizational efficiency. As a fourth branch of government, it had to be accountable, although this did not necessarily mean Webb was going to clear everything he did with others. He took the view that people should judge him by his results rather than by his plans. He did not want senior officers telling him what to do. "I figured it was my responsibility to keep going until the President stopped me," he said, "and to have a program he would want to approve rather than disapprove."[15]

While Webb told his political superiors what he thought they needed to know, he strove for the discretion he regarded as necessary to succeed. This meant he had to satisfy a variety of internal and external constituents that they could realize their interests through him. At the same time, he had to take risks: do what he thought was necessary, justify his actions afterward, and personally absorb the political heat. In the year or so following Kennedy's Apollo speech, Webb made rapid-fire decisions, taking advantage of his honeymoon with political superiors to propel NASA on its trajectory toward the moon, as well as to initiate other items on his agenda.

An early example involved the contract for the guidance system, one of the first and most important Apollo contracts. Although Webb had set up an elaborate Source Evaluation Board procedure to insulate major procurement decisions from external political pressures and to emphasize considerations of technical merit, he was not about to let procedures hold up progress. In this case, he was certain that the best person in the world to design a navigation system to the moon was Stark Draper, leader of MIT's Instrumentation Laboratory. As a former Draper associate, Seamans also saw him as a unique talent, unsurpassed. He had done extraordinary work on guidance systems for the military. Designing the Apollo navigation system, a completely original task, could not be allowed to fail. Before making the final decision, Webb asked Draper if he could really develop a space navigation system that could get a man to the moon and back safely. Draper said he was so confident that he would be willing to make the voyage himself, if Webb would guarantee the propulsion system. That was enough for Webb. In August, NASA awarded a sole-source contract for the Apollo navigation system to MIT. Industry complained, but the process moved forward.[16]

The Apollo decision also meant a vast expansion in NASA facilities. In August, NASA acquired 125 square miles of land on Merritt Island (Cape Canaveral), Florida, for a spaceport, which would eventually grow into a new NASA center headed by Kurt Debus. The next month, NASA selected Michoud, Louisiana, as the production facility for Saturn rockets, and debated the location of the biggest prize of all—the Manned Spacecraft Center (MSC), whose mission would be to develop the spacecraft and create the complex of technical facilities for spacecraft research and development, astronaut training, and flight operations.

When Webb decided to locate the MSC in Texas, he crafted a memo to the president that set forth the technical criteria and explained why a site outside Houston was chosen. Kenneth O'Donnell, presidential appointments secretary and a key Kennedy political operative who favored a Massachusetts site, recalled that "Webb made an excellent argument. The President can read. He said, 'It's a good decision. Let's go through with it.'"[17] Webb told Robert Gilruth, chief of the Space Task Group at the Langley

Center in Virginia, who would be MSC's director, that he and many others would be moving to Texas. He mentioned the technical factors in the decision, but, as Gilruth recalled, also asked, "What did Harry Byrd [senator from Virginia] ever do for you, Bob?" When Gilruth replied, "Nothing," Webb responded, "That's what I mean. We've got to get the power. We've got to get the money, or we can't do this program. And the first thing, we got to move to Texas. Texas is a good place for you to operate. It's in the center of the country. You're on salt water. And it happens to be the home of [Albert Thomas] the man who is the controller of the money."[18]

The contract with MIT, the first of many important contracts NASA let in 1961 for Apollo, was unusual in going sole source to a university. Most of NASA's work would go on a competitive basis to industry, with the bulk of the major contract decisions for Apollo made between September and December. For example, each of the three stages to the Saturn rocket went to a separate firm: in September, the second stage went to North American Aviation; in December, the first stage went to Boeing and the third stage to Douglas Aircraft. In between came the most controversial decision: the contract for the command and service module, the Apollo spacecraft.

The Source Evaluation Board, made up of technical experts drawn from within NASA, in November recommended the Martin Company as "the outstanding source for the Apollo prime contractor." Webb, Dryden, and Seamans, as was their policy, questioned the board carefully, then met in Webb's office for the final decision. When Gilruth and others who would be directing spacecraft development were brought in and asked to comment, they protested the board recommendation, indicating that they spoke also for a number of astronauts; all felt that Martin knew how to build missiles, not machines that flew men. Their choice, rated second by the Source Evaluation Board, was North American, which was able to build "flying machines" and had demonstrated exceptional work on experimental aircraft.[19]

Webb said he wanted to sleep on it over the weekend. His dilemma was that NASA was divided, that his policy was to spread contracts around to diversify the agency's industrial and political base and enhance competition, and that his scouts told him North American was already "strained to the limit" with the Saturn second stage. Should NASA's largest single contract award go to the contractor that already had the most NASA work? Webb had been pressured by Fred Black, North American lobbyist, who had promised North American would expand operations in Oklahoma, thereby helping Senator Kerr—and thus Webb. Webb placed a call to his former

Truman administration associate Robert Lovett, his predecessor as under secretary of state, now a member of the North American board. Could North American assume another huge and technically demanding job? Lovett told him he could "count on this company." On Monday morning Webb told his associates he was going with North American.[20]

Choosing a top technical manager to direct Apollo was another crucial decision, one of the most important Webb made in 1961. Throughout the spring and summer, Webb, Dryden, and Seamans discussed possibilities among themselves and with contacts outside NASA. Two candidates emerged within NASA, Abe Silverstein, head of the Office of Space Flight, and Wernher von Braun, director of the Marshall Space Flight Center (MSFC) in Huntsville, Alabama. Unfortunately, the potential tension between the two men, owing to Silverstein's Jewish heritage and von Braun's service to Hitler in World War II, was a matter that could not be avoided, at least in private conversations. But which should head manned space? Von Braun was summarily rejected by Dryden, who told Webb and Seamans that they could select him, if they insisted, but he would submit his resignation the same day. Webb decided to talk to Silverstein. The conversation did not go well. As Webb saw it, Silverstein wanted to be a czar with virtually complete autonomy, especially in regard to Seamans. Webb looked elsewhere within government. The most successful recent large-scale project was the navy's Polaris, and the deputy to Admiral William Raborn, head of Polaris, had been Captain Levering Smith. The NASA leaders had a good discussion with Smith, and it looked as though he was going to join NASA as Apollo director. But as soon as the navy found out, it promoted Smith to admiral and gave him an assignment he could not refuse.[21]

The NASA triad searched further that fall, outside government, and Seamans came up with D. Brainerd Holmes, of Radio Corporation of America, with whom he had worked in the past and who, at age forty, was considered one of the top technical executives in the country. Holmes had been directing the design and construction of the Ballistic Missiles Early Warning System, which involved massive installations in northern Alaska, Greenland, and Scotland. Executives in industry whose judgments Webb trusted spoke highly of him. Webb met Holmes and decided that he had qualifications that made him a good candidate. By November 1, Holmes was at NASA, taking a huge cut in salary in his move from the private to the public sector as director of the new Office of Manned Space Flight (OMSF).

Reorganizing NASA

At the same time, Webb had reorganized NASA for its new responsibilities, especially Apollo, by creating four program offices: Advanced Research and Technology, Space Science, Applications, and Manned Space Flight. The Office of Advanced Research and Technology essentially encompassed the former NACA enterprise (i.e., the older aeronautics centers). Webb had carved the space component of NASA—mostly under Silverstein's Office of Space Flight—into three rapidly growing entities. That Science and Applications now enjoyed an organizational status equal to that of Manned Space Flight was a deliberate move by Webb to check and balance the inevitable power its funding would give OMSF and to emphasize his view that NASA was more than Apollo. Seaman's authority under the reorganization was greatly enhanced: all program *and* center directors reported to him, and he controlled budgets.[22] When the reorganization was publicly announced, its justification came in the jargon of administrative rationality. At issue in fact was power. Webb had pulled power upward from the centers to headquarters, especially to the triad, to counter centrifugal forces operating at midlevel and to provide a measure of balance among NASA programs. He wanted internal control at this point, when so much was getting started, including a third manned program.

When Holmes joined NASA, he had two manned programs to run—Mercury, well under way, and Apollo, still being planned. As of December 7, he had a third, not even conceived at the time of Kennedy's decision—Gemini. The reasons for Gemini were primarily technical, but they also served Webb's need to consider the political base for Apollo.

Planning for Apollo indicated that "the leap from Mercury to Apollo was prodigious." Apollo would need three astronauts, instead of Mercury's one, to maneuver the large spacecraft; furthermore, one gigantic spaceship/rocket (the proposed Nova) capable of going to and returning from the moon could not be developed in time to meet the president's deadline. This "direct ascent" approach would have to give way to a "rendezvous" method: a smaller (but still large) system would be launched and somehow reassembled outside the earth's gravity for the remainder of the voyage. For the lunar mission to be successful, Apollo's astronauts would need to learn how to use new radars and computers to follow and link up equipment, or "dock."

For Gilruth, it was too risky for NASA to wait the projected four years between the end of Mercury and the first flight tests of the Apollo system. A program had to be devised to give the astronauts experience in all aspects of lunar flight, especially rendezvous. The solution was Gemini, which would use a two-man capsule.[23] In announcing the Gemini decision in December 1961, NASA officially proclaimed it "the training program for Apollo," although Webb privately regarded it as "insurance against a possible Apollo failure." "Mercury would not have led us very far," he noted. "With Gemini, we would have learned a great deal about spaceflight and its capability. If we had an insuperable obstacle and had to stop Apollo, if our equipment wouldn't work or it is too difficult a job, if we really didn't see how to overcome some difficulty in getting to the moon, we would have still done the next most important thing."[24]

Also, Webb appreciated the political dividends. Gemini would keep NASA visible during the hiatus between Mercury and the first Apollo flights, the perfect research and development laboratory for NASA's technologists—an evolutionary machine from which they could learn in moving toward Apollo. McDonnell, the contractor for Mercury, would build it. Webb explained the rationale of Gemini to the president and Congress, who went along with the decision.[25]

While Webb reshaped NASA for Apollo, he also launched what would be known inside and outside NASA as *his* university program. Scientific consultants told him in summer 1961 that the country had scientific needs but questioned NASA's "authority" to supply such requirements. Webb's "eyes lit up," John Simpson, a University of Chicago space scientist, recalled. He said, "That's my job to worry about that. I'll see to it that our charter let's us do what we need to do."[26] Webb's idea of needs went beyond only what was good for science. He wrote Lee DuBridge, president of Caltech, that billions would be channeled through NASA (much of it to the West Coast) over the coming decade to advance science and technology at the most rapid rate, and "to feed it back into our national economy and the fabric of our national life." He sought to interest DuBridge in helping him find a way by which NASA-derived technology could energize urban development, water resources, energy, communications, management, and life sciences. "I know that the lunar objective causes some problems to you," but it would prove its worth "even if we never make the lunar landing."[27] DuBridge and other university presidents to whom Webb communicated no doubt wondered what the exuberant NASA administrator was up to. What did such earthbound issues as urban development, water resources, and energy have to do with going to the moon? Was Webb running NASA or the whole government? And what did universities have to do with all this?

When Webb spoke in general terms to a number of key legislators about a new "university program," few paid much attention or raised objections. They all had universities in their states and districts. If Webb wanted to expand his work with universities, why not? Of course, they wanted to make sure there was sufficient geographical spread in the program. Webb reassured them. This would not be an elitist program.

NASA's revised budget included new authority for NASA to provide facilities to universities, thus remedying one worry Webb's scientific consultants had raised. When the November NASA reorganization was announced, an existing Office of Grants and Research Contracts was moved under Homer Newell, head of the new Office of Space Science. Webb told Newell he would reprogram $12 million from the budget to get the Sustaining University Program (SUP) started this fiscal year and would see about enlarging the program in the next.

Webb knew that President Kennedy wanted to increase funding for science education, including higher education, that Jerome Wiesner had told him of a need for thousands of new scientists and engineers to be produced in the 1960s, and that Kennedy had been rebuffed by Congress in his attempt to increase the number of students trained in science, engineering, and mathematics through other agencies. Webb asked him to consider NASA as an alternative vehicle, noting that NASA was being criticized by Wiesner and others for taking too many scientists and engineers away from more "worthwhile" endeavors. Well, Webb said, he would "fill the tank from which we were drawing." He asked Kennedy to back him up when the budget director challenged him on this, and, as Webb saw it, the president gave him the "go ahead."[28]

In late November, Webb and his budget assistant met with Budget Director David Bell to discuss the next year's budget. Alerted by his staff that Webb had reprogrammed money in 1961 to get into the university business and was proposing to extend its domain in 1962 to the tune of $30 million, Bell asked Webb what this was all about. Webb defended the effort, and when he finished told his assistant to "bury" the university funds within the general NASA budget request. No line item for facility grants, institutional research grants, or training grants (fellowships) would appear, in contrast to the original NASA proposal sent to the Budget Bureau. SUP would be made less visible to Congress and would be funded again through reprogrammed funds. Webb said he had Kennedy's sanction for the program, which Bell could check with the president himself. Although Bell did not debate Webb, he asked for a letter fully explaining his program.[29]

Neutralizing Opposition

The Apollo honeymoon ended in 1962 as challenges to Webb's decisions began. During the first half of the year a spirited technical debate took place within NASA over whether to rendezvous near the earth or in orbit around the moon. Aware of the debate, Webb chose not to micromanage but to make sure technological choices benefited by processes giving all sides a chance to have their say, recognizing this as one of those times when waiting a bit longer would produce a better decision. His desire for consensus also reflected the fact that the technical debate on mode had gradually taken on an institutional complexion. Slowly but steadily Houston solidified around Lunar Orbit Rendezvous (LOR). Huntsville, led by von Braun, favored Earth Orbit Rendezvous (EOR). Because NASA could only go to the moon with its two Apollo development centers in tandem, with Houston responsible for the spaceship and Huntsville the rocket, Webb allowed enormous amounts of NASA time to be poured into the mode issue, a choice generally viewed as superseded in importance only by the president's lunar decision itself. Finally, von Braun announced that Marshall was going to go with LOR, which he felt offered "the highest confidence factors of successful accomplishment within this decade."[30] His shift essentially ended the debate within NASA.

Pleased with the process, Webb accepted the judgment of his organization only to discover that the president's science adviser, Jerome Wiesner, felt LOR was "the worst mistake in the world," one that was "risking these guys like mad." Throughout the summer and into the fall, NASA and Wiesner's office debated the technological choice. President Kennedy, Wiesner, and various dignitaries toured NASA facilities in September. At Huntsville, von Braun showed them a mock-up of the first stage of the moon rocket, the *Saturn 5.* "I understand you and Jerry disagree about the right way to go to the moon," the president said. "Yes, that's true," said von Braun. "We were having an intelligent discussion," Wiesner later recalled. "I was starting to tell Kennedy why I thought they were wrong when Jim Webb came up, saw us talking, thought we were arguing, and began hammering away at me for being on the wrong side of the issue. And then I began to argue with Webb." The vociferous dispute occurred in front of the president and the media accompanying him. On the way back to the president's plane, Sir Solly Zuckerman, science adviser to the British prime minister, who was part of the entourage, asked Kennedy how the dispute would come out in the end. "Jerry's going to lose, it's obvious," said Kennedy. "Why?" the Englishman inquired. "Webb's got all the money," Kennedy said, "and Jerry's only got me."[31]

In October, Webb informed Wiesner that NASA had studied the mode decision long enough and was going ahead. This would mean award of a contract to Grumman Engineering Corporation to build a small lunar module that would detach from the mother ship circling the moon, land on the moon, and then return to the mother ship. It would be up to Wiesner to stop him. In early November, Webb and Wiesner met in a tense confrontation before Kennedy in the White House, where Webb cast the issue in terms of who was in charge of getting to the moon. "Mr. Webb," the president said, "you're running NASA—you make the decision."[32] On November 7, Webb announced that the LOR program would go forward.

Webb fought internal as well as external battles during 1962–63, at times simultaneously, reinforcing his authority within as well as outside the organization. One of his most difficult internal problems concerned the original seven Mercury astronauts. As celebrities, they had a constituency of their own that included the president. They had signed contracts with *Life* magazine (prior to Webb's appointment) allowing them to supplement their government incomes with "exclusive" stories. In May word seeped back to Webb that the astronauts might be overstepping the bounds of propriety. They were being offered free homes by real estate interests in Houston, and some of them had no intention of living in the houses but intended to sell them and pocket the money. Webb anticipated a major threat to NASA's image unless he reigned in the astronauts, fast. When Kennedy heard about the venture, and that some media people were trying to link the White House to the astronauts' financial rewards, he called Webb, saying he could not understand how the White House had been dragged into the affair. Webb said he did not know how either, "but I can tell you how to get out of it. Just tell [the media] the Administrator of NASA is handling that."[33] Webb summoned the seven astronauts and Gilruth, their nominal superior at Houston, to Washington. Shortly thereafter, word went out that the astronauts had refused the gift of homes.[34]

The Mercury astronauts, however, had one more challenge for Webb. After the Gordon Cooper flight brought the Mercury series to a close in May 1963, the seven astronauts pressed for "one more" Mercury flight in the gap pending the first Gemini flight, not scheduled for some time. Webb told them that it was time to turn NASA's attention to the next step in going to the moon—Gemini. When the astronauts informed Webb they were going to take their case to the president, he told them to go ahead. He soon got a call from Kennedy. "You know who's going to make this decision, don't you?" he asked. Webb replied, "I think I do," and the president said, "You're going to make it." Webb then sent Seamans down to Houston to publicly state—in front of the astronauts—that Mercury was over, and it was on to Gemini.[35]

Far more serious than the astronauts as an internal test of Webb's authority was his relation to the man he had chosen to lead the Apollo project, D. Brainerd Holmes. Although Webb presided over the four divisions of NASA, Holmes's division, the Office of Manned Space Flight, controlled at least three-quarters of the budget, with Mercury, Gemini, and Apollo under its aegis, as well as by far the most people. Aggressive, determined, and immensely capable, Holmes expected utmost loyalty and did not mince words. Barely two weeks on the job, in November 1961, he stormed into Webb's office and demanded independence from Seamans. Webb refused.[36]

Webb and Holmes operated on different wavelengths. Holmes came out of meetings with Webb, saying, "I can't understand that man at all."[37] He never stopped pushing for more power and more resources and, although he was not necessarily wrong in his assessments of what was good for Apollo, his style grated on Webb. In 1962, NASA headquarters moved into two new buildings, one on and one near Independence Avenue, Holmes in one building, Webb in the other. The separation not only reflected the scale of Holmes's operation but also symbolized the distance growing between the two men.

Holmes, meanwhile, was becoming famous as the Apollo "czar," a term Webb hated, and *Time* magazine featured him on its cover August 10, 1962.[38] Holmes consciously cultivated Congress, much as Webb did. The NASA administrator tolerated the actions of his OMSF director, aware that he could not get to the moon without a hard-driving executive behind Apollo. His basic philosophy about strong and difficult people was that you had to take the bitter with the better.

By late summer Holmes felt the Apollo schedule was slipping—possibly four to six months behind schedule—and he determined he needed $400 million more than the original estimates to catch up. Since Congress was still in session, he asked Webb to request a supplemental appropriation for the project, funded at $2.2 billion for fiscal year 1963. Webb said he could not go back to Congress, a move that would harm his own credibility with legislators. Well then, said Holmes, why don't you simply transfer the money from these less important, nonmanned programs? Webb was even more adamant about cannibalizing the science, applications, and SUP efforts to get the $400 million. Holmes was angry. He believed Webb was placing Apollo—and Holmes's own chances of succeeding—in jeopardy.[39] Failing to make his case inside, Holmes secretly began talking with supporters in Congress and with the media, unaware that Webb's contacts kept him apprised of these activities.

The issue came to a head when Holmes sought an interview with *Time* magazine in which he discussed the dispute over priorities. In an advance copy of the story made available to a member of the Webb staff, *Time*'s editors had excised a quote from Holmes: "The major stumbling block of getting to the moon is James E. Webb. He won't fight for our program." The editors felt that Holmes had let the original cover story "go to his head," and that he was "out to get Webb."[40]

The *Time* article came out on November 23 depicting Apollo's alleged money problems, schedule slippages, and the disagreement between Holmes and Webb. Contrasting Webb's view that Apollo was only part of the space program with Holmes's perspective that "it's the top priority program within NASA," the article also mentioned that Holmes blamed Webb for letting the Apollo program lag four to six months behind schedule.[41] The story triggered attention in the *New York Times* and elsewhere.

Soon afterward, Kennedy called a meeting at the White House, where Webb and Holmes verbally fought it out in front of the president. Webb said he could not take responsibility for a space program that was not "balanced," waxing at length on the various facets of the space program and how all were critical to the country. When he was finished, Kennedy expressed his concern that he and his NASA administrator might not be in accord on Apollo's priority. He said that the manned lunar landing was the most important U.S. objective. Webb said, no, the objective was to be "preeminent in space." After Webb stated his position again, at Kennedy's request, the president said he was "still not sure" they saw "eye-to-eye." He asked Webb for his position in writing so he could be certain if they were working together or not.[42]

In a nine-page response, Webb wrote:

> The objective of our national space program is to become preeminent in all important aspects of this endeavor and to conduct the program in such a manner that our emerging scientific, technological, and operational competence in space is clearly evident. . . .
>   Consequently, the manned lunar program provides currently a national focus for the development of national capability in space, and,

in addition, will provide a clear demonstration to the world of our accomplishment in space. The program is the largest single effort within
NASA, constituting three-fourths of our budget, and is being executed
with extreme urgency. All major activities of NASA, both in Headquarters and in the field, are involved in this effort, either partially or
full time.

While manned space had the "highest national priority," he went on, it
would "not by itself create the preeminent position we seek." He described
how the other space activities contributed to preeminence, and the importance of a "well-balanced space program." He would not recommend taking
funds from these other areas for the manned lunar landing. Finally, he
pointed out that he was discussing with BOB a NASA budget in FY 1964
that would increase the $3.7 billion appropriated in FY 1963 to $6.2 billion.
Webb said he would rather wait for the regular budget-approval process
with Congress, but that if the president determined that a supplemental appropriation for the current year was the way to go, he and his colleagues at
NASA would do their best to present the case on Capitol Hill.[43]

Kennedy thought Webb was going too far beyond Apollo with some
of his "preeminence" interests and in his heart of hearts was closer to
Holmes's view.[44] But he would trust the NASA administrator. Webb recalled having a conversation around this time in which he told the president
that if they stuck together, things would work out all right, but if they disagreed, Webb could not guarantee that would be the case. The president assured him of his intent to "stick with" Webb.[45] He sent no formal response
to Webb's letter.

At a NASA celebration that accompanied the end of the Mercury program in May 1963, Webb pointedly and publicly omitted Holmes from a
long list of those he lauded for NASA's success in manned space flight.
Livid, Holmes burst out to Seamans, "It's me or Jim." Seamans reported to
Dryden and Webb that NASA could not get to the moon with Holmes and
Webb at loggerheads, then went back to Holmes. "You said it yourself," he
told him. "Webb and you can't live in the same house. And Webb's not
about to leave." Holmes resigned in June. Under enormous pressure to hire
a new manned space director, Webb called friends in industry. The name
that surfaced was that of George E. Mueller (pronounced "Miller"), vice
president of Space Technology Laboratories, a subsidiary of Thompson
Ramo Wooldridge, Inc. After consulting with Dryden, Webb called Sea-

mans, who was then away on vacation, to make sure he also thought well of Mueller.[46]

Joining NASA officially on September 1, 1963, the forty-five-year-old Mueller knew the program was the target of criticism and exacted from Webb the understanding that he would have a relatively free hand managing Apollo.[47] Virtually everyone agreed he was a first-rate engineer, and, as much a workaholic as Webb, he labored seven days a week and expected others to do so, scheduling important meetings on Sundays and holidays, calling the technical shots as he saw them, and seldom worrying if his decisions or manner of making them ruffled the feathers of subordinates.[48] He fastened on the lunar deadline and became its guardian.

Mueller profited from what had happened to Holmes. As determined as Holmes, he was circumspect with Webb and usually careful about what he said in reference to the administrator and to whom he said it. Bureaucratically adept, he found ways to get what he wanted without confronting those in superior positions. A man who neither sought nor received the attention Holmes did, he was content with the power his position afforded and quickly made a difference at NASA.

Shortly after he arrived, Mueller ordered an intense study made of where Apollo stood and found that Holmes had been right: Apollo was falling behind. Even with budgetary reprogramming and additional funds from the president and Congress, the program would have trouble making the Kennedy deadline. A lunar journey might not take place until 1971. Mueller thought he had a solution to the problem. As he saw it, NASA was overtesting. Von Braun's "German model" called for testing virtually every item connected with the rocket and spaceship separately and with painstaking detail, an approach with which Gilruth was not unsympathetic, since he worried constantly about the safety of the astronauts under his authority at Houston. The German model meant a long sequence of launches testing various parts of the Apollo configuration in space. But testing a number of the components together and launching them together as a complete system would eliminate many of the tests of individual stages and modules.[49]

Although von Braun and Gilruth opposed his approach as too risky, Mueller did not believe that simultaneous testing posed a much greater risk than testing separate components sequentially. Even if it did, how else to get to the moon by 1969? There had to be an "all-up" decision, as it came to be called, and Mueller held firm. This meant that the first flight of a *Saturn 5*, the moon rocket, would also be the first flight for various stages and modules now scheduled for separate tests. They would all be tested in flight at once.

When Webb decided to let Mueller proceed, the director informed a meeting of Houston and Huntsville officials of his all-up concept. Two days later, he sent a priority teletype message to relevant NASA groups, spelling out a new flight schedule, asking for responses in ten days and announcing his intention to post "an official schedule reflecting the philosophy outlined here" in three weeks. Webb strengthened Mueller's hand by a second reorganization of NASA, reversing the 1961 decision to put the centers under control of Seamans, already partially negated in 1962 for OMSF, as Webb sought to placate Holmes. Now, Webb made an across-the-board decision to shift power he had kept in the triad to program directors. Thus, Marshall, the Manned Space Center, and the Launch Operations Center (rechristened Kennedy Space Center in December) became solely Mueller's responsibility; Goddard Space Flight Center, the Jet Propulsion Laboratory, and certain other installations went to Newell, head of the Office of Space Science and Applications (OSSA); and the four former NACA labs—Langley, Ames, Lewis, and Flight—fell to Raymond Bisplinghoff, head of the Office of Advanced Research and Technology (OART). Whatever else it did, the reorganization sent a strong message to von Braun, Gilruth, and others that Webb was enlarging the influence of the program directors, now called associate administrators. In particular, it put Mueller in a good position to get his way if Gilruth and von Braun decided to fight the all-up decision. They chose not to do so, and the decision stood.[50]

In a meeting with Webb and Seamans, Mueller meanwhile said he needed more strong technical managers in headquarters, reporting to himself, to make Apollo a success. He produced a list of individuals, most of whom were in the air force. Seamans and Webb agreed, and, working primarily through a personal friend, General William F. "Bozo" McKee, deputy chief of staff of the air force, Webb maneuvered the necessary transfers.[51] General Samuel C. Phillips, one of the air force's top technical managers, was soon detailed to NASA as director of Apollo, under Mueller, and was later joined by twenty other able air force officers.[52] The crisis in Apollo leadership that had begun in 1962 with Holmes's mutiny thus ended in 1963 with an astute new manned space director, a stronger overall Apollo management team, and decisive steps to get Apollo back on schedule.

Clashing with McNamara

Another threat to Webb's control of the space program in the 1962-63 period came from Secretary of Defense Robert S. McNamara. Along with a basic institutional cooperation between DOD and NASA was an institutional rivalry—the air force wanted to be a manned space agency—as well as a personal competition between Webb and McNamara. They employed very different administrative styles toward a common end—control over their domain. The issue was the boundary of those domains, for both men had imperialistic tendencies.

In December 1962, McNamara began probing Webb to see how far he could go in establishing a DOD manned presence in space through Gemini. The air force argued that the near-earth activities Gemini would pioneer could have military significance in terms of manned reconnaissance, and McNamara agreed. He began by suggesting a basic division of labor: DOD would "take over all manned flights in earth orbit; NASA, all flights beyond earth orbit." This meant DOD would control space near earth, and NASA around the moon and beyond. Informally, McNamara proposed "a merger of NASA-DOD manned space programs under DOD management." When Webb objected, he formally proposed "a joint program."[53]

Webb saw the stakes as nothing short of NASA's independence as an agency. If McNamara took over Gemini, what would be next? Moreover, McNamara's proposal interfered with Apollo. "Gemini had been planned to meet the needs of NASA's manned program; it had been under way since December 1961." While NASA had designed Gemini with potential military applications "in mind," transferring Gemini might divert its being used as a building block for Apollo. "There were also compelling [international] political reasons for Gemini to remain within NASA, since the arrangement by which NASA operated tracking stations in Mexico, Nigeria, Zanzibar, and Spain prohibited their use to support military programs." If McNamara's terms were accepted, these stations "would be unavailable and the existence of a joint civilian-military program would jeopardize negotiations for tracking stations elsewhere. The effect of transferring Gemini to DOD would be to place in doubt NASA's image as a civilian agency dedicated to the peaceful exploration of space."[54]

Webb met with McNamara on the Gemini question in mid-January. McNamara's approach to negotiation, Webb said, was to "knock you down on the floor with a sledge-hammer, and then, while you're down, ask you to sign off on a particular decision." They had clashed before, and Webb felt personally slighted by the defense secretary's brusque style. He certainly had gone to some lengths to avoid dealing with McNamara, establishing various NASA-DOD liaison mechanisms to facilitate agreement short of the Webb-McNamara level. But the Gemini question (Air Force reportedly spoke of a "Blue Gemini" program under its auspices) was too important to be settled anywhere besides the top of the two agencies. In the meeting, Webb made it clear to McNamara that NASA control of Gemini was not negotiable. However, he would agree to Gemini's carrying certain military experiments. McNamara decided not to push Webb further, and the two men hammered out a pact. Under terms of the Gemini agreement, announced January 21, 1963, "Gemini was not to be thought of as a joint program, but rather as a program serving common needs, with the Department of Defense paying for the military features, NASA in full charge of the program, and the role of the [Gemini Program Planning] board [to plan experiments for NASA and DOD] strictly advisory." In addition, the agreement held that "DOD and NASA will initiate major new programs or projects in the field of manned space flight aimed chiefly at the attainment of experimental or other capabilities in near-earth orbit only by mutual agreement."[55]

That manned space was of primary interest to Webb and of secondary interest to McNamara gave Webb leverage in bargaining. If anything, McNamara was ambivalent about how far he wanted DOD (i.e., the air force) to move in this direction. He wanted both to extend his reach and to hold the air force in check. Webb understood this. NASA could not indefinitely keep DOD out of manned space, but Webb would try to limit and channel military ambitions so they did not hamper NASA's program. As Seamans put it, "McNamara was more powerful than Webb. But Webb had more guile."[56]

Challenges came as well from outside the executive branch. For two years after the Apollo decision Congress had been relatively docile. But in 1963, with Kennedy calling for a huge increase in NASA's budget, Congress decided to take a hard look at agency spending. In the midst of defending the NASA budget request, Webb found himself placed in a difficult position by Kennedy. The president, in a fall address to the UN General Assembly, declared that in the field of space there was room for U.S.-USSR "cooperation," for "joint efforts," including the possibility of a "joint expedition to the moon."

Kennedy had personally alerted Webb to his proposal and asked the NASA administrator to control his organization lest it undermine a possible foreign policy initiative. Webb had passed the word to his lieutenants that they hold to the line of presidential policy—an action for which the president was grateful. However, the Kennedy speech offered ammunition to those who wanted to cut the NASA budget. The House had already agreed to cut the president's proposed budget by $600 million. Now, the Democratic chair of the House Appropriations Committee, Clarence Cannon of Missouri, decided to join with the Republicans on the Thomas subcommittee to cut NASA's appropriation an additional $900 million, which might have seriously "crippled" Apollo. Webb and Representative Thomas worked furiously behind the scenes to prevent the additional damage. The president contributed to their effort by stressing that a strong space program was essential to any cooperative endeavor. The prospect of a U.S.-USSR joint program eventually faded, and Webb and Thomas defeated the Cannon foray. In the end, the original request of $5.7 billion was cut to $5.1 billion, much more than the preceding year but less than Webb believed was needed. It was not clear who Congress was teaching a lesson, Webb or Kennedy.[57] What was clear was the necessity of having Thomas as an ally on the Appropriations Committee.

Two other disputes that came up in 1963 conveyed the message that Congress could no longer be taken for granted. The first concerned the final jewel in NASA's diadem of in-house facilities—the Electronics Research Center (ERC). Webb wanted this established in Cambridge, Massachusetts, near Harvard, MIT, and the Route 128 electronics complex, a key to his strategy of maximizing NASA's ability to create regional government-industry-university alliances for a stronger technological America. Many critics in Congress saw ERC as a payoff to supporters of President Kennedy and aid to his brother Edward, who had recently run for the Senate under the banner "I can do more for Massachusetts." The intense congressional controversy forced Webb to conduct a nationwide search for a site and to report in detail the rationale for his choice. In the end, ERC still went to Massachusetts.[58]

Similarly, the Sustaining University Program came under congressional fire in 1963. SUP had of necessity surfaced as a line item for the first time in the FY 1964 budget submission, for *Science* magazine had claimed that its level of spending made NASA the "biggest [agency] in graduate aid." Senator Gordon Allott, ranking Republican on the Appropriations subcommittee funding NASA, complained about millions of dollars going "into a program that no one had even heard of before." The Senate Appropriations Committee said it would not fund SUP unless NASA fully justified it. Special hearings by the Senate Space Committee had to be held on the program, and SUP was subsequently legitimated by Congress, two years after its birth.[59]

That Webb had to work hard to win his congressional battles in 1963 was partly related to the death in January of Senator Kerr, who was replaced as Space Committee chair by Senator Clinton P. Anderson, Democrat from New Mexico, a significant shift. During the Truman years, Anderson, as secretary of agriculture, had insisted that Webb, then budget director, come to *his* office to negotiate Agriculture's budget. Webb had refused, saying he worked for the president, not for Anderson. As a New Mexico senator, Anderson showed the same drive to control. Intellectually sharp and personally testy, he was perhaps the strongest senator on the Joint Committee on Atomic Energy, using that group to exercise unusually close influence over the Atomic Energy Commission. By the time he became chair of the Space Committee, however, he was in poor health, suffering from Parkinson's disease and other ailments that sapped his energy and made him unpredictable but did not change his will to control.

Various sources warned Webb that Anderson would try to find a way to bring him to heel.[60] Sure enough, Anderson challenged him on his reprogramming of funds already appropriated—particularly the shift of $400 million from Nova to Saturn. A hearing followed, during which Webb came under fire for excessive reprogramming and had his authority to shift funds subsequently narrowed. Afterward, Anderson walked up to him. "Well now, you've done all right," he told Webb. "You're going to get along just fine. We've known each other a long time, and we're going to get along just fine." Webb replied, "I'm sure glad to hear you say that, Senator, because several of my friends have said you told them that you were going to cut my throat, if you could. I didn't believe it, Senator, because we've been friends such a long time."[61]

If he did not stand up to the crusty senator right at the beginning, Webb realized, Anderson would push him into the ground, as he had done to some leaders of the Atomic Energy Commission. Although Webb was used to dealing with tough men who liked to exert power, Kerr among them, he and Kerr had been friends. Webb and Anderson never would be. In fact, Webb knew that, although Anderson supported NASA, he would have preferred someone else as administrator. He was just waiting for Webb to make the big mistake, Webb said later, so he could go for "the short hairs."[62]

Balancing Anderson to some extent was the strongest Republican on the Senate Space Committee, Margaret Chase Smith of Maine. The only woman in the Senate, Smith had shown her remarkable blend of courage and independence when she became the first senator to actively speak out against Senator Joseph McCarthy in the 1950s. While staunchly conservative and critical of the Democrats, she voted her conscience. Webb went out of his way from the beginning to cultivate Senator Smith, using SUP to advantage, and they developed a strong mutual respect. She was important to the bipartisan image he wanted for NASA, and absolutely critical to bolstering the at-best-lukewarm support Webb got from Anderson.[63]

Using various strategies to win friends and maintain his authority, Webb neutralized opposition inside and outside NASA in these early years. Tested by the air force, the president's science adviser, his own Apollo director, astronauts, the secretary of defense, and Congress, he kept NASA on course—his course. As a result, by the end of 1963, NASA possessed not only the technical competence but the political clout to take America to the moon.

Webb as a young pilot in the U.S. Marine Corps Reserve poses beside his aircraft during a weekend of active duty in 1933. *Courtesy of Mrs. James E. Webb.*

Budget Director Webb, President Truman, and Treasury Secretary John Snyder
prepare for a news conference in 1948. *Courtesy of Mrs. James E. Webb.*

John Glenn's successful earth orbit in February 1962 provided President Kennedy and Webb as NASA administrator with one of their earliest triumphs. *Courtesy of Mrs. James E. Webb.*

Leaders of the Kennedy administration's space program visit the Marshall Space Flight Center in Alabama in mid-September 1962. *From left to right:* President Kennedy; center director Wernher von Braun; NASA administrator Webb; Vice President Johnson; Secretary of Defense McNamara; science advisor to the president Jerome B. Wiesner; and director of defense research and engineering (and future defense secretary) Harold Brown. In the course of the visit Webb and Wiesner engaged in a heated discussion of lunar-rendezvous strategy, a dispute Kennedy witnessed with much interest. *Courtesy of NASA.*

Webb stands behind Hugh L. Dryden *(left)*, deputy administrator, and powerful Oklahoma senator Robert S. Kerr *(right)*, chair of the Senate Space Committee and a strong Webb supporter, at a press conference following the successful *Mariner 2* space-survey mission to Venus in December 1962. *Courtesy of NASA.*

Webb and President Johnson, along with astronauts L. Gordon Cooper *(left)* and Walter M. Schirra and Florida congressman Claude Pepper, face the glare of television cameras during a briefing at NASA Mission Control Center, Houston, in mid-September 1964. *Courtesy of NASA.*

Webb makes a point with President Johnson during a discussion of the space program circa 1968. *Courtesy of Mrs. James E. Webb.*

Apollo 11 astronauts Neil A. Armstrong, Michael Collins, and Edwin E. Aldrin, Jr., aboard the *Apollo/Saturn 5* space vehicle, lift off from Kennedy Space Center Launch Complex 39A the morning of July 16, 1969. Four days later Armstrong and Aldrin descended to the moon's surface while Collins piloted the command module in lunar orbit. *Courtesy of NASA.*

THE STRUGGLE TO
MAINTAIN MOMENTUM

Between 1964 and 1966 NASA stopped growing, and Webb sought some-how to maintain momentum in the space program. While his relation-ship with President Kennedy had been positive and quite straightforward, his association with Johnson was infinitely more complex. They were ap-proximately the same age and had similar backgrounds and political philosophies. After Kennedy was assassinated in November 1963, Webb had direct access to President Johnson whenever necessary. He had more per-sonal rapport with Johnson than with Kennedy and knew that LBJ re-spected him as a sounding board and source of advice. But the two were not close. Both wanted room to operate, to maneuver, which brought a certain wariness to all their relationships. When it came to Johnson, Webb was es-pecially careful.

The Johnson Transition

Johnson's declaration when he assumed the presidency that he would fulfill the goals of the fallen Kennedy went double when it came to Apollo. Johnson regarded himself as the founding father of the space program, and the appointment of Webb as one of his best decisions.[1] In an early discus-sion with President Johnson about Apollo, Webb pointed out how the con-gressional cut during 1963 had put the goal at risk. In spite of Webb's aver-sion to supplementals, he and Johnson agreed to have Congress add funds to the existing fiscal year appropriation, as well as seek an increase the com-ing year. With Johnson's backing, Webb largely prevailed. In August 1964,

Johnson signed NASA's appropriation for FY 1965 of $5.25 billion, with a $72.5 million supplemental to FY 1964, a $150 million raise from the year before.

Grateful that Johnson had emphasized continuity of presidential support in the early months of 1964, Webb assisted the new president in ways he could appreciate, putting his influence behind the civil rights act Johnson wanted to get through Congress in 1964. As a southern politician, Webb talked to a number of key senators, including the leader of the southern coalition fighting the bill, Richard Russell of Georgia.[2] Prior to the 1964 presidential election, Webb also helped Johnson counter a political adversary. In late October, when Governor George Wallace of Alabama was taking a hard line against civil rights *and* Johnson, Webb went to Alabama and let it be known that NASA was concerned about the attitudes down there, which made it difficult to recruit top people. In public, he did not discuss race but spoke instead of a "hate federal government doctrine" and implied that at least part of NASA's Marshall Space Flight Center might be moved elsewhere. Wernher von Braun's operation at Huntsville was a source of pride to Alabama, and to Wallace. Should he take Webb seriously? When Louisiana's representative Hale Boggs publicly indicated an interest in receiving the Space Flight Center, including von Braun, Governor Wallace denounced Webb on *Meet the Press.* Webb went to Alabama and repeated his argument that Alabama had to change its image if it wanted to get good people to come there and to develop as a state.[3]

When Johnson easily defeated Senator Barry Goldwater in the 1964 election, Webb assumed he would have a White House anxious to maintain the momentum of the space program. Capitol Hill was a different matter. January 30, 1964, marked the sixth straight failure of a Ranger flight, unmanned rockets sent to the moon to take television pictures of the lunar surface to help find a landing site for Apollo. Congress wanted to know what went wrong. Was the NASA center responsible for Ranger, the Jet Propulsion Laboratory (JPL), capable of running the program? Webb knew he had problems but did not want Congress reaching into his management prerogatives.

He found himself in "an extremely delicate situation, much like walking down Fifth Avenue in your BVDs."[4] At the time of the Ranger mishap, he was locked in a dispute with Lee A. DuBridge, president of Caltech, the institution responsible for JPL. The contract under which Caltech managed JPL for NASA was up for renewal. Webb felt DuBridge was not taking the supervisory responsibility seriously, in spite of the handsome fee NASA paid Caltech to run JPL on its behalf. Webb needed JPL to get on top of the Ranger project but worried that a congressional investigation could weaken JPL and thus hurt Apollo. Watching closely from the sidelines was Congressman Albert Thomas, who could not understand why the work NASA had performed "for a fee" at JPL could not be done by civil servants at "his" center in Houston.[5] Using the hearings to pressure JPL without letting them get out of hand, Webb praised JPL in his testimony, assured Congress he could correct the problems, and implored its members not to legislate management solutions that would drive away the lab's best people.

The House Space subcommittee conducting the investigation criticized NASA and JPL, but especially the latter, strengthening Webb's hand by citing JPL's "extraordinary show of independence" as a problem afflicting Ranger. It called for firmer control by NASA, but left the strategy to Webb's discretion. To NASA's delight (and possibly at Webb's instigation) the subcommittee called for a strong general manager as deputy director, a reform NASA had wanted which JPL and DuBridge had strongly opposed.[6]

By not signing the contract, Webb had kept pressure on JPL to "shape up." Now Caltech's board of trustees began asserting themselves, and DuBridge and JPL yielded. In June 1964, it was announced that Alvin Luedecke would be hired as deputy director of the laboratory. A major general in the air force, Luedecke was retiring as general manager of the Atomic Energy Commission. At this point, Webb was dealing directly with Arnold Beckman, chair of Caltech's board.[7] Eventually, he signed a new contract symbolizing a more responsive JPL and a management setup more reflective of the requirements of Apollo.

What mattered most in the short term was *Ranger 7*. In July 1964, *Ranger 7* took off from Cape Kennedy for a flawless flight; the cameras worked perfectly, taking pictures of the moon "a thousand-fold more detailed than any that could be obtained through ground-based telescopes."[8]

Throughout the 1964–66 period, Gemini dominated NASA. While serving as a stepping stone to Apollo, Gemini also helped Webb keep NASA before the public eye as the country was moving on to other priorities. Television, enhanced by the now operational communication satellite, became an increasing asset to Webb, allowing millions of people all over the world to witness one Gemini flight success after another. Webb was not the only person who saw the political and public relations value of Gemini. As it became apparent that Johnson wished to use it for his purposes, Webb tried to control how that happened.

At particular issue were the Gemini astronauts, who were demonstrating skill and courage in "extravehicular activity" (space walks) and other achievements. Johnson wanted to send them abroad as his own ambassadors of goodwill, to emphasize his interest in peace at a time his Vietnam policy was under fire. Webb resisted as much as possible. He was happy to have the president "point to space as a peaceful development," but wanted no one using astronauts for political purposes unless he was calling the shots. The dispute came to a head at the Johnson ranch in Texas. The Russians were going to have at least one cosmonaut, Yuri Gagarin, at the Paris Air Show, and the United States, said Johnson, *had* to be represented following the next Gemini launch. The president would not take no for an answer and started reading Webb a press release. Webb interrupted, saying they could not assume a successful launch; problems were possible. The president changed the press release to read "After the worst launch of all time . . . ," and so it went. Webb resisted all the way, and then acceded. When the two *Gemini 4* astronauts went to the Paris Air Show, Webb went along.[9]

As Gemini developed, Webb steered the political rewards of his choosing in LBJ's direction. In October 1965, a technical mishap forced one mission to be redesigned. Two Gemini capsules would rendezvous in space, a remarkable feat at the time, conceived, designed, and approved within three days. Webb made sure that the announcement of the rendezvous flight came from the Texas White House so Johnson could get the publicity and credit.[10]

By the time the last Gemini flight—that of *Gemini 12*—took place in mid-November 1966, Johnson was basking in its glory and proclaiming the United States had "caught up" with the Russians and was "pulling ahead."[11] The Gemini series had been so successful in realizing its goals that it finished ahead of schedule. As with Mercury, many of those associated with Gemini, especially the astronauts, wanted "one more flight." Astronaut Gordon Cooper mentioned the possibility to Webb at a dinner in Houston. Webb cut him off sharply. "We're focusing on Apollo. We don't want Gemini extended."[12]

On the surface, all looked well with NASA, Apollo, and Webb. But times had changed. In two areas, momentum was a problem—SUP and post-Apollo planning.

SUP and the Great Society

In November 1964, Webb told President Johnson that he knew "of no area where the inspirational thrust toward doing everything required of a great society can be better provided on a proven base of competence, and with so many practical additional benefits to be derived, than through the space program. . . . The space program lies in your first area of building the great society, for it is truly an imaginative new program based on new ideas and new capabilities."[13] He could wax eloquent at any time about the spinoffs from space and pushed hard for technology transfer, but he was after more in the way of social uplift, and this was where SUP came in. For better or worse, Webb in 1961 had fixed his eye on the university as his principal vehicle for relating NASA to larger domestic purposes and building a Space Age America. When Johnson discussed his Great Society in 1964, Webb raised SUP as an example of what NASA was already doing to help. Definitely intrigued by SUP's geographical spread concept, in 1965 the president directed all science and technology–intensive agencies to begin or augment "science development" programs to strengthen universities across the country so they could leverage further change.[14]

No program revealed Webb's administrative ambition more than SUP. Throughout the mid-1960s, Webb probably gave more of his personal time to this small component of NASA's overall effort than to any other non-manned space activity. Johnson's science adviser, Donald F. Hornig, recalled the unbridled enthusiasm with which Webb discussed his hopes for SUP.[15] By 1966, however, Webb's disillusionment with the program had turned him almost bitter about the response of the nation's university presidents.

Like many others of his generation who had seen universities mobilized by government for service in World War II, Webb shared the "technocratic temptation" to envision the university as a repository of knowledge that could be harnessed to public goals and general problem solving.[16] But, in Webb's managerial eyes, the university, to be a more perfect partner of government, had to become better organized and more service oriented. To get universities to change, Webb had tied his largest prizes, new-building grants, to Memoranda of Understanding (MOUs) between himself and university presidents. It was an exchange for Webb, a quid pro quo. He assumed the presidents were serious when they signed the memos and promised to become more interdisciplinary and problem oriented. Few universities refused to become a part of SUP because their presidents chafed at the MOU. Most presidents, including leaders of many of the most prestigious institutions in the country, happily signed the memos and took the money. By mid-1964, twenty-five facility grants and MOUs were in effect. NASA-funded space centers were going up all over the country.

Webb did not hesitate to tell university presidents how to use the NASA funding he provided. He wrote Julius Stratton, president of MIT, that the work being funded at MIT under SUP would not achieve its full potential unless all the resources of the university were brought to bear on questions of how science and technology could be most useful. He told Stratton that the current studies would "benefit from a little closer following by a man with your perspective and perception of the great issues of the time." He suggested that Stratton get James Killian involved and also Jerome Wiesner, two former presidential science advisers now back at MIT. He told Stratton he had himself urged Wiesner to see "how the total resources of the university could be applied to specific areas of research that are urgently needed," and to the "problems of the New England region in relation to the translation of the capacity that MIT has for helping the leaders solve these problems."[17] Nearly a year later, Stratton sent Webb a bundle of material indicating twenty-three ways MIT was interacting with industry. Webb was not impressed. Expressing his annoyance to an associate, he asked, What was going on? Was Stratton giving him "a snow job"?[18]

In September 1965, Herman Wells, retired president of the University of Indiana, whom Webb had hired as a consultant ("scout"), reported on a tour he had taken of certain key SUP universities. The prevailing attitude, he informed Webb, held that the MOU "might help NASA justify its position, but it did not add any additional obligations to the universities." Webb was dumbfounded. This was not "window dressing," he declared in response to Wells's findings. He expected a "positive reaction." After all, he was providing new buildings and "flexible money" for interdisciplinary research and fellowships, allowing university presidents to find their own way to respond to the SUP philosophy. The next time a facility grant award came up to him to approve (and SUP was a program Webb personally oversaw), Webb refused to sign it until the university backed up the application with a letter detailing specifically how it would carry out the MOU.

Part of the problem lay within NASA, Webb felt—Tom Smull, the head of the program, simply did not understand that Webb was interested in raising government-university relations to a level of partnership worthy of a Great Society. He had in 1962 hired George Simpson, a University of North Carolina (Chapel Hill) sociologist active in the research triangle enterprise, to serve as assistant administrator of technology utilization and policy planning. The research triangle, a regional economic development activity in the area bordered by the University of North Carolina, Duke University, and North Carolina State, appeared to Webb a useful model for SUP that could be replicated throughout the country. Simpson had many responsibilities, however, and had to deal with Smull through Homer

Newell, to whom Smull reported. Newell gave lip service but little else to Webb's vision. Moreover, Simpson was gone from NASA by 1965. In October of that year Webb transferred Smull to special assistant to the administrator, on leave from his SUP job. He wanted Smull to learn what Webb wanted out of this program, close enough so he could not claim any communication gap. At the same time, he asked William Hagerty, president of Drexel Institute of Technology, to head a group of outside consultants and NASA officials evaluating SUP.[19]

Webb expected SUP to catalyze interaction between disciplines, between the space center and the rest of the university, between the university and its region. He expected the presidents of universities to do what they said they would do in the MOU: exercise leadership on behalf of the Webb vision. He told senators and members of Congress he would work with them to develop their states via SUP, and he anticipated help from the universities. Where were the institutional innovations, the technological and societal spin-offs? Advisers urged him to be patient. In August 1966, he received the evaluation report from Hagerty, which found SUP a success by virtually every conventional standard: fellowships, research, facilities. By Webb's standard, however, progress was slow. Major obstacles and perhaps ultimate limits would prevent achieving the service-oriented goals he wanted. Not only did the university presidents fail to appreciate the degree to which Webb was serious about the MOUs, most faculty members who had benefited from SUP did not even know the MOUs existed.

Webb reacted with a mix of defensiveness, disappointment, anger, and, most of all, frustration. He had never expected *all* the universities to come through with innovative activities, he said, but he had thought a few would, and these would show the way to others. In September, Smull went back to managing SUP, presumably educated in the Webb perspective but monitored by the secretariat. That winter, Webb and President Johnson dealt with the upcoming budget. With Vietnam expenditures putting a ceiling on what Johnson was willing to provide NASA, Webb had to consider priorities. Little evidence backed up his rhetoric about NASA and the Great Society. As a linkage mechanism, SUP had failed in the short run, and the president told him to let it go. A lot had happened since 1965, when Johnson had cited SUP's geographical-spread feature as a model for government-university relations. Universities were now the focus of anti-Vietnam protests. Why should Johnson provide funds to the sources of his problems? The president spoke privately of student demonstrators against Vietnam as "little bastards."[20] He wanted agencies like NASA "out of the education business."

Webb got the president to agree to let him phase down rather than immediately terminate the program, for he wanted to use SUP to initiate some low-cost experimental programs aiding black colleges and the development of public administration as a field. He also had to cut $10 million from the $41 million already provided SUP in fiscal year 1967. The Webb-Johnson understanding became even plainer the next year when only $20 million was requested for this program, which went downhill thereafter and was officially killed in 1970.[21]

Selling Post-Apollo

The other area where momentum had slowed was in planning for NASA's future beyond Apollo. Shortly after becoming president, Johnson directed Webb to move forward on an agenda of post-Apollo options. By 1965, however, Johnson did not want to hear about the possibilities, nor did he particularly want Congress to hear them. He deferred decisions on post-Apollo, even though he gave the go-ahead to Secretary of Defense McNamara in August to develop a DOD version of Gemini, the Manned Orbital Laboratory (MOL). Webb now found himself having to distinguish NASA's goal—a large, multipurpose space station—from the small, military-only space station of DOD.

Aware that Johnson would not approve a major national goal like Apollo, Webb made the centerpiece of his post-Apollo package what became known as the Apollo Applications Program (AAP), an interim program that would make maximum use of Apollo hardware and keep industrial production lines going so that a national decision for a space station or Mars expedition could be possible later. (Much downsized, AAP became Skylab in the early 1970s.)

Selling post-Apollo became a higher priority for Webb from 1964 to 1966. The issue went beyond maintaining existing programs to maintaining NASA. In fiscal year 1965, NASA appropriations peaked at $5.25 billion and then began a slow decline. Johnson kept putting Webb off on a post-Apollo decision. Testifying before the House Space Committee in February 1966, Webb said that the FY 1967 budget request of $5 billion "reflects the President's determination to hold open for another year the major decisions on future programs—decisions on whether to make use of the space operational systems, space know-how, and facilities we have worked so hard to build up, or to begin their liquidation."[22] "Caught uncomfortably between an Administration decision against commitments to major post-Apollo programs and increasingly critical attacks in Congress on a lack of definitive planning for the future," Webb argued that NASA needed decisions, and that the president and Congress must make them.[23] Several legislators responded that he should recommend specific courses of action, which Webb had done in private, only to have Johnson turn them down—at least for now. Webb grew more and more anguished.

In May 1966, he risked his relation with the president by granting an interview to the *New York Times* and warning that the nation faced a "crisis in space planning." A decision on post-Apollo programs had to be made within a year, he said, long before the actual moon-landing attempt. "It is extremely important not to think you can postpone the decision again," he said. "I think it is imperative to have a thorough-going national debate on whether we want to go past the point of no return." Webb emphasized that only so many Apollo space capsules and Saturn rockets were being developed; when they were gone, that would end the production line unless new equipment was ordered now. Without such orders, some of the contractors associated with Apollo would have to lay people off. The NASA-industry space machine was already slowing, he said, and after July, forty to sixty thousand aerospace employees would be cut.[24]

In speeches to influential groups around the country, Webb attacked the view that the race was over, stressing that the Soviets had demonstrated an ability to lift weights superior to that of the United States. Speaking to the media prior to an address to the National Security Industrial Association in October 1966, he said it would "be at least another year or two before we catch up in areas of booster rockets and payload capabilities." The Saturn rocket could not even be tested in flight until 1967. At present, the Soviets "are undoubtedly ahead of us in terms of a manned fly-by of the moon and may be ahead of us in terms of a lunar landing."[25]

In December, Webb took his cause to a meeting of the National League of Cities, where he received a chilly reception. The mayors had no interest in celebrating NASA or hearing about post-Apollo plans, only in passing resolutions seeking more money for cities. Webb was shocked by the degree to which NASA was made a scapegoat for the mayors' anger about lack of support for the Great Society. Apollo and the urban slums were contrasted in terms of misplaced national priorities.[26] The conference turned into a confrontation between the values of the Great Society and those of space, between domestic priorities and those of the Cold War. While Webb was his usual combative self, he was jarred by the experience.[27]

Throughout 1965–66, Webb had become increasingly locked in struggle with the budget director, Charles Schultze, over NASA expenditures. While Webb could always see Johnson, he still had to face the budget director, and, pressed by Vietnam, Johnson had let Schultze become more powerful, a buffer between himself and all non-Vietnam spending claims. Schultze was unmoved by Webb's concern about layoffs. "The space program is not a WPA [Works Progress Administration]," he wrote Johnson in September 1966. By mid-December, however, Schultze finally agreed with Webb that "we cannot postpone decisions any longer" lest there be a gap in the space program after Apollo. They still disagreed on how much was enough to get post-Apollo activity launched, and Webb now knew Johnson would go with the minimal Schultze figure.[28]

As 1966 ended, Webb saw the consensus underlying Apollo and NASA rapidly eroding, and the highly visible successes of Gemini making Congress, the president, and Americans in general complacent. Fearing that the president was losing interest in space as his other problems grew, Webb reminded Johnson how he "had almost had to drive me" to recommend the Apollo decision to Kennedy in 1961.[29] Johnson was not backing away from Apollo, but he was not supporting Webb on post-Apollo. In the past, Webb could seek advice, and some solace, in conversations with Hugh Dryden, his deputy. But Dryden had died of cancer in December 1965. Webb lost a wise friend and trusted confidant and could not replace him. At Webb's urging, Johnson had made Seamans deputy administrator—a position Seamans added while keeping his general manager's hat. The dyad, once a triad, also symbolized for Webb the sudden shift in fortune with which he had to cope.[30]

His strategies to maintain NASA, Apollo, and other programs had succeeded *and* failed in the 1964–66 time frame. He kept up overall momentum for Apollo, and the media and public watched one Gemini space achievement after another, but NASA's budget was cut back, SUP began to phase down, post-Apollo was delayed, and Webb saw his own power to persuade start to slip.[31]

THE APOLLO FIRE

As 1967 began, NASA technical officials felt upbeat. NASA checkout for its upcoming mission, the first Apollo manned flight, was gaining momentum. Although development woes remained, every problem that had arisen was being resolved. Even Webb had reason to be more optimistic. While he could not get the money he wanted, his three-year struggle to persuade Johnson to make a decision on post-Apollo was over. Johnson had concluded that either he made a decision now or the manned space program would come to a virtual halt after the moon landing.

The president authorized Webb to include $454.7 million for the Apollo Applications Program (AAP) in the FY 1968 budget that went to Congress in late January. The *New York Times* reported that NASA's post-Apollo plans called for putting astronauts on the moon for two-week stays and into earth orbit for up to one year. The funds would pay for new launch vehicles and spacecraft and for modifying the hardware so that additional astronauts could be aboard an orbiting laboratory. As was typical of Webb, he let others announce the good news at a press conference, where OMSF director George Mueller and other NASA officials discussed and answered questions about the new post-Apollo program. The short-term future of NASA beyond Apollo seemed assured.

Responding to Disaster

Into the early morning hours of Friday, January 27, Webb worked on various issues concerned with NASA's budget. Exceedingly pleased that

Johnson had at last given an affirmative to AAP, he still expected a major fight with Congress, for which he must prepare a strong defense, a persuasive presentation to win congressional support. He knew that the President's Science Advisory Committee (PSAC) was working on a study of post-Apollo plans. While he did not expect it to influence Johnson, it might complicate his situation with Congress. At 3:30 A.M., he went to bed.[1]

At 1:00 P.M., astronauts Virgil Grissom, Edward White, and Roger Chaffee, wearing their silvery space suits, climbed into the three seats of the capsule atop a two-hundred-foot *Saturn 1-B* launch vehicle, in training for the first manned Apollo flight. Called *Apollo/Saturn 204*, it was scheduled to launch on February 21 on a two-week sojourn around Earth. The astronauts went through a full-scale simulation of a launching, while officials watched on a closed-circuit television monitor. Some problems arose with the environmental control and communication systems, but nothing to indicate major trouble. The afternoon wore on. At 5:00 P.M., the three men were still inside the capsule running tests.

At the same time, the Outer Space Treaty was signed at the White House by representatives of sixty nations, including the USSR, pledging that space would be a domain of peace. The receiving line included President and Mrs. Johnson, Chief Justice and Mrs. Earl Warren, UN Ambassador and Mrs. Arthur Goldberg, and Vice President and Mrs. Hubert Humphrey. Webb, George Mueller, Wernher von Braun, Robert Gilruth, and Robert Seamans, among others representing NASA, soon left for the International Club, where Mueller had arranged a dinner for Apollo and Gemini business executives. Seamans was hosting a smaller dinner at his Georgetown home and so left the main NASA group. Stark Draper, director of MIT's Instrumentation Laboratory and principal designer of Apollo's guidance system, was to be among his dinner guests. The president moved from the treaty-signing ceremony to another White House event involving Secretary of Commerce John Connor, who was leaving government service. It was now after 6:00 P.M.

At the Cape, the astronauts continued the testing, simulating a launch. At 6:31 P.M., with but ten minutes to go before "lift-off" and the end of an arduous workday, a spark ignited. One of the astronauts yelled, "We've got a fire in the cockpit." Flames flashed through the capsule. As workers at the pad pushed up the gantry to the spacecraft in a high-speed elevator, fire engulfed the capsule. Asphyxiated, the crewmen died in seconds.[2]

The dinner at the International Club was about to begin when Webb received word from Cape Kennedy. He went to the nearest telephone to call the president. Johnson and Lady Bird were at the reception for Connor, who had just proposed a toast, when Johnson was handed a note by one of his aides. Webb had "reported that the first Apollo crew was under test at Cape Kennedy and a fire broke out in the capsule and all three were killed. He does not know whether it was the primary or backup crew, but believes it was the primary crew of Grissom, White, and Chaffee."[3]

Webb did not cancel the dinner, but he and other senior NASA officials excused themselves as soon as they could to return to NASA headquarters for more information and to confer on decisions that had to be made. Webb also wanted to be sure the leaders of the Senate and House Space Committees were informed. Soon, Webb, Mueller, and Seamans (who had heard at home and left his dinner party) were together at headquarters, where they agreed that NASA was best qualified to handle the inevitable investigation. However, this was a decision the president would make. Although NASA had a procedure for dealing with disasters, the fire was unlike any NASA had experienced, because three astronauts had been lost. The Apollo program manager, Sam Phillips, should go at once to the scene of the accident, take charge of the situation, and impound all information; there should be a temporary blackout of all but the most general NASA statements to the press until more was known; Seamans and Mueller should select members of a NASA review board, subject to Webb's agreement.

Meanwhile, Webb would contact Johnson and senior members of Congress and get their concurrence on the proper way to proceed. No discussion arose about the conduct of an external investigation. Seamans recalled that "there was absolutely none as far as I was concerned. I assumed we were going to follow our own guidelines."[4] One of the first aides with whom Webb conferred was Julian Scheer, head of NASA Public Affairs. Scheer recalled Webb telling him, "This is an event we have to control. I'm going to see the president. I'll tell him he'll be insulated from this. We will conduct the investigation. We will get answers. There will be no holds barred. We'll issue a report that can stand up to scrutiny by anybody."[5]

That evening Webb telephoned Johnson to talk about the fire and its implications. Although both had anticipated setbacks, and Webb had reminded Johnson of this fact only days before, the reality of the astronauts' deaths shocked them. Also, they both knew there would be questions. As Webb told Johnson, critics would ask what had happened. "Could the fire have been prevented? Were we going ahead too fast? Were we pushing too hard?" Webb "wondered how the nation would regard its space adventure now that disaster had fallen." Johnson feared that the tragedy might replace the sense of national excitement with national despondency. Webb felt the agony of the accident deeply. As Johnson would recall, Webb said, in effect: Mr. president, all we can do is what's right, and we know what we are doing is right. We cannot be discouraged and depressed to the point that we throw up our hands. We are going to find out what went wrong and we are going to correct it. But we are going to continue.[6]

While Webb was busy on the phone with the president and then with senior legislators, Seamans and Mueller selected members for the NASA review board, consulting with others in person or on the phone. They agreed that Floyd "Tommy" Thompson, director of the Langley Research Center, something of an elder statesman at NASA, and not intimately connected with Apollo, had the confidence of all concerned and was well suited to chair the board. An astronaut should serve, and they decided on Frank Borman, one of the most intelligent and articulate, to represent that group. In addition to six NASA specialists, they chose a U.S. Air Force colonel, an explosives expert from the Bureau of Mines, and a nongovernmental scientist, chemist Franklyn Long of Cornell University. (Long had to resign when it turned out he did not have the time for what was, for a period, virtually a full-time assignment. Other experts were later added, and the board eventually had fifteen members.)

Seamans confirmed the initial board members and procedures late that night with Webb, then went home, packed a suitcase, and left Washington at dawn for Cape Kennedy. On the way, his plane stopped at Langley Field in Virginia to pick up Tommy Thompson. As day broke in Florida on January 28, the two men joined Phillips, who had left the previous evening and had already impounded all data and physical evidence. Phillips had made some initial statements to the media but barred them from the accident site. A number of other NASA officials had also converged on the Cape from Houston and Washington, and J. Leland "Lee" Atwood, president of North American, had flown down. Most NASA senior managers, including Webb, had slept little, if at all, the night of January 27.

Webb remained in Washington. Agitated and saddened as he was, he would not let his agency or the lunar goal be derailed. "The effect of the fire on me was that we had to find out what happened and fix it and move ahead," he said later, "that we had to do that expeditiously and we had to maintain our support while we were doing it, and particularly we had to be very careful not to destroy the system that gave us success."[7] He could only achieve these goals, however, by maintaining some control over fast-breaking events. He anticipated demands for an "independent" investigation from, perhaps, the president's science adviser, Donald Hornig. He expected that many in Washington—in Congress, DOD, the media, and even among disgruntled NASA employees—would use the disaster to further their own interests.

As Seamans, Thompson, and Phillips took command at the Cape on January 28, Webb moved to steer decisions in Washington. He knew whose choices mattered most. In the early afternoon, he met with President Johnson at the White House. As was the president's habit, he had changed into his pajamas after lunch and was in his bedroom resting. There, the two men discussed the situation. "They're calling for investigations," Webb explained to the president. "The science advisory group in the White House is being pointed to as the proper body. A lot of people think it's a real issue for the future, and that you ought to have a presidential commission to be clear of all influences. You can have any investigation you want, with my full cooperation."[8]

He went on to emphasize that such investigations could get out of hand, exceed their specific purposes, damage not only NASA but Johnson. The alleged influence peddling of North American lobbyist Fred Black and the rumored involvement in the award of the Apollo contract of onetime Johnson aide and Washington wheeler dealer Bobby Baker would be dredged up. Some would want to use the tragedy to get at Webb and embarrass the president politically. Webb advised Johnson to take all this into account in deciding how to handle the investigation.[9]

"Well, what do you think we should do?" the president asked. "If you want me to do it," Webb replied, "I'll tell you what I think the job is—to find out what caused this fire and the loss of life, fix it, and fly again so we can complete the Apollo mission. If you want me to do that, I'll do it. NASA is the best organization [to do the investigation]." After weighing the options, Johnson gave Webb his okay. "In that case," said Webb, "there is just one stipulation I want to lay down, and that is that you are not bound to this decision. You can change it at any time you want, but I want to be told first." Johnson and Webb shook hands. They had struck a bargain.

Webb fully understood the significance of this meeting, later called "one of the crucial political decisions of the Apollo years. It was also typical of Johnson's brand of personalized deal-making, and Webb was supremely capable of taking maximum advantage of such intimate power-brokering."[10] He got what he wanted. The president hadn't known that NASA had already designated the membership of an investigative board and that preparations for the investigation were at that moment under way at the Cape.

Next, Webb spoke to the chairs of the two Space Committees and other key individuals in Congress, explaining that the president had placed the investigation in NASA's hands and promising to provide information to Congress as the inquiry developed. To protect the integrity of the accident review board, however, and to avoid even the appearance that he or anyone else was influencing the result, the inquiry would take place at the Cape behind closed doors. Webb said he would establish a procedure under which Seamans would visit the board each week for an update on its progress and submit a brief review of his findings to Webb, who would send it to the White House and Congress and then release it to the media. The committee chairs guardedly went along with this procedure, in return agreeing to delay a full congressional inquiry until NASA's review was complete. Thus, within twenty-four hours of the fire, the major decision had been made and approved as to who was going to conduct the initial investigation and the procedures to be implemented.

Taking on the Critics

NASA officials recalled that Webb remained very cool in the first hours and days after the fire, a general in command of his troops and poised to defend NASA. "A combative bureaucrat who guarded his turf with canine ferocity," Webb would not "stand by while outsiders vivisected Apollo."[11] At the same time, he let NASA insiders know that he was angry. What went wrong? he wanted to know. Who was to blame? It was not just a search for villains or scapegoats, recalled James Beggs, who worked for Webb in the late 1960s and later became NASA administrator under President Ronald Reagan. He believes Webb felt a special pain. He had tried to create "the perfect management system," said Beggs.[12] Did that system fail, or certain people in the system? Webb had to know.

He needed to get the facts for himself, not wait for the formal process of the review board, which would take perhaps two months to complete its work. Also, given its makeup, the board would emphasize the technical aspects of what went wrong. Webb's interest lay in the larger management issues, as well as whether specific individuals were at fault. In the congressional investigation following the NASA review, he knew critics would be out to hang somebody, which meant he had to be personally prepared for charges. Above all, he did not want to be surprised. He directed Paul Dembling, newly appointed NASA general counsel, to gather every shred of information pertaining to the decision-making process that led to the fire.

Anything relevant would go to the review board. He wanted to know if NASA's closet hid any skeletons.

Dembling put four NASA lawyers full time on the Webb investigation, while Webb deployed other staff from his office to help, including one assistant to study the role of the secretariat in steering information within NASA. What did Webb not know that he should have? Why not? Who did not tell him what he should have been told? If Webb was going to effectively represent his agency and Apollo against critics, he had to know the truth.

Meanwhile, President Johnson, Vice President Humphrey, Senator Anderson, and California Democrat George P. Miller, chair of the House Space Committee, all said publicly that the Apollo program "must be continued" in spite of the accident.[13] But it was not long before the critics spoke up. Webb had expected the media to aim their guns at NASA, and they soon mounted a steady volley around the theme that NASA's urgency had led to risky shortcuts. The media in general were unhappy with Webb, who had at first barred them from the scene of the accident and had put NASA officials under strict orders to say as little as possible publicly. Not until January 30 was one representative of the media allowed to view the pad where the men had died. Gradually thereafter, restrictions relaxed, but NASA and contractor personnel were directed not to speculate on the causes of the fire. Webb wanted to make sure the media got the facts through "appropriate" channels, namely the Seamans reports he would provide.

Reporters worked all the harder to get information through other channels. On January 31, the day of the astronauts' burial, the *New York Times* broke the story about the existence of tapes of the voices of the astronauts, suggesting there may have been time for an exit from the capsule, as opposed to NASA claims.[14] A furious Webb met in Washington with Mueller, Gilruth, Scheer, and others, demanding to know how the *Times* got the story about the tapes and why he had to find out about the astronauts' last ten seconds through the newspapers. He insisted that the public information officer at the Cape be fired, but he was not. Webb was upset also because the initial NASA statement had said the astronauts had died instantaneously, and apparently they had lived some seconds, suggesting NASA was not providing accurate information. Contradictions had appeared in other statements, most of which came not from headquarters but from the Cape. Webb wanted NASA to say only what it *knew* to be truth, nothing more. He had refused suggestions from Scheer that he appear on television, partly to avoid information coming out piecemeal.

By February 1, the *Apollo 204* Review Board was hearing witnesses to the fire and calling in experts in fuels, propulsion, and explosives. The next day, Seamans spent time at the Cape, talking with the review board and other key personnel involved in the investigation of the *Apollo 204* accident. He summed up in a report for Webb what was going on in terms of the investigation, clarified some of the statements made immediately after the event that were either incorrect or imprecise, emphasized that no specific cause of the fire had been determined, and noted the review board's procedures. Finally, he related the sequence of events just prior to and during the fire, as they could best be determined.[15] To make the report as matter-of-fact as possible, Webb directed Seamans to eliminate what Webb saw as emotional wording. He then sent the report to the president, and then to Anderson and Miller, and, once they had it, to the media. The *New York Times* published the report in full.

No doubt Webb hoped that these reports from NASA would satisfy Congress in the near term, pending the outcome of the formal review board inquiry. But many legislators, mindful of feeling in their home districts and prodded by the media, struck a more assertive note. When Republican John Wydler of New York, a member of the House Space Committee, urged a joint investigation by both House and Senate into the Apollo accident, he was overruled by senior colleagues. Texas Democrat Olin E. Teague, chair of the House Manned Space Flight Subcommittee, argued that such an investigation would be an "insult" to NASA's board of inquiry.[16]

Senator Anderson, however, felt differently, at least in regard to what his committee should do. Although a strong supporter of NASA, he was not necessarily in Webb's corner, for Webb had denied him the increased influence over NASA he wanted. The two had always been like rattlesnakes eyeing one another, Seamans recalled. Now, one of the rattlesnakes saw an advantage. Anderson, who had at first gone along with the Webb procedure, now wished to have at least some preliminary hearings on interim findings, insisting that his full committee have an opportunity to question Seamans. With Webb's concurrence, in a closed executive session, Anderson and thirteen other members of the Senate Space Committee questioned Seamans about what was known so far. Afterward, Anderson told reporters he was still solidly behind NASA. "The space program must continue [and] can continue," he said; he had not heard anything that indicated the lunar goal would not be met.[17] Anderson told Webb that he expected to be informed of significant milestones in the investigation, as they occurred; Webb said he would cooperate.

Meanwhile, criticism came from within NASA. Two NASA test engineers, in papers presented at a technical conference at Cape Kennedy, said that the pressure of meeting schedules had tempted workers to take short-cuts. The two men, employed by Marshall Space Flight Center, had prepared their paper before the fire occurred. The same day, the NASA review board heard testimony from another engineer, a former North American employee who had been fired for being a "disruptive influence," who enumerated a list of alleged quality shortcomings in the checkout of the Apollo spacecraft.[18] Such reports, appearing in the media, made NASA look negligent and worked against Webb's attempt to present information through NASA's "responsible" sources.

Seamans met again with members of the *Apollo 204* Review Board at Cape Kennedy in mid-February to discuss their progress in the investigation of the accident. The memo he prepared on the plane back to Washington went the same route as the first: to Webb, then the president and Congress, and on to the media. In a separate communication to Webb, Seamans recommended that OMSF develop plans to move Apollo forward by taking early advantage of the findings of the review board. Carefully selected individuals from NASA, he suggested, should be permitted to observe the board's proceedings. This access was arranged, but Webb ordered that public affairs personnel be excluded, lest he be open to later charges of trying to put a cosmetic stamp on the findings.

Meanwhile, Anderson turned up the congressional pressure, requesting information on NASA's earlier problems with equipment, which Webb supplied. Seamans met with the review board again, and his third interim report then circulated in accord with the now established routine. This time when he released the Seamans report to the media, Webb provided a statement of his own. In addition to the three Seamans reports, he said, he had had "the benefit of a review by three members of the Board—the Chairman, Dr. Floyd Thompson, astronaut Frank Borman, and Department of Interior combustion expert Dr. Robert van Dolah," who had come to Washington to brief him in person. He had concluded the following thus far:

> (1) The risk of fire that could not be controlled or from which escape could not be made was considerably greater than was recognized when the procedures for the conduct of the test were established. . . .

> (2) [There were placed] in the Apollo 204 capsule such items as Velcro pads to which frequently used items could be easily attached and removed, protective covers on wire bundles, nylon netting. . . . Tests con-

ducted in an Apollo-type chamber since the accident have shown that an oxygen fire in the capsule will spread along the surface of Velcro and along the edges of nylon netting much faster than through the material itself.

(3) Soldered joints in piping carrying both oxygen and fluids were melted away, with resultant leakage contributing to the spread of the fire.

(4) The bursting of the capsule happened in such a way that the flames, as they rushed toward the rupture and exhausted through it, travelled over and around the astronauts' couches. Under these conditions, and with just a few seconds of time available, the astronauts could not reach the hatch and open it.

(5) This fire indicates that a number of items related to the design and performance of the environmental control unit will require the most careful examination and may require redesign.

Webb pointed out that Borman had told him "that he would not have been concerned to enter the capsule at the time Grissom, White, and Chaffee did so for the test, and would not at that time have regarded the operation as involving substantial hazard." However, said Webb, Borman's work on the board had "convinced him [Borman] that there were hazards present beyond the understanding of either NASA's engineers or astronauts."[19]

This statement from Webb failed to satisfy Anderson, who scheduled an open hearing in late February on the preliminary findings of the board and actions to be taken by NASA. Miller, however, said the House Space Committee would hold hearings after the board's work was complete, at which time the committee's Oversight Subcommittee, chaired by Congressman Teague, would conduct the investigation for the full committee.

The Phillips Report

At the Senate hearings, Webb sat opposite the committee, Mueller on his right and Seamans on his left. Mueller, given the lead role, read a prepared statement indicating that NASA acknowledged inadequacies in standards and that the agency was working to correct the problems. The source of the spark that started the fire was still unknown. Previous successes had dulled the alertness of NASA and its contractors to the possibility of a fire.[20] He outlined a new program of testing, redesign, and procedural changes; a new escape hatch would be built and other modifications studied.

Most of the senators' questions addressed what caused the problem, how the "race" had contributed to the disaster, and what NASA was doing to get the program back on track. In response to questions about delay, NASA officials said no firm estimate was possible before April, when the review board completed its work, although Webb did indicate the flight to the moon might be pushed back into 1970.

Minnesota Democrat Walter F. Mondale, a relatively junior senator on the committee who in 1984 would run for president, was more interested in domestic social problems than in space and had paid scant attention to NASA up to this time. Ambitious to establish a national reputation as well as to get at the truth, he decided to play the devil's advocate, and Anderson let him. Mondale had information from Jules Bergman, an NBC television reporter who had been leaked a copy of the cover letter and back-up materials Phillips had used to brief North American on the results of an investigation he had led of that company in late 1965.

NASA had then been having considerable trouble with North American, the contractor with the largest role in Apollo, responsible for both the Apollo spacecraft and Saturn rocket second stage (S-2). Schedule slippages and other problems had brought tensions to a point where Phillips in December 1965 had assembled a "tiger team"—a group of top NASA specialists—to go to North American and find out what was going wrong and why. After talking with both North American management and working engineers, Phillips had written Mueller an angry memo on December 18, 1965, filled with specific complaints and naming people he regarded as at fault. While he did not name North American's president, Lee Atwood, he left no doubt that Atwood's "passive role" was responsible for the situation. Such passivity was unacceptable to Phillips, in view of the inept performance of the head of Space and Information Division (S&ID), the key North American man running NASA's work, Harrison Storms. Phillips did not mince words: "I would recommend that Harrison Storms be removed as president of S&ID and be replaced by a man who will be able to quickly provide effective and unquestionable leadership for the organization to bring the Division out of trouble and into the position where program commitments will be met." Unless North American was "responsive to these concerns of ours," Phillips said, "I strongly recommend that our only alternative is to move the work not being done well elsewhere."[21]

The next day, Phillips had conveyed his views, considerably sanitized from the standpoint of specific personalities, to Atwood and Storms. Charges of technical and managerial inadequacy came in the form of "briefing and notes." (These materials, when assembled, would become known as the "Phillips report.") To underline NASA's concern, Mueller had also written Atwood "on a personal basis," to suggest that both the S-2 and spacecraft projects needed his attention and that he "take a hard look at the competence and effectiveness of individuals, especially in the upper echelons of the organization; and move out those who are not really contributing, due either to the organization or their own competence." Mueller had emphasized that because the "present situation" was "intolerable," Atwood must take "drastic action." Phillips's tiger team would be maintained and would visit North American again "to see if progress is consistent with that required to achieve program objectives."[22]

Atwood had responded by hiring a new manager, Robert Greer, a retired air force general, to help deal with various technical problems Phillips had uncovered.[23] By April 1966, it had appeared to NASA manned space officials that the company was working to correct its deficiencies, and hence they had decided to take no action against the company.[24] Atwood would not remove Storms, however, who continued in charge of North American's work for NASA.

NBC's Bergman had told Senator Mondale what he knew about NASA's conflict with North American and the "report" on those troubles. At the hearings, Mondale asked the NASA officials if the agency had considered turning to another contractor. Seamans indicated that there had been no thought given to transferring the spacecraft contract, but there had been consideration regarding shift of some of the engine work at one time. What about the Phillips report? Mondale asked Webb, taking the NASA administrator by surprise. For the first time in the hearings (and perhaps in his tenure at NASA), Webb was unsure what to say.

"When I asked Webb about it, you should have seen the look on his face," Mondale later recalled. "It was clear to me that this was the one thing they didn't want to happen." Webb said as little as possible. He knew of no such report, nor could Mueller recall a document with that name. Seamans said there had been field surveys, but NASA had not thought of these as reports. After the hearings, Webb went up to the senator. "You should know enough to ask the chairman of the committee before you ask a question like that," he said. "I'm a Democrat and you're a Democrat."[25]

As Webb and his associates drove back to NASA following the hearings, he cranked up the window separating them from the chauffeur. He was visibly upset, blasting Seamans for volunteering information on the inability of the astronauts to open the hatch. Did he not realize that "millions of dollars were at stake and you don't want to answer any questions unless you're asked"? Seamans said little, except that he was "concerned" about the Phillips report. So was Webb.[26]

At the close of work that afternoon, a farewell party was being given in the general counsel's office for a senior NASA official who was leaving the agency. Seamans left the party early and went back to his office with a large glass of bourbon. As he sipped his drink, Paul Dembling came in carrying a document. In response to the Mondale question, Dembling had made an inquiry, and there it was—the Phillips report. It consisted of a cover letter and collection of notes on Phillips's findings placed in a loose-leaf binder, the package Phillips had sent Atwood in December 1965 following his verbal briefing to the North American chief executive. Seamans told Dembling to "take it to Webb."[27]

When Dembling handed Webb the report, the NASA administrator was aghast. He had intended to write to Mondale confirming that no Phillips report existed. He had certainly given the impression at the hearings that he was either unaware of the document or prevaricating. Dembling recalled Webb saying, "They kept asking me and I told them we didn't have anything. I'd never seen anything. And there was no such report."[28]

From Webb's perspective, Mondale was not just a liberal Democrat who spoke for mayors and others who would rather see NASA money going to cities and the Great Society, he was also the spear carrier for other Minnesota Democrats who wanted to pressure Webb: Joseph Karth in the House and Hubert Humphrey, vice president and head of the Space Council. They had their personal differences with one another but were united in their desire to get Webb to give them more attention and do more for Minnesota. Webb had clashed with Karth over the Electronics Research Center decision, with Humphrey over the vice president's desire to show he could help Minnesota, via NASA's budget, from his Space Council position. Webb thus saw Mondale, rightly or wrongly, as representing larger and more powerful forces, including Anderson, who would savor Webb's discomfort and let the junior senator have his day. Webb's critics had at last found a chink in his armor. Mondale had reason to believe Webb had lied to him about the Phillips report. Or, if he had not known about it, he should have. Maybe Webb was not the great administrator he was cracked up to be. Either way, Mondale and those he represented had a club to wield, and Webb knew it.

Webb called in Mueller, Seamans, and Phillips and upbraided them over the Phillips report. They defended themselves, saying they really did not think of these materials, collected together in a loose-leaf binder, as a "report." Maybe not, but the word "report" was on the front page. Why didn't he know about this?

In the days following the Senate public hearings, the media concentrated criticism of NASA on its "acknowledged shortcomings" and apparent willingness to risk lives for the sake of a race in space. Webb's mind, however, stayed on the Phillips report. He asked Colonel Lawrence Vogel, his onetime executive assistant, who had returned to the army, to temporarily rejoin his staff. He needed help from someone he fully trusted. Vogel agreed, and the necessary arrangements were made.

As the general counsel, Dembling, continued his sweep of documents in headquarters and centers, Webb directed him to give new emphasis to the North American connection. The general counsel's office wrote Phillips that it wanted everything possible in regard to NASA–North American discussions, not only documents but also records of telephone conversations.[29] Webb would not tolerate any more surprises on the witness stand. He wrote Vogel on March 7 to let him know that Dembling had designated one of his staff, S. Neil Hosenball, to work full time with him in acquiring and categorizing information. Regarding the problem of material in the files that the contractor had supplied on the understanding it would not become public, he asked Vogel to work with Hosenball to lay out options.[30]

In mid-March, Webb held a general strategy session with senior NASA officials and various aides to plan for the future congressional investigation, particularly as it touched on NASA–North American relations. In discussing the upcoming legislative hearings on the fire with Dembling, Webb had made it clear that NASA was about to run the gauntlet. Some members of Congress would come at the agency like prosecutors. He told his general counsel to prepare for the hearings as though he were getting ready for a case in court.

Independently of the larger group, Mueller and Webb discussed the Phillips report. Unaware of how much Mondale or others really knew, they believed they had a responsibility to protect North American from full disclosure. Mueller suggested he summarize the report for the committee, while Webb's position was to resist giving out any more than they had to. To protect the report, Webb had Dembling and Hosenball take it to the General Accounting Office, headed by Webb's longtime friend and former BOB assistant Elmer Staats. Although Webb suspected Mondale already had a copy, he was not supposed to, since it was confidential. As an investigative arm of Congress, Webb suggested, GAO could act as custodian of the report and Mondale could inspect it there. When Staats said he could not do this,

Webb and his legislative affairs director, Richard Callaghan, paid Mondale a visit; Webb told the senator he could have the Phillips report on the condition that he not show it to anyone outside government. Mondale refused to make any deals. He made it clear he did not believe Webb was playing straight with him, and he intended to press him hard, the Apollo goal notwithstanding. The meeting was more confrontation than discussion, and neither man gave an inch.[31]

On the bottom of a March 22 memo discussing NASA's legislative strategy, Webb scribbled a handwritten note. We at NASA are "now at [a] turning point regarding Congress—DOD—others," he wrote. NASA was "a new institution" that has had "to establish its legitimacy [as] to function (R&D) and as to method of operation (use of industry with proper safeguards)." NASA had to carry out its work with industry in a manner accountable to Congress and the congressional "need-to-know." However, this accountability had to be exercised "within agreed safeguards."[32]

Even if copies of the Phillips report had already been leaked, Webb decided, if he did not take a stand on it, Congress and the media would want to penetrate even further into NASA's organizational troubles. Congress was already pressuring him for North American's performance records. Another factor weighed heavily on him: he had been told that Phillips would resign if Webb did not defend the integrity of his communications with industry. Phillips felt he had to be absolutely forthright in what he told contractors, and he did not see how he could be effective as a manager if he pulled his punches. Webb did not want to lose Phillips at this critical juncture of the Apollo program. If Phillips went, others might also, and the program management team could unravel.

The centers had problems too, especially MSC, where the three dead astronauts had been not just national celebrities but personal friends. Many of the astronauts, MSC executives, and contractor employees in Houston were drinking heavily in their grief and concern over what they did or did not do that contributed to the deaths. There was finger pointing. Astronaut Thomas Stafford, an Oklahoman, concerned that Webb was not being informed of the situation through channels, called Webb's former associate and friend in Oklahoma, Jamie McWilliams. "I want you to get a message to Webb," he said. "Tell him that if something is not done to straighten out the problems down here, several of us will pull out of the program. I want you to get Webb to do something."[33]

McWilliams flew to Washington, went directly to Webb's office, and transmitted the message. The conversation lasted only a few minutes. The message reminded the NASA administrator that he had to worry not only about the external constituency, but also his internal forces. Would they hold together at this critical moment? His administrative philosophy depended on teamwork. Now that team was showing severe strains.

With such high stakes, Webb knew he had to change his key people in a way that would help the organization recover. He had to act in the short run with an eye to the long run, and he had to do it surgically, decisively, humanely, and quickly. He could not wait.

Reorganizing NASA

The primary issue in the short term was Joe Shea, in charge of Apollo spacecraft development. The Webb-initiated sweep of NASA documents had turned up a "smoking gun" in Shea's possession, a letter Shea had received from Hilliard Paige, an executive with General Electric, on September 29, 1966. To provide technical support to NASA for Apollo, GE worked primarily with the centers and devoted considerable attention to issues of safety and reliability. GE made up part of Webb's management system—checking and balancing technical views of NASA and its prime contractors, intended to provide feedback to various levels of the agency. In the letter, Paige said his people were very concerned about the danger of fire breaking out in the capsule. Since NASA used a pure oxygen atmosphere and certain materials, like Velcro, that were exceedingly flammable, fire would spread rapidly, probably too fast to extinguish. After watching his staff run a test simulating what would happen, Paige was alarmed enough to write the letter. He later recalled this communication as an unusual action on his part. He regarded this as more than just another problem, and he wanted Shea to give the warning his attention as the spacecraft's technical manager.[34] Shea turned the letter over to the safety and reliability engineers in his office to get their opinion. Three weeks later he received a memo from William Bland, chief of the Reliability, Quality, and Test Division of the Apollo Spacecraft Program Office, who noted that his group had been pressed "with more significant problems" and hence had been slow getting back to Shea on the fire issue. The "inherent hazards from fire in the spacecraft are low," he felt, and he saw no need to hold up any spacecraft flight.[35] Shea followed up with a response to Paige on December 5, thanking him for his concern and reassuring him that his office believed there was an "adequate margin of safety." He appended this handwritten postscript: "The problem is sticky—we think we have enough margin to keep fire from starting—if one ever does, we do have problems. Suitable extinguishing agents are not yet developed."[36]

That was that. The correspondence was filed, and neither Shea nor Paige took the fire issue to higher authorities, although Paige considered doing so. He could have gotten the information to higher-ups in NASA, even to Webb, but this would amount to blowing the whistle on Shea. He concluded that GE had to get along with Shea and Houston generally, and he did not want to injure the personal and institutional relationships that had been established with considerable difficulty.[37] The Webb system of checks and balances and multiple channels of information upward in this case did not work as Webb intended.

Whatever else might be said, Shea had made a mistake. Moreover, his relation with Gilruth, never close, was now deteriorating. Convinced that Shea had not kept him adequately informed of problems, Gilruth also worried that Shea was heading for a nervous breakdown.[38] An executive with a contractor closely associated with the program in Houston already had cracked under the pressure. In fact Shea was terribly devastated by the astronauts' deaths. He blamed himself. Reports came to Webb and others in headquarters that he was drinking excessively and driving at breakneck speeds on narrow roads at the Cape, that he was not sleeping much and was totally exhausted. Shea did not share this view of his condition.

Deeply conscious of his responsibility to NASA, Webb also remembered what Shea had done for the agency—he had helped steer the LOR decision to a conclusion and then had run the spacecraft development office well until the fire. He did not want Shea testifying before Congress in his current emotional state. He could not take a hard grilling, Webb thought, and Mondale was saying NASA was guilty of "criminal negligence." In mid-March, Shea and his wife went to Washington, where Shea was to deliver a Goddard lecture, a significant address within the space community. Webb was appalled by the title of the lecture, "The Crucible of Development." Because he and Gilruth had forbidden Shea to talk about Apollo, Shea had used historical analogies to communicate his message "that technological development is a 'severe, searching test'—a dictionary definition of 'crucible'—and the fire had been such a test." But Webb saw crucible "with its connotations of fire and molten metal." He "called Shea to his office and persuaded him to change the title to 'Research and Development in Perspective.' Shea consented, reluctantly. He in turn was frustrated with Webb, Gilruth, and the rest—in his view, he at least was trying to confront the larger truths of what had happened. The others were trying to back away from it."[39]

In his effort to contain the damage to NASA that the fire had caused, Webb wanted to use images that would soften, not exacerbate, feelings. As he told Seamans, referring to Shea's speech, NASA was for many the embodiment of technology, and technology was not as popular as it had been in the early 1960s. In 1967, technology was associated with Vietnam and industrial pollution. NASA must avoid images "such as that of feeling we are apostles of a new ideology—as a new semi-religion of technology." The agency had to take a different stance in the present environment, made worse by the fire, and send a more humble message: "We are workmen at a hard job, needing to overcome a setback and in that role we will hold our support."[40]

Although Shea's speech, even with a new title, had not been what Webb had in mind, he believed that Shea was in fragile condition and had to be handled carefully for his own protection, as well as the good of NASA. When the Sheas arrived in Washington for the lecture, Webb picked them up at the airport and persuaded them to stay at his home. "Shea had come without his topcoat and it was still cold in Washington. Webb insisted he take an old topcoat from Webb's State Department days, an elegant black one."[41]

At the same time, Webb was orchestrating a legislative strategy for NASA that would keep Shea from testifying. He and NASA's chief physician at Houston, Charles Berry, had insisted that Shea take a vacation, and shortly after returning to Houston from Washington, he had done so. Within a week, however, Webb sent Seamans to Houston to confer with Berry, who went to Shea's vacation retreat in central Texas and told him to take an extended leave. An announcement to that effect would be released the following morning. Shea refused. He was all right, he said, not sick, and anxious to get Apollo moving again. It was the people above him who were in shock, not the troops. Nevertheless, he agreed to have two psychiatrists chosen by NASA examine him that evening. They found Shea under strain, but not psychotic. He might have had his problems right after the fire, but he was in control of himself now. Shea therefore continued to refuse to take a leave, and the planned announcement was canceled.

This turn of events did not make relations between Shea and his superiors at Houston any easier. Nor did his view that the Apollo spacecraft was basically sound and that little needed to be done to get it back on schedule.

Other technical people at the center and in headquarters believed a much more drastic overhaul was needed. A week after the examination, in late March, George Mueller asked Shea to come to Washington as his deputy. Seamans called and added pressure. Then came Webb. You have spent enough time at the detail level, said Webb. The time has come for you to play a role in policy. Webb knew how to take people up on the mountain-top, Shea later recalled. He accepted the offer, believing that he was being moved up. He was, but also out of the spacecraft directorship and out of the line of political fire.[42]

On the trip to Houston, Seamans had discussed Shea's replacement with Gilruth and his deputy, George Low. In early April, Gilruth and Low sat in Webb's Washington office with Seamans, Mueller, and Phillips, again discussing who could handle this all-important assignment. Webb wished to couple the announcement of Shea's new job with the name of his successor. Low and Gilruth had left for National Airport and were about to take off when a call came from Webb, saying "Hold everything. We are coming." He arrived shortly thereafter, Seamans, Mueller, and Phillips in tow. He knew who he wanted to take Shea's job, he said—Low; the others immediately urged him to accept. Low would have to demote himself—the position of director of the Apollo Spacecraft Program Office had a bureaucratic rank below that of deputy director of MSC—and he would be taking the place of a man he respected for the job he had done in managing the spacecraft program. But he gave in. "I was overwhelmed," he later recalled.[43] The next day, his appointment was announced, along with the reassignment of Shea to Washington to serve as deputy associate administrator for Manned Space Flight.

On the following day, NASA announced a reorganization at head-quarters that had been in the works prior to the fire. An Office of Organization and Management, headed by Harold Finger, would run all the "functional" offices: industry affairs, technology utilization, defense affairs, university affairs, and the Office of Program Plans and Analysis. Nominally, Finger reported to Seamans, the deputy administrator. In the postfire reality, Finger reported to Webb, and Seamans's role was reduced, or at least that was how Seamans, tense and exhausted, saw the situation.

The reorganization, and its announcement at this time, reflected Webb's sense that he had to take action now to strengthen NASA's organizational setup. These personnel and organizational decisions not only represented internal moves critical to the message Webb was sending to the watchers inside and outside NASA but also reflected his dissatisfaction with the organization. The personal investigation he had launched was turning up a range of problems. One of the lawyers conducting the investigation told him, "It's pretty bad. You don't want to know any more."[44] Webb learned that whatever the merits of his administrative system, some people had not done what they were supposed to do. Because the accident had occurred with the spacecraft and the spotlight was on Houston and Shea, the question of removing Gilruth was discussed and rejected. But problems had also surfaced with the Saturn 2, and the investigation illuminated troublesome errors of management at the Marshall center. At one point, an irate Webb told a staff meeting that a lot had gone on about which he did not know, and that was not going to happen again.

What bothered him above all was his sense that the men he trusted most—his senior officials at headquarters—had let him down. They had allowed problems with North American to fester too long. The Phillips report to Atwood was mild compared to what Webb was finding out, especially about NASA views pertaining to Storms. Seamans and Mueller should have brought North American in line, should have communicated to Webb how serious were the problems between agency and contractor. In Webb's view, Mueller had deliberately presented a filtered picture of the situation, and Seamans had failed to press him on it. Mueller was running an independent operation. "You have to penetrate the [OMSF] system," an angry Webb told Seamans. "Don't let Mueller get away with bullshit."[45]

It came to Webb that his external efforts with the president, Congress, and universities, coupled with his faith in Seamans and Mueller, had caused him to neglect his own internal management of Apollo. It was not the "Webb system" that had failed, but certain people who had not done their jobs: Mueller had failed to share unpleasant information upward; Seamans had failed to probe and supervise Mueller enough; Shea had failed to communicate problems to Gilruth; Paige had failed to go beyond Shea in alerting NASA to the danger of fire in the capsule; and Webb had let his outside role dominate his inside responsibilities.

If Webb was part of the problem, he was going to be part of the solution. He reasserted control of the Apollo program with a vengeance. Shunting Mueller and Seamans aside, he took direct charge of the North American question, an intervention essential, in his view, not only because he had lost confidence in Seamans and Mueller, but also because he sensed that the NASA–North American relation would be the primary focus of the upcoming congressional investigation. The Phillips report assured that. As he made changes in NASA—replacing Shea with Low, upgrading Finger at the expense of Seamans—he noted, with dismay bordering on alarm, an absence of parallel action by Atwood at North American.

By Saturday, April 8, the *Apollo 204* Review Board had finished its work. Its report would be delivered Sunday at noon to Webb's office, with congressional hearings scheduled for Monday, at which Webb would be the lead-off witness. Although the exact schedule remained to be worked out, Atwood would testify Tuesday. Would he be ready? Webb told Atwood on Saturday that he had no knowledge of what was in the final board report apart from the interim reports he had received from Seamans, which had been released to the media. His intent, he said, was to release the report, immediately upon receiving it, to the president, Congress, and the media at the same time. He would study it in preparation for the hearings, and he urged Atwood, who would be in Washington Sunday, to have a representative at his office to get the report as soon as possible. It was important, said Webb, for NASA and North American to make whatever management changes were necessary in their relationship expeditiously, in order to recover rapidly from the Apollo disaster and resume manned space flight. He expected Atwood personally to be involved in these negotiations, he said. "It will be my purpose to enter these discussions with a clear objective and to expect your fullest cooperation."[46]

Atwood responded that he and other North American officials would indeed review the report immediately. He would also meet with Webb "at the earliest possible moment" to work out any necessary issues. "You have my personal assurance that the full resources of North American and its personnel are dedicated to the successful and timely accomplishment of the Apollo program, and that we will do everything which appears necessary to that end."[47]

The Review Board Report

Early Sunday morning, the carefully guarded review board report traveled by jet from Kennedy Space Center to Washington. Three thousand pages long, the result of a ten-week, $4 million investigation, it had been prepared under strictest secrecy. Webb's plan to let the media, president, Congress, and NASA have it simultaneously would, he hoped, "prevent a reporter going up to someone and getting that other individual to pop off, because the person would not have read the report." It would force the media "to focus on the substance of the report," rather than to ask some political or administrative official to brief them.[48] It was, in short, a strategy for controlling information flow, if not the information itself.

While Webb knew generally what the report would say, he was surprised at the sharpness of the criticism. Atwood had the same reaction. While the report did not fault particular officials, it strongly castigated both NASA and North American for "many deficiencies" and called for safety improvements. It identified the probable cause of the fire as a faulty electrical wire, and pointed to "deficiencies in design and engineering, manufacture, and quality control," to engineering shortcomings and lax procedures.

Unable to pinpoint the exact cause, the board listed the conditions that led to the tragedy:

— a sealed cabin, pressurized with pure oxygen atmosphere

— an extensive distribution of combustible materials in the cabin

— vulnerable wiring carrying spacecraft power

— vulnerable plumbing carrying a combustible and corrosive coolant

— inadequate provision for the crew to escape

— inadequate provisions for rescue or medical assistance

Furthermore, "careful consideration" of how the fire could have happened "leads the board to the conclusion that in its devotion to the many difficult problems of space travel, the Apollo team failed to give adequate attention to certain mundane but equally vital questions of crew safety." Indicative of the sloppiness in the manufacture process, the board cited a wrench socket inadvertently left between two bundles of wiring. Among its numerous recommendations, the board called for a new escape hatch (which NASA already had decided to develop) and serious study of the possibility of replacing the pure oxygen system, which "feeds a fire with blast-furnace intensity," with a two-gas system—mixing nitrogen with oxygen to create an atmosphere more like ordinary air. However, the two-gas system would mean a larger spacecraft and spacecraft walls capable of standing greater internal pressure in the vacuum of space.[49]

The criticism in the report obviated any charges of a whitewash. It made clear that the deaths were avoidable, a result of human error. But the board did not go beyond its technical focus to larger management problems such as NASA–North American relations, or, say, the GE-MSC relationship, and it did not blame specific individuals. Olin Teague, chair of the House subcommittee charged with conducting the investigation, declared the report "a broad indictment of NASA and North American and the whole program." He was "disappointed and surprised," he said, at the laxity of those participating in the project, and he would hold hearings right away, mornings, afternoons, and evenings, to get at the issues. Some of the "carelessness" indicated in the report he found "unbelievable."[50]

FROM CRISIS
TO RECOVERY

A_s *Webb prepared* for the congressional hearings and media blitz associated with the fire, outwardly a man in control, inside he was distraught. He wanted desperately to succeed with Apollo and saw his response to the fire at this critical moment as crucial to the future of the program.

Defending NASA on Capitol Hill

On April 10, 1967, House hearings on the Apollo fire began at 9:00 A.M. and lasted well into the evening in a room packed with Apollo project officials, contractor representatives, the media, and other interested observers.[1] Webb led off. He declared that those involved with the Apollo project could correct their errors and fulfill their goal of placing a man on the moon by 1970. "Whatever our faults," he said, "we are an able-bodied team." When several members of the subcommittee argued for a reexamination of the Apollo project, Webb said that, in his opinion, the board had "overstated the case." "We will take our part of the blame for what we have done or left undone," he declared, "but I believe this committee can have confidence that NASA and its contractors have capability to overcome every deficiency required to proceed on and to successfully fly the Apollo-Saturn system and accomplish its objectives." He had spoken to the head of the review board on Sunday night, he said, and had asked him to say frankly whether he thought the basic design of the Apollo system could be made to work; he had also asked Frank Borman, the astronaut on the review board, his opinion. Both men felt that the problems the board had found could be overcome.

As always, Webb's delivery was rapid-fire. But John Noble Wilford, who covered the hearings for the *New York Times,* noted that Webb's voice quickened when he asked, with emotion, "for whom the Apollo bell tolls." He went on to convey his own sense of what was at stake in the Apollo investigation:

> If any man in this room asks for whom the Apollo bell tolls, it tolls for him and me, as well as for Grissom, White, and Chaffee.
>
> It tolls for every astronaut test pilot who will lose his life in the space simulated vacuum of a test chamber or the real vacuum of space.
>
> It tolls for every astronaut scientist who will lose his life on some lonely hill on the moon or Mars.
>
> It tolls for an open program continuously evaluated by opinion makers with little time for second thought—operating in the brilliant color and brutal glare of real-time, worldwide mass media with the speed of the television, from euphoria to exaggerated detail.
>
> In my view NASA's senior officials and the members of your committee have a grave responsibility to work together to purge what is bad in the systems we together have created and supported.
>
> We have perhaps an even graver responsibility to so act as to preserve what is good and represents, still at this hour, a high point in all mankind's vision of a new day on earth because the rocket engine makes it possible, but just possible, to explore and use that vast and unlimited region that separates us from our sun and other planets—that region we call space.[2]

If Webb's words sounded a clarion call for Congress, media, and others to raise their vision to larger responsibilities, they did not deter panel members from attacking him and NASA. Republican Donald Rumsfeld of Illinois, who had introduced a bill to create an independent review board, declared that the *Apollo 204* Review Board, most of whose members were NASA employees, could not be sufficiently candid. Behind the fire lay fundamental management problems, he charged. Webb denied that the review board had pulled punches, claiming its members to be the best qualified individuals to conduct the investigation. Representative Ken Hechler, a West Virginia Democrat, suggested it might be necessary to revise and resubmit NASA's budget. "I don't agree with that," Webb retorted sharply. He "sat on the edge of the leather [witness] chair and leaned toward the microphone on the witness table," Wilford wrote.[3] While willing to admit error, he was intent on defending his agency.

The next day's *New York Times*, in its editorial verdict, found NASA and North American guilty of "incompetence and negligence." The *Times* saw "incredible complacency" in the "disgraceful and disheartening findings of the Review Board," whose report it called "candid and hard-hitting" and whose authors it commended, even though "they quailed before the challenge of identifying the basic cause of the failures they found." The real problem, said the *Times*, "was the whole irrational public relations environment of the space program with its technically senseless—and, as the Apollo tragedy proved, highly dangerous—dedication to the meaningless time table of putting a man on the moon by 1970." In the name of a "politically set schedule," "enormous risks were run that cost the lives of astronauts Grissom, White, and Chaffee." The *Times* demanded "that safety, not public relations . . . dominate future NASA policy under a new leadership."[4] In calling for "new leadership," the *New York Times* said indirectly what a number of his detractors demanded directly: Webb had to go. It was he for whom the bell tolls.

That Webb seemed to snap at certain legislative critics worsened already strained relations, but as he explained to a legislative supporter, he had to come on strong in the hearings in responding to particular questions to prevent "any kind of an attack [that might] begin to build momentum."[5] While none of the other NASA officials attempted such a stance, Webb felt his role was to meet force with force.

The House committee met from April 10 to April 12, day and night. On the last evening, members probed the NASA–North American relationship and the Phillips report. In his testimony, Phillips said that during the period of his tiger team effort, he thought about taking part of the space contract away from North American and giving the work to one of NASA's own centers. Seamans, however, said that this had never been formally recommended.

The next day, as the House committee paused in its hearings, the Senate Space Committee got under way, its focus the NASA–North American relation. Seamans and OMSF officials disclosed that they had indeed been unhappy with North American in late 1965. Seamans pointed out that North American had approximately 25 percent of the Apollo work. However, the company had made reforms in response to NASA complaints, and Seamans and Phillips tried to clarify the earlier remarks by denying that they had ever considered bringing in a new contractor.

The next hearings were set for Monday, April 17. In the interim, Webb met privately with senior members of both committees, working feverishly to win their support. He candidly admitted faults, managerial as well as procedural, took full responsibility for mistakes, and said he would correct the problems, not only in NASA but in North American. He would testify on Monday, he said, but asked for two weeks after that date to review the report more intensively and make necessary decisions. He would then be in a position to give Congress a plan for recovery. He wanted Congress to trust him.

The committees went along with Webb. They could wait two weeks. In fact, everyone needed more time to digest the review board's report and the initial testimony. Meanwhile, Webb supplied Teague with the memo he requested—seven and a half pages that summarized the Phillips report and steps taken subsequently to correct the problems—and said he would do the same for the Senate.[6]

In winning the two-week reprieve, Webb impressed some observers with his powers of persuasion with Congress. Still, Evert Clark, who reported on NASA for the *New York Times*, perceived a change. "The tough effusive optimist who has bulldozed his agency along the road to the moon so successfully until now" seemed "wounded." "The fire has faced the space program with a crisis of confidence for the first time. From the President down to the lowest-paid National Aeronautics and Space Administration public relations man, the image projected for the program in the past was one of near-perfection—systematized, computerized, and almost infallible." Clark was correct. Webb had consciously created this image from the moment he was sworn in. This was to be the best-managed agency ever, and he had worked at the reality and image as part of his strategy to keep Congress and the White House from trying to run the space program. Now, wrote Clark, the NASA "facade" had been "broken."[7]

What Webb had going for him, Clark pointed out, was the Soviet Union. After a two-year hiatus, mounting evidence indicated that the Russians wanted back in the space race and were "developing a rocket larger than the Saturn V." That helped explain congressional willingness to give Webb time. Congressional desires to seek the jugular were "tempered by the fear of further damaging an important national program."[8]

On April 17, Webb made his first appearance before the Senate Space Committee investigators. Twice, he was pressed for details of NASA's relation with North American. Other NASA officials, in testimony the previous week, had strongly criticized North American's performance. Had he ever considered canceling the $3.3 billion contract? Webb said he preferred not to answer, for such public disclosure might set a precedent that could destroy the "intimate and confidential" nature of dealings between NASA and its contractors. He told the senators he would, if requested, give his answer in "a non-public way." "I will say this," he noted. "It was never recommended to me that I change contractors away from North American." Webb seemed to defend North American when one of the senators accused the company of negligence. "I don't think you can call it negligence," he said, "if somebody is unable to operate at 100 percent. They did not do all the things they should have done, but I can say the same things for all of us at NASA."[9]

That evening, five astronauts, led by Borman, were to testify before the House committee. Before going to the Hill, Borman met privately with Webb in his office. "Frank," Webb said, "the American people need to understand what happened just as we now understand. You are not to try in any way to hold back facts or color your testimony in NASA's favor. Just tell them exactly what your investigating group found, no holds barred, even if it makes NASA look bad." They rode over to Congress in Webb's car. As they were about to walk into the committee room, Webb took Borman's arm. "Remember, tell the whole truth," he said quietly.[10]

Borman did. "None of us gave real concern to a fire in the spacecraft [during a test on the pad] and this is the crux of the problem," he said. But "you are asking us do we have confidence in the spacecraft management, our own training, and do we have confidence in our leaders. I am embarrassed because it appears to be a party line. The response we have given is the truth. We are trying to tell you that we are confident in our management and in ourselves. I think the question is really are you confident in us?"[11] Borman's testimony, in the judgment of many, including that of Chairman Teague, swung votes on the House committee. Some had been ready to call for a delay in the space program by as much as five years, but if the men whose lives were on the line had confidence in NASA management, maybe the legislators should also. As an astronaut and member of the review board, Borman had a special credibility. He was known as one of the "straight arrows" in the astronaut corps.

Ironically, Webb's testimony earlier in the day had hurt NASA with the Senate Space Committee. His strategy—to say as little as possible, at least in public, and to counterpunch aggressively in defense of NASA and even North American—bothered some of the senators. It was not his aggressiveness as much as his evasiveness that caused them consternation.

But if the senators were bothered, the media were even more frustrated. The *New York Times,* in particular, found Webb less than forthcoming. The word went around that NASA stood for "never a straight answer." "I have found that while NASA has more information than a dog has fleas while all is going well," observed William Hines, a NASA critic on the *Washington Evening Star,* "the experts tend to pull back for regrouping when things go wrong." Mary McGrory, writing in the same paper, found Webb to be his usual garrulous self in the hearings, except concerning the Phillips report. "His method of dealing with difficult questions," she wrote, was "simplicity itself. He does not answer them." McGrory described how Webb dealt with Senator Howard Cannon, Democrat from Nevada, who asked if he had ever considered canceling the contract with North American. Webb "raised a hand." "Is it wise," he inquired, "to make that kind of statement in public here—getting into that kind of detail, whatever the situation is?" "North American and I," he continued, "are determined to find a relation on which we can go forward. I would prefer not to start the precedent of discussing this. It affects the rights of many people in this room." Just then, McGrory noted, the bell for a Senate vote was rung.[12]

Negotiating with North American

Webb was both protective of North American before Congress and dictatorial in his direct dealings with the company. In between hearing appearances and informal meetings with legislators, he was locked in conflict with Lee Atwood. During the initial set of hearings on the report, when Atwood was in town to testify, he met with Webb at NASA for an hour and convinced Webb that he did not intend to make changes, especially in regard to Storms.[13]

Within NASA, Storms was controversial. Aptly nicknamed "Stormy," he was exceedingly strong-willed, a trait that helped and hurt him. Many of Webb's top associates regarded him as stubborn, and Phillips and Mueller questioned his competence. Mueller felt that the Apollo spacecraft was too complex a machine for Storms, whose approach to management he described as "basically to yell at people to go fix things." After the fire, Webb became convinced that Storms had to be replaced, not least because Storms, like Shea, resisted making major changes in the spacecraft. "There's not a goddam thing wrong with those spacecraft," he said after the fire. "If they want to fly one this December, just fly what we've got." Few in NASA agreed.[14]

In April, Webb told Atwood that he was not satisfied with the "hand-shake on December 28, 1966," the informal agreement between NASA and North American negotiators on a new North American contract. Since November, the company had been working on a "letter contract," a situation Webb found deplorable. That handshake was based on a NASA confidence in North American that Webb no longer felt. NASA and North American would have to work out a new relationship. Such a relationship involved more than contracts and dates, Webb said. It entailed confidence. NASA could not inspect quality into North American products. Webb told Atwood that he personally would lead NASA negotiations for a new contract, and he wanted Atwood to do the same, both assisted by appropriate specialists.[15] Furthermore, Webb wrote several days later, "when we meet we must, in my view, come right to grips with the real problems which must be solved if NASA and North American are to have a continuing relationship on which the success of the Apollo program can rest." Some conversations between NASA and North American in the past had not really made any difference, in Webb's view. "The time has passed for this kind of exchange."[16]

Hence, when Webb testified before the Senate a few days later, on April 17, he had no intention of divulging his position with respect to North American. He preferred to settle matters in private rather than make a case before Congress and in the media. He had made changes in NASA and expected North American to do the same. In public, he called North American "our wonderful associates." In private, he called the company something else.

Atwood wrote Webb on April 18 that he was establishing a group to assist him, and he would be ready to enter into negotiations. "It will be our objective to demonstrate that a valid basis exists which would warrant NASA's full confidence in North American, both in the contract area and in other aspects of the program." Webb's own preparations for the negotiations were intense. His staff analyzed options, including the possibility of removing work from North American, and the costs and benefits of doing so. In studying the criticisms North American might make of NASA and devising NASA responses, the staff came up with quite a few possibilities, for example, "There was no single face in our dealings with NASA; there were differing philosophies of contract management in the two centers [MSC and MSFC]; funding was sporadic and often resulted in short-term contractual arrangements; there were differences in MSC and MSFC specifications; there were long delays in approval of specifications by MSFC."[17]

To make sure Atwood would take the negotiations seriously, Webb called Robert Lovett, the former Truman administration official and current director of North American, whose advice about the company Webb had obtained prior to his choosing North American for the Apollo spacecraft award. Webb explained his position, sent Lovett a copy of his letter to Atwood detailing NASA–North American problems and their need to resolve them, and asked Lovett to show it to Atwood's board or at least the executive committee. This unusual step, pressuring an executive through his board, was one Webb had used during the Ranger investigation to get DuBridge to listen. It had worked then. Webb hoped it would work now.

Webb met Atwood in Washington on April 24. Assisted by lawyers and procurement specialists, the two negotiated for four and a half hours. The meeting was confrontational, with the faults of both sides put squarely on the table. Afterward, Webb concluded "that the management of the company, right up to Mr. Atwood himself, does not have a realistic approach to either understanding or solving the problems which exist. . . . I saw no evidence that would give me confidence that NASA will not have to act to either terminate the present contract and re-advertise the work or work with the management to bring in stronger men who can give leadership to a work force that does have certain measures of strength, or, alternatively, separate the NASA work in the S&I Division from the rest of the company and endeavor to find some consortium that can operate it to the completion of the present contracts. . . . NASA's problem today is to get equipment moving forward, incorporating the necessary changes, and getting ready to fly again."[18]

Webb and Atwood continued to meet over the next two days. During the course of the discussions and arguments, Atwood showed Webb a number of letters written to NASA which he said hadn't been answered. Webb ordered an immediate search, and the accumulated letters turned up, unanswered, at the Apollo Spacecraft Office in Houston. Atwood's case had merit, but Webb had made meaningful changes in Houston. Joe Shea was gone; George Low was in his place. What was Atwood going to do about Harrison Storms? He was, at this point, resisting making the key personnel change Webb demanded.

According to Atwood, Storms's background and enthusiasm made him "the ideal focal point and leader" of North American's space operation. "He always reached for the maximum in performance, and, from an engineering point of view, he had become a prime candidate for our most valuable player."[19] Atwood valued loyalty and did not intend to let Webb make a scapegoat of Storms. After a mild heart attack in 1966, Storms had come back strong; his performance on the job was excellent. Less interested in close management supervision than in engineering issues, and currently engaged in discussions with the Rockwell Corporation, Atwood had relied heavily on Storms and was convinced that Storms had served him well. Like Webb, Atwood could be gentlemanly in manner. But inside he was iron-willed, more than capable of defending his position. Storms himself knew he was an issue and believed he was being "unjustifiably crucified."[20] He thought Webb was trying to protect NASA by casting the blame on North American.

For Webb, Atwood was a frustration. He did not seem remotely aware of the seriousness of the situation for NASA, his own company, and the space program. Refusing to admit there was a problem in appearance as well as fact, Atwood was insensitive to the politics of the moment, in sharp contrast to Webb. For the NASA administrator, both the political problem and the technical issues demanded a response, and he saw Atwood as unwilling to address either. For Atwood, Webb was an enigma. Where was the issue of "fairness" in this discussion? Atwood wanted to know. He would not budge on the matter of Storms. The two men—equally convinced of their respective positions, totally different in approach—talked at and past one another.

Atwood also was holding firm against other changes Webb wanted. Webb was adamant about penalizing North American financially for the fire. As Dembling recalled, Webb told Atwood, "I'm not going to pay you any bonuses [as the company was due under its arrangement with NASA]. I can't face the American people and tell them we're going to pay the contractor bonuses after three people got burned up. You can sue me. You can do whatever the hell you want. I am not going to pay you. We're going to enter into a new contract." He did not believe North American had dealt with the government in good faith in the earlier contract negotiations. "They had a lot of people out there who didn't want to do it our way," recalled Webb, "but our way had to prevail if we were really going forward with Apollo. . . . I told them they had to do certain things. . . . They said we are not going to do them and I stood up at the table and I said, 'All right, Lee, these are not negotiable, if you are not going to do them I am going to take away every goddam contract work you have with us if I can and give it to somebody else.'"[21]

On Friday, April 28, the negotiations at a standstill, Atwood returned to California. Webb and Seamans discussed the situation. Webb had made a threat. Now what? Seamans doubted that NASA could cancel the spacecraft contract and still attain the lunar goal. Nevertheless, he suggested, "Why not invite Lockheed and Boeing, and lay our cards on the table? Tell North American we [are] doing it. See if we don't get some action." The next day, Webb drafted a memo to the Boeing Company. NASA was not satisfied with North American, he said. He wanted to know if Boeing, among other companies, could help get Apollo moving again.[22]

A letter to Atwood followed. As far as he could tell, Webb said, Atwood had interpreted the review Phillips had conducted in fall 1965 as concerned strictly with engineering problems. A great deal more than that was involved, however, and Atwood had not dealt with the management issues. Moreover, "your view that the Apollo 204 review board misjudged the quality of workmanship being provided by North American is not shared." Hence, he said, "I am asking senior officials of those companies with well recognized capabilities, including particularly Boeing, Lockheed, Martin, McDonnell, and General Electric, to give me their frank judgment as to whether there are resources in the country that can help us get the Apollo program moving forward in a better way than I now feel we can with the present pattern with its heavy reliance on North American."[23]

Webb had played his strongest card by risking the Apollo goal, for replacing North American would inevitably add delays and cause the program to slip well beyond 1970. He handed the letter to Larry Greene, a Washington representative of North American, who flew to California and delivered it to Atwood. Atwood had been agonizing over the choices. The financial aspects were negotiable in his view. NASA was his biggest customer. In the midst of negotiations with another giant corporation, Rockwell, on a merger, the fire had created terrible image and morale problems. Although he wanted to protect Storms and other executives associated with Apollo, the Webb letter reaffirmed what Webb had said to him in Washington— either North American would comply or Webb would go elsewhere. Was Webb bluffing?

Atwood decided he could not take the chance. He told Storms that he would have to transfer him from the NASA work to another assignment in North American. Then he called Bill Bergen, corporate vice-president at North American for the Space and Propulsion Group, a position higher than Storms's. Bergen had only recently joined North American after thirty years with Martin, the company NASA's Source Evaluation Board had originally recommended for the contract in 1961. He volunteered to give up the Space and Propulsion Group and take over the Space Division—to demote himself, just as NASA's George Low had demoted himself for the good of Apollo. "God bless you," said Atwood.[24]

In a letter to Webb dated Sunday, April 30, Atwood conceded to all his demands. He would replace Storms with Bergen, make numerous other organizational changes, and "personally . . . focus all the Corporation's resources in support of Bill Bergen." Also, "to symbolize that the Division will be wholly dedicated to space work, we are designating it as a Space Division." He included a memo of understanding between North American and NASA aimed at showing his approach to a strong cooperative relationship with NASA.[25] Greene flew back to Washington that evening with the letter, to get it on Webb's desk Monday morning. The weekend was one Webb and Atwood would remember. Atwood later said that he realized that some management changes had to be made, but he remained bitter about replacing Storms, who he felt "had done a good job in most respects." He did not know that Storms had failed technically. Still, "he had lost communication with NASA, fire or no fire."[26]

The official announcement of the changes in North American came on May 1. In addition to the Bergen-Storms shift, Ralph Rand, corporate vice president in charge of manufacturing, was named executive vice president of the renamed Space Division, replacing William Snelling, who was moved to another post. The following day, Atwood sent Webb a list of implementing actions, a follow-up to his memo. Webb replied that Atwood's actions were "late, but may not be too late," although NASA was talking with other contractors. He advised Atwood to be candid and not worry about NASA's reaction in his testimony when Senate hearings resumed. The basic system NASA had created for getting the job done had to be protected, and that was the key issue. "Whether or not American industry and NASA emerge from the legislative process we are going through with increased capability and know-how, and, in addition, a basic understanding on the part of those who must feel confidence in the operation for it to succeed, is in many ways the major question involved in the examination of the facts related to the Apollo 204 fire."[27]

NASA would keep its relation with North American, Webb decided, but he wanted an extra check on the California company. Boeing was already serving in a dual capacity, developing one of the Saturn stages and also performing work involved in linking the three stages into a system. Why not extend the Boeing contract to tie together the rocket and spacecraft? This "integration" contract would superimpose Boeing over North

American and give an extra incentive to North American to shape up.

Bill Allen, president of Boeing, came to Webb's office with two of his top executives. Webb regarded him as a friend and someone he trusted. Allen made it clear that Boeing, already very busy, did not "covet this work" of coordinating the contractors; if Boeing took on this task, it would want to work directly with Sam Phillips. Given Webb's feelings about Mueller and Seamans at this moment, giving Phillips more authority had its attractions. A few days later he called Allen in Seattle. "Bill, I'm going before the Senate subcommittee investigating the pad fire later today, and I want you to listen to a statement I'm reading to the subcommittee."

"Go ahead," Allen said.

"I have just hired the Boeing Company to perform an Apollo technical integration and evaluation program." Webb paused. "Bill, you've got to do this for us."

"I told you we don't covet this," Allen said, "but if it's in the national interest we'll do it." He subsequently gave George Stoner, director of the Boeing Space Division, the new NASA assignment. The chain of command, de facto, ran from Stoner to Phillips to Webb.[28]

Redeeming Apollo and Webb

In areas other than the dealings with North American and Boeing, the period between Webb's congressional appearances (April 17–May 9) proved eventful. Congressman Teague and several others on the House Space Committee flew to Kennedy Space Center to examine the accident site and talk with NASA officials. Having been told Shea was not in condition to testify, Teague also wanted to determine for himself whether Shea could be called. He concluded he should not.[29] Days later, a Soviet cosmonaut, Vladimir Komarov, died on April 23, as he tried to bring his *Soyuz 1* spacecraft back to earth after an aborted flight. The announcement of the death not only proved that the Soviet Union was still in the space race but also underlined the inherently hazardous nature of the space enterprise and took some of the edge off the Apollo fire as a singular U.S. accident.

On April 30, New York Democrat William Fitz Ryan, an outspoken Webb opponent on the House Space Committee, made public a copy of the Phillips report. Although its text was highly critical of North American, it revealed nothing that was not already known, in more general ways, from earlier hearings, other leaks, and newspaper reports.[30] Ryan nevertheless called for a full-scale investigation of NASA. Teague (who NASA believed also had obtained a copy of the report) disagreed, commenting cuttingly that "the members of this committee who have worked actively in the space program have no complaints."[31]

At this critical moment, Margaret Chase Smith, leading Republican on the Senate Space Committee, proved Webb's ally. She asked Elmer Staats, head of the General Accounting Office, to obtain the Phillips report so she could look at it. This was the method Webb had wanted to establish in the first place, and he sent it to Staats, who now felt he could go along with the procedure at the request of Smith. Webb again stated his position that the information in the document was gathered in part from interviews of company employees, to which the company had agreed on the understanding that the information gathered would remain confidential, a principle that was critical to preserve. Webb needed Senator Smith on his side. He had almost lost her support through a careless slip in the April hearings, when, in response to her question, he had said North American had been NASA's top choice, skirting the edges of the truth. The Source Evaluation Board had favored Martin, and Webb had selected North American. When his misstatement came to light, Webb had spent time between hearings mending fences with Senator Smith.[32] She trusted and respected Webb, who turned his southern charm on her, but she was under pressure herself, as the senior Republican involved in the investigation, to be hard-nosed with him. The Republicans were looking for ways to embarrass the Johnson administration, with a presidential election not far away.

Webb's continuing problems with Anderson, chair of the Senate Space Committee, made Smith's support even more valuable. Webb wrote Anderson on May 8 expressing dismay that he and others on the Senate committee were unhappy with his testimony. The hearings were set to resume the next day, and Webb said he wanted to find a way by which "the Committee could reestablish the confidence in NASA it formerly had."[33]

When Webb went before Congress on May 9 and 10, two issues appeared on the agenda that had emerged from the initial hearings, both Webb's doing. The first was a report on what NASA and North American were going to do to get Apollo back on track. The second, indirectly Webb's responsibility, grew out of his performance at the hearings—his resistance to revealing the Phillips report, his answers (and nonanswers) to other questions. *He* was now an issue.

To the extent the focus was on him, however, it was less on NASA, and many in the agency believed Webb had deliberately steered the agenda of the hearings in this direction, setting himself up as the lightning rod. They thought he was using the Phillips report now as a diversionary tactic to protect his organization. His attitude at this time, they noted, was a defiant "Come and get me." And he also had friends on the Space Committees: Teague in the House, as well as the chair of the full committee, and on the Senate side, powerful individuals with whom he had had close relations back to the Truman administration, such as Stuart Symington. His most important advocate, however, was Margaret Chase Smith, who prevented the attack on Webb from becoming a partisan issue.

These hearings constituted a second legislative phase. Where the first had seen a general probing by Congress for issues, this one focused on key issues, Webb himself among them. His detractors held that Webb's administrative power had gotten too great, and Congress had to assert its influence over Apollo at Webb's expense.

Webb and senior NASA associates testified before both the House and Senate Space Committees, announcing "sweeping Apollo revisions." The new flight schedule set the first manned Apollo flight at March 1968, at the earliest. Changes in headquarters and field included a new office of flight safety reporting directly to Mueller, and an expanded flight safety office at Kennedy Space Center that would augment the emergency training of relevant NASA personnel. The North American contract would be renegotiated, minus the incentive fees previously planned. North American would retain responsibility as prime contractor for the spacecraft, but Boeing would have a new assignment integrating the North American work with the total Saturn/Apollo system. NASA would consider other forms of contractor assistance as necessary. North American would not be contracted for post-Apollo work that could constitute a diversion from its Apollo task. Finally, participation of the astronaut group in future key decisions would be assured by new responsibilities assigned to such astronauts as Frank Borman, who would chair an engineering group based at North American's Downey, California, plant. NASA was assuming $75 million as the cost of the Apollo spacecraft redesign, which would include a new escape hatch, fireproof materials, and better distribution and protection of flammable materials. The spacesuit would be made virtually fireproof, Velcro and other combustible materials replaced. NASA would continue to study the option of conducting ground tests with a two-gas atmosphere in place of pure oxygen; a decision would follow the other design changes.[34]

The Space Committees took no particular issue with any of the management and technical matters, welcoming them all. But what about Webb? Senator Smith gave him the opportunity to clarify the question of North

American's being the first choice. It was not the choice of the Source Evaluation Board, he said, but his own. In the House hearings, Ryan pointed out that "the Phillips report is now part of public knowledge, though not for any thanks to NASA." Webb suggested that the Phillips report failed to show that after the report was made to North American, NASA had gone over the deficiencies with North American, and, by April 1966, most of the troubles had been cleared up. "That's not the issue," said Ryan. "It may be," responded Webb, "that the issue is whether you want to distort the truth about the program."[35]

The issue of truth held center stage. Webb's performance on "the Webb issue" received, at best, a mixed reception. The *New York Times* found him, not Ryan, at fault. "NASA Candor Needed," it editorialized in response to the second round of hearings, reminding readers that in April Webb had said North American was first choice. Now, he was saying Martin was first, until overruled. No wonder, said the *Times*, cynics had raised the possibility that the notorious Bobby Baker had had something to do with the award. The *Times* demanded, as had Ryan, a full investigation by Congress.[36]

Other newspapers leveled similar criticisms. "NASA Accused of Covering Up Troubles," read a *Washington Post* headline on May 11, followed by "Webb Issues 3rd Version of Apollo" the next day. "Honeymoon Over," *Aviation Week and Space Technology* commented, claiming Webb's credibility had been further damaged by his recent testimony and noting that the "usual critics were joined by traditionally friendly members from both parties who accused Webb of not keeping them informed of NASA problems" and that "some congressmen . . . would not take Webb's testimony at face value again and vowed the strictest future surveillance of the space program."[37] Webb was especially bothered by stories in the *Washington Evening Star*, which featured articles on various NASA problems, based on leaks of documents. Webb believed the paper was getting its information by bribing its way into NASA files, and he said as much to others.

In fact NASA's decision making had created plenty of problems—inevitable given the complex, large-scale, and fast-paced effort that was Apollo. The question was how much Congress should know, and who was to determine what it knew, how, and when. Webb obviously felt it best for the program if *he* determined the flow of information to Congress. His interest, at this point, was in damage control.

Some members of Congress continued to probe. If the Phillips report was not that unusual, as NASA said, then there must be other "Phillips reports," and Congress wanted to see them. In fact, it wanted to know about all the other NASA-contractor problems. And what about this Bobby Baker business? No evidence supported the gossip that Bobby Baker and lobbyist Fred Black had influenced the North American award through Senator Robert Kerr; the problems lay with appearances. Webb had stock in the Oklahoma City bank that had allegedly profited indirectly from some Kerr-Black-Baker–North American connection. He had helped bring the Kerr-McGee interests into the Fidelity National Bank and Trust Company of Oklahoma City, he had served as bank director, and he still owned a large amount of stock in the bank. In the wake of the fire, he learned that after North American received the multibillion-dollar Apollo contract, it transferred large amounts to the bank, thereby presumably advantaging Kerr-McGee—and himself.[38]

If Webb considered resigning, as some speculated at the time, he said nothing about doing so. In fact, he later recalled his attitude as one of fighting harder—"pushing the accelerator to the floor" in terms of his own personal effort. In 1966, he had averaged a speech a week. In the first four months of 1967, he made twenty-seven speeches to audiences ranging from the Huntington, West Virginia, Rotary Club to the National War College in Washington.[39]

Webb saw the momentum building against him and disliked his own children's reading about this shady political operator who was their father. His son, studying at Princeton, wrote asking how he could stand the barrage of criticism. Webb was determined to end the rumor, innuendo, and finger pointing, to clear his own name and NASA's, where morale was plunging as the attacks continued. At this point Senator Smith told him that a top North American lobbyist had been talking out against Webb, warning that he was going to have to be "cut down to size." Smith had told him she was backing Webb, but Webb foresaw a problem, especially with Anderson.[40]

Showdown with the Senate Space Committee

Webb decided to force a showdown and asked Anderson for an executive session, during which he would answer any and all questions. Anderson was at first reluctant, but Webb would not back off. To pressure Anderson, he contacted each member of the Senate Space Committee, asking for an executive session. He would bring all materials having to do with North American and other contractors with problems; he would bring his associates; he would answer any questions senators had about him personally. Nothing would be held back. He wanted to put this matter to rest.

Under the circumstances, Anderson had little choice. He asked the committee's professional staff to review the original notes concerning the Phillips report in their entirety, together with "any documents, letters, or reports which resulted from the decision by NASA in April 1966 that the problems encountered by the Phillips team were being overcome." To safeguard the material, NASA could have observers present during the time the staff considered the documents.[41] Webb had the documents made available and told Miller, chair of the House Space Committee, that the same procedures could apply on his side of the Capitol. Staats gave Senator Smith an analysis of the "Sam Phillips report and its context," reviewing the situation that engendered the report and the actions taken afterward. His letter included little criticism, essentially verifying what Webb had told her and other legislators.[42]

Anderson scheduled Webb's executive session for June 12, reprimanding him for not informing the committee earlier of the North American problems; he wanted to know of any other "extremely serious situations" now existing with NASA contractors.[43] Webb also received a list of "apparent ambiguities in NASA testimony" he was to consider in preparation for the executive session. The senators wanted to know, "If the performance of the company improved so much from December 1965 until the time of the accident, why were such major changes in key management personnel and organization in the S(&I) Division necessary this year? Were these changes at NASA's insistence?"[44]

Webb and various senior associates met on June 9 to discuss strategy, including answers to these "apparent ambiguities." Virtually all the key headquarters officials would be present at the executive session, along with all necessary documents. Phillips would discuss the Phillips report and specific corrective actions that followed. Bernie Moritz, the procurement official working directly with Webb on the renegotiation, would discuss the North American contract. Webb would speak on the total NASA–North American relationship, including the impacts on NASA of the proposed merger of North American and Rockwell. Mueller and others would discuss other projects and NASA-contractor difficulties. For example, as there was a Phillips report, so there were other "reports." The NASA-Grumman relationship, with respect to the Lunar Excursion Module, the device that would actually land on the moon, had problems. In addition, NASA officials would be ready to discuss source selection—North American and others. Finally, Seamans had prepared a lengthy memo on the North American selection, which went to Anderson and Smith. On this same day, Anderson released a public statement claiming that NASA should have informed the Space Committee of problems with the contractor, but he would nevertheless continue to support the agency.

At the executive session, a great deal was vented. Walter Mondale, Republican Charles Percy of Illinois, Massachusetts Democrat Edward Brooke, and other Webb critics had a chance to ask their questions, and Webb had his opportunity, as he put it, to set them straight where they were wrong. Had there been any political pressure in the North American award? Of course, said Webb. Senator Kerr, chair of the Senate Space Committee, had asked him to listen to the North American lobbyist, Fred Black. Although he did in fact listen to him, Webb said, what he had to say did not influence the North American award. The chair of the Senate Space Committee (and any legislator) had a right to ask an administrator to listen to a lobbyist, noted Webb, and the administrator had a responsibility to make decisions based on the facts as he saw them. "Anderson believed that where there was smoke, there was fire," Webb later recollected, "and if they just probed a little deeper, they'd find Bobby Baker and bury me. But there was no smoking gun to be found."[45]

George Mueller briefed the House investigators on June 13 on the previous day's discussion in the Senate Space Committee's executive session as it related to NASA, as contrasted with Webb personally. The tone of the meeting was relatively friendly. Connecticut Democrat Emilio Daddario, who had been among the critics, said he felt previous briefings had not pointed out serious problems as much as they had shown an idealized version of reality. Representative Rumsfeld said that NASA should not "downplay" such matters as the Phillips report but display them as examples of the effectiveness of the NASA management system. Teague wanted to know about the morale of NASA workers. The tone of the hearings had distinctly changed.[46]

A week later, Webb gave Teague a letter answering the charges against him. He said he had no connection with Bobby Baker, that he had resigned some time ago from the directorship of the Fidelity National Bank and Trust Company in Oklahoma City, where he had continued as a stockholder, with no knowledge of bank business other than that received by all stockholders. He had met three times with Fred Black since becoming administrator of NASA, including the meeting initiated by Senator Kerr that he had mentioned to the Senate committee. In no case had Black influenced his decisions. Webb also enclosed a statement outlining the rationale for selecting North American.[47]

Although the investigation had not ended, its momentum was spent, its most obvious outcome the agreement by Webb to keep both Space Committees better informed on problems. Otherwise, as Seamans wrote to Thompson, head of the NASA review board, on June 21, "discussion with the congressional committees indicates no further interest in the Apollo 204 related materials."[48]

Webb's personal negotiator, Bernie Moritz, concluded his arrangements with North American at the end of June with agreement on a new contract and on the penalties due to the accident. In renegotiating the contract, NASA had insisted on and received a cost-plus, fixed-fee arrangement rather than the more lucrative incentive agreements under which North American had been working by letter contract since December 3. North American would forgo all claims to incentives—some of which it had already received—on the capsule destroyed in the fire. The cost to North American attributable to the fire would be $15 million. NASA also insisted that the space agency would hereafter "unilaterally decide" whether to make special awards for "management achievement." North American's maximum possible profit for Apollo, as a result, would be substantially lower than under the old contract, and its management of the program would be highly supervised by Boeing, now assigned integration of the spacecraft and launch vehicle.[49] Webb informed leaders of the Senate and House Space Committees of all these modifications.

Webb took the Fourth of July off, his first holiday since the fire. Since January 27, he had worked seven days a week, week in, week out, in spite of occasional migraines. Now, he could rest—a bit. At this point, six months after the tragedy, Evert Clark of the *New York Times* took stock. He found the space program "just emerging from the shock." General Phillips felt they were "over the peak," although Webb saw the agency as "still in a time of testing." Clark believed they were both correct. From interviews with many inside and outside the agency, he found that the "worst was over and the program to land men on the moon has been retrieved, but also that the fire and its aftermath have not yet passed into history." Webb's view was that NASA would not fully recover "until we make a couple of these birds fly." Clark found that most concern lay in the area of congressional confidence rather than in managerial or technical problems. Many on the congressional committees felt they and the public had been deliberately kept in the dark about the longstanding NASA–North American problems exemplified by the Phillips report and that Webb had been evasive in his testimony.[50]

The immediate impact of the fire had been to postpone not only the Apollo schedule, but also consideration of post-Apollo funding. The usual congressional process, on hold until the investigation was over, by July, was getting back to normal, but with a difference: Congress seemed out to punish NASA—and Webb. It was in a cutting mood. Alluding to intelligence reports, Webb told the Senate Space Committee that the Soviets "are preparing to launch a booster with an appropriate large payload that will be larger than the Saturn V and that will give them an image and capability for the next several years of being ahead of the U.S. program. So at the time we are reducing at the rate of 5,000 per month in manpower, they are increasing." Most in Congress were not impressed. The administrator's critics were skeptical of Webb's claims of a big Soviet rocket and ridiculed it as "Webb's giant."[51] At the end of July, the authorization process ended with a substantial cut for NASA, with further cuts looming when the Appropriations Committees acted.

Webb found many former supporters abandoning the lunar deadline. Robert Hotz wrote in *Aviation Week and Space Technology* in early August that this was a "new era for NASA." In view of the war and urban turmoil, Webb had to be sensible, Hotz suggested. While the Apollo goal was "still valid," Hotz no longer saw "any political appeal or technical logic in the slogan of doing it 'before the end of the decade.'" It was "evident even before the Apollo fire that this program had been harnessed to a schedule that was becoming more unrealistic in relation to genuine technical progress with each passing month." While Webb was not surprised that a man often critical of NASA, Representative Karth, would accuse the agency of an "ostrichlike, head-in-the-sand approach," he was disturbed when a strong advocate, Edward Welsh, executive director of the Space Council, declared that "this is not 1961."[52] Northern liberals looking for money for social programs were joining fiscal conservatives anxious to reduce expenditures in an alliance aimed at NASA.

Still, Webb thought he had President Johnson on his side. In an article in the August *Fortune*, writer John Mecklin pointed out that NASA's controversial administrator only recently had been described by Johnson as "the best administrator I've got."[53] Maybe so, but on August 21, the president signed the NASA authorization bill, announcing that the House Appropriations Committee had recommended a half-billion-dollar reduction in his request for NASA and that he would not oppose such a cut. Conditions had greatly changed since he had submitted his budget request back in January, Johnson said, noting that the federal deficit for the fiscal year might run as high as $29 billion, instead of the $8.1 billion estimated. Hard choices had to be made, and the test was "to distinguish between the necessary and the desirable."[54] Although Webb had pleaded with Johnson not to make an announcement endorsing the cuts, saying it would undercut NASA's supporters in Congress as well as NASA, Johnson felt he had to show Congress he would cut space to get his tax bill (a 10 percent tax increase). Senator Smith was furious and charged that Johnson had "literally pulled the rug out from under those who direct the space program."[55]

Johnson's statement "was greeted with gloom by NASA officials," but Webb had little recourse.[56] The president explained to him that he did not "choose or prefer to take one dime from [his] budget for space appropriations this year and agreed to do so only because [the House Committee on] Ways and Means in effect forced [him] to agree to effect some reductions or lose the tax bill."[57] The president's action made it easier for other traditional supporters of NASA, particularly in the Senate, to back off. Usually, when the House cut back on NASA's authorization and appropriation bills, the Senate restored the funds, and, in conference, the two reached a compromise. Not this year. The president's action sealed NASA's fate in favor of the House decision. Instead of the $5.1 billion requested for this fiscal year, NASA wound up with $4.6 billion.

The budget director, Charles Schultze, joined the chorus of those who wanted to let the 1969 Apollo deadline slip and divert Apollo money to post-Apollo programs to smooth the transition. "Why not make a virtue out of necessity?" he asked. But neither Webb nor Johnson intended to take this direction, at least not yet.[58] Although Webb protected Apollo, post-Apollo programs took a pounding. So did he. When he was forced to defend the president's action before the Senate Appropriations hearing, Democratic senator Spessard Holland of Florida remarked sarcastically, "It seems you are throwing in the sponge. I thought you were a fighter."[59]

Meanwhile, within NASA, Seamans decided to leave. Webb had taken much of his own frustration out on his top associate, bypassing Seamans more and more to take command of NASA's recovery effort. Seamans also felt that during the fire investigation he had made a crucial mistake for which Webb had not forgiven him. While Webb was out of town, Seamans, in an effort to cooperate with the media, had granted what he thought was an off-the-record interview and had said the astronauts couldn't escape because the hatch to the capsule opened from the outside in. Webb hit the ceiling. He had an understanding with the president and Congress that they were not to be surprised by new information in the media; they wanted to know first. "From then on, it was downhill with Webb," recalled Seamans.[60]

Seamans heard that Webb was criticizing him to others and noted that he was being left out of important decisions. At one meeting, when Seamans pointed out to Webb that he had something to contribute on a matter Webb had assigned another man, Webb snapped, "Let's not have any of that kind of talk."[61] While Seamans understood the pressure under which Webb worked, he felt unfairly treated. He too was exhausted from the Apollo fire experience. He had worked hard and loyally for many years. In late September, demoralized, Seamans did some soul-searching, and the next month he placed his letter of resignation on the administrator's desk. Webb read it, looked up at him, and asked, "What will your peers say about the job you did at NASA?" Taken aback by this question, Seamans stammered that he thought "they will say I did a good job."[62] Webb immediately arranged to see the president, and on October 2, Seamans's resignation was announced, effective January 5, 1968.

Sensing a big story, the media came after Seamans, who said he would not be airing his grievances. A few days later, at a press conference, Webb was asked whether his agency might be coming apart. The individual raising the question had asked the same thing in 1963, Webb pointed out, after Brainerd Holmes was fired. "You will recall that I told you that a year later you might have a different opinion." Webb suggested the same situation applied today.[63]

Apollo 4

Nothing mattered more that fall, Webb knew, than a dramatic demonstration that NASA was back in space. Rhetoric would not do the trick; the country needed evidence. Webb told his agency he was ready if the technical people were. On October 26, NASA announced that the first *Saturn 5* test was set for early November. A week later the agency released a new schedule, revised due to the fire and its aftermath. To the surprise of many, it revealed a plan of Apollo flights over the next two years that would lead to a lunar landing in late 1969. This schedule assumed success followed by success followed by success, right up until the flight to the moon. Beginning with the Saturn flight, now scheduled for November 9, there could be no failures. It was a bold gamble.[64]

As the date approached, Webb received frequent reports on the flight, both in terms of technical readiness and congressional and public relations aspects. He knew that the Apollo program's 1969 goal was on the line, and it was by no means certain NASA would succeed.

This flight—known as *Apollo 4*—was critical and risky not only as the first major launch since the fire, but as the first launch of a *Saturn 5* rocket and the first from the pad at Kennedy Space Center that had been specially constructed for Apollo.[65] Most important, *Apollo 4* was the first test of the "all-up" concept that Mueller had instituted when he became director of OMSF and that many in NASA doubted would work. These included Arthur Rudolph, the man under Wernher von Braun most responsible for *Saturn 5* development. When he had initially expressed his misgivings to Mueller, the OMSF director had responded, "So what?" Now, years later, the day of reckoning had arrived.

As was his custom, Webb stayed in Washington to deal with the political fall-out of a failed launch. No astronauts were on board *Apollo 4*, but the stakes for NASA could hardly have been higher. Early the morning of November 9, a large assemblage of government, industry, media, and the general public gathered three and one-half miles from the launch pad. The roar of the Saturn was so great that no one was permitted much closer. For von Braun, it was the moment toward which his technical skills had pointed him for a lifetime: the launch of the first moon rocket. Topped by an Apollo spacecraft, at 363 feet it towered six stories higher than the Statue of Liberty. It weighed 6 million pounds and would generate 7.5 million pounds of thrust.[66]

At 7:00 A.M., right on schedule, the restraints on the rocket fell away, and *Saturn 5* rose slowly off the pad. Watching on television, in Washington, Webb knew that NASA had broken not just a technical barrier, but a psychological and political one. *Apollo 4*'s success made possible Apollo's recovery from the fire.

In the days that followed, *Apollo 4* was celebrated everywhere in the United States and among its allies for the remarkable technological achievement it was. *Aviation Week and Space Technology* called the test "flawless." The *New York Times* reported that the test had achieved all its objectives and was the most significant step in the moon program to date. But observers could not convey what those who worked in NASA sensed. "Only a few years earlier, many of them had been hesitantly trying, often failing, to launch rockets with a single, small engine in each stage. Today, in its first trial, they had launched a rocket the size and weight of a Navy destroyer, carrying eleven new engines, new fuels, new pumps, new technology of all kinds, and had done it perfectly." Most important, the launch meant that the decision Mueller had made and Webb had backed had paid off. The all-up concept worked and "had opened the way to the moon."[67]

The Senate Space Committee did not publish a report on the Apollo fire until January 30, 1968, and the House committee never did publish a report summarizing its findings. While the Senate report contained the critical comments of a minority of members, it found no evidence that the urgency of the Apollo program had led to the astronauts' deaths. In fact, the first of the committee's recommendations was that NASA continue to move the Apollo program forward toward its goal.[68]

Last Hurrah at NASA

Webb in early 1968 faced the challenge of maintaining Apollo on a course to reach the Kennedy goal despite upheaval in the country. The most turbulent year of a tumultuous decade began with the shock of the Tet Offensive in Vietnam, followed by Johnson's announcement not to run for reelection. Then would come the assassinations of Martin Luther King, Jr., and Robert F. Kennedy, a wave of urban riots, and the Soviet invasion of Czechoslovakia.

Reconstituting Leadership

At NASA, Robert Seamans left to return to MIT. Webb called him a "one-man band"—brilliant, versatile, and with an enormous work capacity—who could handle any problem or assignment, be it policy, administration, science, or technology.[1] His departure on January 1 left a large gap at NASA. With Webb's acquiescence, the head of the Civil Service Commission, John Macy, led the search for a replacement. It was not easy to find someone from outside NASA who could take over as deputy administrator at this very late date in the Johnson administration. Both the president and Webb felt they must find someone capable of assuming NASA leadership in case anything happened to Webb.

Also, Webb worried about his control of the Office of Manned Space Flight (OMSF). Without Hugh Dryden and Bob Seamans, he was alone, a nontechnical man at the helm of a huge technological agency with one of the most demanding projects to run in history. He needed a deputy and

general manager he could trust. While respecting George Mueller's technical ability—reflected in the success of the all-up decision—he no longer
trusted him personally. During the postfire turmoil, with his own future in
jeopardy, Webb had heard from a *Washington Post* reporter that Mueller
was angling to get his job if the NASA administrator went. Johnson had told
Webb there was nothing to this, and Webb had kept quiet, subordinating
his personal feelings to the Apollo objective, for which Mueller was important. But he remained on guard, planning to form a collective leadership in
which Mueller would literally be "surrounded."[2]

Part of this collective leadership was Homer Newell, who had been
appointed to the number three position (associate administrator) in September 1967. A quiet and introspective scientist-administrator, lacking Dryden's standing in the scientific community and NASA, he was hardly capable of directing the various program managers and center directors. In
contrast to Mueller, whom Webb had to restrain, Newell needed prodding.
He was important, nevertheless. As a civil servant, he would be part of the
continuity to keep NASA strong in the 1970s. He also represented the scientists who would be users of the capability NASA was creating in the 1960s;
Webb wanted that capability put to work, starting with the Apollo Applications Program (AAP). Finally, Newell counterbalanced Mueller, for the two
men did not get along. Newell was not a "general manager" in the sense
Seamans had been, but Webb felt that he had relied too much on Seamans,
who had provided him with a consensus view and had allowed Mueller to
hide some of the real problems with North American. Webb now wanted
senior people "around the table," more-or-less equals who would thrash
out issues and make them visible to him.[3]

In January, Newell established a NASA Management Council, which
would be attended by representatives of all headquarters program and
functional offices. Even as Webb ruled, he talked about "participative management."[4] Among those around the table was Harold Finger, head of the
Office of Organization and Management. In Webb's chain of command,
"administrative" concerns would be wedded more closely to the substance
of program offices. He sent all program officials a revised system for project
approval and control: a NASA operating plan would serve as an official
statement of resource plans for the current year, based on funds actually
made available by Congress; each item in the plan would be reviewed by
Finger. Webb explained that in NASA's increasingly constrained financial
environment, program administrators should not complain about the bu-

reaucratic "system" and try to insist that the technical program must come ahead of administrative requirements. Both were important.[5] Also, he intended "to continually assess the degree to which I may need to increase or decrease my own personal participation in these decision and action systems," his way of saying he was going to start delegating again, but if he saw anything he did not like, he would take back power.[6] He was watching. He asked Charles Mathews, head of AAP, who was under Mueller, to be Mueller's deputy—and a spy for Webb, part of Webb's "surrounding" strategy, and a means to keep control of Apollo.[7]

His primary avenue of control, even as he created a collective leadership and intoned participation, was through the budget. Where Mueller had enjoyed his own budget function independent of Seamans, after the fire, Webb reassigned Mueller's key budget official, William E. Lilly, to himself. The Webb-Lilly alliance was quite powerful; Lilly was, in effect, comptroller for the agency. In the elevator one day, Lilly asked Webb what was going on. Why all these meetings, all this emphasis on participation and collective leadership? Webb said it was part of the education process, a way to elevate people, to help them learn and get ready for more responsibility. Lilly worried that with all this participation NASA might never reach a decision on a particular matter. Webb told him not to worry. In the end, "You and I will make the decision." As Lilly recalled, with Webb, there were "purposes within purposes within purposes."[8]

NASA was recovering, and the team was working together, although everyone chafed at the enhanced paperwork, the growing bureaucracy, as Webb emphasized "supervision" from the top down in the same breath as "participation."[9] In mid-January, Macy called Webb with a candidate for the deputy administrator and general manager spot. Thomas Paine, forty-seven, was an engineering graduate of Brown University who had served as a submarine officer in the Pacific during World War II. He had a Ph.D. in physical metallurgy from Stanford and from 1963 to 1968 had managed General Electric's Tempo Center for Advanced Studies, an interdisciplinary study group. He had not dealt much with NASA but had been active with DOD over the years and was regarded not only as able in technical management but also as an especially bold and imaginative planner. "Send him over," Webb directed, and Paine was whisked to NASA in a White House limousine.

Webb told Paine he had only half an hour to talk with him because he had to testify before Congress shortly. As Paine recalled the half hour:

He used the smartest technique to get to know someone I ever saw. He said: "I'm going to call out a list of people in Washington. I want to know what you think of these guys. Give me your candid response." He then went down a list of people. These were people in the State Department, on the Hill, in the executive branch generally. I didn't know half of them. The other half I knew.

I remembered considering one in particular, an old boss. This was J. Herbert Hollomon. He was the number two man in the Department of Commerce. I was an admirer of him. But I also knew his weak points. On the whole, I guess my assessment was negative. At the end of this time, Webb said, "I've got to go to the Hill to testify." He said, "Your reactions are the same as mine." He said he appreciated my candor. I told him I would not accept the job unless he wanted me. I repeated that. Webb responded, "On that basis, I want you to take the job." I said, "I will consider it."[10]

Paine met with Johnson, agreed to be deputy administrator, and on February 1, the same day his nomination was submitted to the Senate, was introduced by Webb to various NASA senior staff. Later, Webb took him to visit with a number of legislative leaders, and they had lunch with Donald Hornig, Johnson's science adviser. Webb also called Mathews from his car phone to tell him about Paine. "I want you to know," he said, "I have Tom Paine as my deputy." Mathews had been fretting considerably about the assignment to help Webb "monitor" Mueller, and he knew that Webb was letting him know he could relax; he was off the hook. Paine was confirmed by the Senate on February 7 and sworn into office on March 25.[11]

The combination of Webb, Paine, and Newell now gave NASA something resembling a leadership triad once again. While Webb said he hoped the three could work as a team, given the situation in 1968, the personalities involved, and Paine's newness to NASA, the triad was much looser and less formidable than in the Webb-Dryden-Seamans era. It was also clear that, while Webb might have wanted to disengage from the tight controls he had held since the fire, he would not let go. The external politics were too uncertain, the internal stresses too obvious. His organization needed a post-Apollo program, but he was convinced the country needed Apollo to succeed more than ever. With Vietnam a disaster and Johnson's Great Society falling apart, space remained the one positive legacy from the Kennedy-Johnson years.

Sacrificing Post-Apollo

If Apollo had recovered from the Apollo fire setback, the Apollo Applications Program had not. The FY 1969 budget request for AAP, $439 million, was 16 percent less than the submission to the Budget Bureau the previous fall, and less than half of what had been anticipated in the FY 1968 budget. With a sharply curtailed budget, Webb concluded that he could not keep Apollo on schedule and at the same time move AAP forward, as he had originally hoped, and "nothing would interfere—or even seem to interfere—with the lunar landing."[12] He felt that if he went at post-Apollo too hard, he might lose Apollo. Moreover, AAP was in trouble politically, administratively, and technically.

The program had little support from the president and Congress. Now obsessed with Vietnam, Johnson had told Webb he supported him on AAP, and that he would personally lobby with Congress to help Webb on this front, but he could not, given his other problems. Despondent, he surrendered to congressional budget decisions on space in 1968, as he had in 1967. Webb still had access to him, but the president's mind was not on NASA. He was phasing out of the presidency, content to let his successor handle the next step in space.

Congress chose budget cutting as its top priority in 1968 and saw NASA as easy to cut, politically. Despite a residual of support for NASA, few legislators saw much incentive in going to bat for AAP. Indeed, many saw political gains in cutting NASA as a frill the country could not afford at this time. That AAP seemed to duplicate the air force's Manned Orbital Laboratory made it even easier to justify cuts.

Even as he sought to open up new channels of cooperation with DOD, Webb fought this legislative mood. The replacement in March of his rival, Robert McNamara, totally spent by Vietnam, with his former Truman colleague Clark Clifford provided an opening for a new relationship between NASA and DOD. Perhaps, Webb thought, he would be able to negotiate a deal with DOD that would allow NASA more leeway in post-Apollo. But as Clifford's assistant, George Elsey, later recalled, "Clifford was working 200 percent of his time on the war."[13] Webb lobbied Elsey, but time was running out. Also, Webb remained cautious with respect to the air force. "The military people were still hoping that we would stumble and drop the basket of groceries and they would pick them up," he told an interviewer later. "So they were not above tripping us up."[14]

Perhaps most frustrating was the lack of cohesion in his own organization with respect to AAP and post-Apollo planning in general. As he delved deeper into the technical side of NASA management, he found more and more disagreement over AAP. He saw Mueller pushing ahead as fast as he could, with as large an AAP program as he could get, thereby protecting OMSF and its centers, especially Marshall. He saw Robert Gilruth opposing Mueller's concept of AAP on technical grounds (and maybe because of his competition with Wernher von Braun). He saw Newell and Mueller in bitter conflict over the scientific experiments to go on AAP, and over whether space science or manned flight offices would dominate decisions. Where Apollo and ample funds had brought people together, post-Apollo and inadequate resources were pulling them apart.

Aware of "the depth and breadth of criticism of AAP," Webb sought a consensus on it inside his agency.[15] He asked Floyd Thompson, who had distinguished himself by his handling of the Apollo fire, and who was about to retire after forty-two years in government, to examine AAP on his behalf.[16] He followed this request up with a directive to Newell that he launch an agencywide effort in long-range planning that would draw the embattled elements of NASA together. Whatever NASA did, he wanted consensus behind it.

Thompson and the group he brought together conducted their review during the first three months of 1968. AAP was trying to do too much, too soon, Thompson reported to Webb. The "objectives for manned space flight in earth orbit . . . must focus on deepening our understanding of man's capabilities and needs in a weightless space environment for extended periods of time." The Newell exercise, which bogged down in a multiplicity of working groups, produced studies that resolved very little. As Newell later noted, the exercise assuredly did not forward the Webb objective of getting an internal consensus, especially between manned space and space science. Mueller went along with it, said Newell, but not in a serious way. With his drive to run his own operation, Mueller maintained parallel planning studies even as he and his organization were nominally giving full support to the agencywide effort. "The problem with manned space flight," wrote Newell, "was that they were in the habit of going it alone, they wanted to go it alone, and they intended to go it alone."[17] Competition, not cooperation, marked long-range planning in NASA in 1968. Under the impact of budget cuts, redesign became a way of life for AAP. Whose ox was gored in the process became the key issue. By mid-1968, according to the official history of the program, AAP "seemed about to come apart at the seams."[18]

To resolve these tensions, Webb put Newell in a leadership position for planning and spoke to Mueller himself about cooperation. But he had never been sanguine that planning would solve NASA's problems. Now willing to let decisions on AAP slip a bit, he could use the planning exercise within NASA as an excuse to delay spending on the program.

The funding situation went from bad to worse. The House debate on the NASA budget filled sixty-seven pages of the *Congressional Record*. In the Senate, a bill to slice $1 billion from NASA, thereby decimating Apollo, failed by only five votes. Webb called spring 1968 a time when NASA suffered "a mass walkout of congressional support." In June, NASA was authorized to spend just over $4 billion, with $253 million for AAP. With the appropriations process ahead, Johnson ordered Webb not to try to get additional funds but instead to expect a further cut under the Revenue and Expenditure Control Act, which required the president to cut another $6 billion from his agencies *after* Congress had made its decisions. Knowing that NASA would thus have to drop below $4 billion, Webb maintained strict control of spending decisions in this difficult period. For AAP, he used month-to-month letter contracts, a device he generally deplored but which gave him greater power to keep AAP far away from dollars he intended for Apollo. Apollo Applications, he told center directors in June, was nothing more than "a surge tank for Apollo." He personally cut parts of AAP and would have cut even deeper had not various subordinates pleaded for the program. By August, NASA had its authorization, but not the appropriations bill. Webb told NASA officials that it would be several more months before NASA had a final budget. Given Johnson's $4 billion limit and expected further cuts, he set a spending level of $3.8 billion and proceeded on a "course of peril," as he termed it.[19] He did not want the congressional-executive budget negotiations to determine the pace of Apollo. His organization needed to move as fast as possible, at least in regard to Apollo, and he would make the necessary trade-offs later if the funding came up short.

This working budget meant that the Saturn production line would now be shut down, a decision Webb deeply regretted and hoped would mean only a temporary halt. Gilruth and others pressed him to save some of the Saturns NASA had already procured for Apollo for a space station program after getting to the moon. Mueller and von Braun argued that many of the technical disputes over AAP would be alleviated if Webb would let AAP have just one *Saturn 5*, which could launch into orbit a large AAP laboratory facility equipped on the ground. Without a *Saturn 5*, smaller rockets would have to send the facility into space and equip it later.

This "wet workshop" concept, as the idea to equip AAP in space was termed, raised difficulties and technical objections a *Saturn 5* would obviate. But "it had taken all of James Webb's power of persuasion to convince Congress and the BOB that Apollo required at least 15 Saturn V launch vehicles," the number NASA had bought, and Webb "would tolerate no suggestion that any could be used for something else." Until the Apollo lunar mission was successful—and as long as Webb was administrator—AAP was told not to plan for the use of a *Saturn 5*.[20]

Webb subsequently came under heavy criticism for letting AAP drift and for failing to push for closure on a firm post-Apollo goal. "NASA leadership faltered," Newell charged in a 1980 book. But Webb felt he did not have the resources and political support for both Apollo and AAP in 1968, and he would place Apollo at risk if he diverted his own and the agency's energies to set a new long-range goal that would only make Apollo seem less important.[21]

Pushing Apollo around the Moon

Sensitive to his political environment and NASA's vulnerability in Congress, Webb buffered his Apollo organization from their pressures as best he could. Charles Murray and Catherine Bly Cox noted how insulated many of the technical people were, especially in Houston, Huntsville, and the Cape, even in 1968. In March, when Johnson announced he would not seek reelection, had one of NASA's flight controllers at Houston "been asked about the most important event so far of 1968, he would probably have said that it had occurred on January 22, when the unmanned Apollo V had carried a lunar module on its first test flight."[22]

At the turn of 1963, Webb had put his job on the line for a "balanced" program. But not in 1968. Whatever NASA needed from him for Apollo in money, equipment, attention, and decisions, it got. Always available to anyone in his formal or informal chain of command for Apollo recovery, he had Boeing report to him every two weeks and spoke to Sam Phillips regularly. When Frank Borman, supervising aspects of recovery at North American's plant in California, saw an administrative snag or had problems with the formal chain of command, he called Webb directly to get the matter straightened out.[23]

The unmanned *Apollo 6*, another test of the Saturn rocket, was launched on April 4. At 125 seconds into its flight, severe "lengthwise oscillations [occurred] in the launch vehicle, producing a chugging motion like a car with bad spark plugs, decelerating and accelerating," a kind of vibration "known to rocket scientists as 'pogo,' after the motion of a pogo stick." Pogo had been encountered before, but never in so severe a way. Engine failures occurred. NASA "managed to complete most of the maneuvers in the flight plan, and the spacecraft was returned safely to Earth, but there remained two sobering, unassailable facts: the pogo in the first stage was so severe that a crew might have been injured, had to abort, or both; and three separate engines had failed."[24]

The tragic day's events had only begun. In the early afternoon, Martin Luther King, Jr., was shot and killed on the balcony of the Lorraine Motel in Memphis. Black people in cities across the country demonstrated; some started fires to vent their anger and frustration. Stokely Carmichael and other militant leaders urged blacks to arm themselves and take to the streets in retaliation for the murder. As rioting continued through the night, President Johnson postponed his planned Vietnam conference in Hawaii and went on television to appeal for reason. The next morning, as dark smoke from burning buildings filled the sky over Washington and Johnson watched armed troops patrol the streets of the nation's capital for the first time since the Civil War, he wondered what the country was coming to.[25]

Few outside NASA paid attention to the *Apollo 6* flight, and few inside let themselves be distracted by the terrible events in the country. *Apollo 6* looked like a success, and NASA truthfully announced that all of the mission's major flight-test objectives had been achieved, but "within NASA, *Apollo 6* was deeply disquieting." Webb put Paine, his new deputy administrator, to work on the *Apollo 6* problems to see how severe they were. Mueller and Phillips were also fully engaged. As each of *Apollo 6*'s malfunctions "slowly . . . yielded an explanation," it became apparent that no serious problem existed, although the various "diagnoses and fixes took many weeks—NASA later calculated that 125 engineers and 400 technicians spent 31,000 man-hours on the pogo problem alone."[26]

In fact, the feeling within the OMSF leadership, which Paine shared, was that NASA should accelerate its schedule. Paine was proving a bold administrator, willing to take risks and think expansively. Unlike those at NASA in 1967, he had not been chastened by the Apollo fire. But Webb was instinctively more cautious now, and especially wary of optimistic OMSF claims. Hence, Paine's opinion mattered to him. But Webb had the ultimate responsibility to decide to go or not go.

In late April, Webb had to choose between a third unmanned test of Saturn to prove it was safe for astronauts and a manned test of the rocket. With the advice from his organization mixed, Webb approved a change in schedule that went with a manned Saturn as the next flight. *Aviation Week and Space Technology* reported that NASA's united front concealed "violent disagreement, particularly from the Manned Spacecraft Center (MSC) at Houston, over the desirability of putting astronauts aboard before one more unmanned checkout."[27] But the headquarters program officials, supported by Paine, argued in favor of moving ahead with a manned flight, and Webb went along. A flight was scheduled for October.

Mueller announced in May that, in view of the decision on *Apollo 6*, a new sequence of flights would culminate, if all went well, with the lunar landing itself, possibly as early as mid-1969. In the fall, *Apollo 7* would "man-rate" both the Saturn and redesigned Apollo capsule, flying together. If successful, this test would be followed by another manned flight, *Apollo 8*, in December, that would add the final part of the manned space system—the Lunar Excursion Module (LEM).

By late summer, however, with work on the LEM behind schedule, it now looked as though the program might have to be delayed. Every test from here on was essential—NASA was down to its "success-oriented" schedule—but one of the subsequent missions called for sending men out to deep space, possibly even to an orbit around the moon. Why not, suggested George Low, the spacecraft director in Houston, switch the LEM test in earth orbit with a manned test in lunar orbit? This seemed incredibly risky, performing a test in late 1968 that was barely in the planning stage for 1969. But Low believed a circumlunar flight to be technically possible, even necessary—a major milestone in the quest for the lunar landing goal.

Low mulled over the options, mainly to himself, and in early August returned from vacation ready to push NASA to change the schedule. A circumlunar flight seemed audacious; before Webb would approve, Low knew, he had to line up a phalanx of support within the agency.[28] As Webb had just told NASA officials in Washington that he was himself setting NASA spending at $3.8 billion, and that the agency was now proceeding on a "course of peril," it did not seem a propitious time to raise that peril to an even higher level.[29]

With others at MSC on their side, Low and Gilruth met with von Braun, Phillips, and others at Huntsville. Low argued that a lunar orbit mission flown in December might be the only way to meet the fast-approaching lunar landing deadline.[30] Von Braun and Phillips agreed. Three days later, most of the principals at the Huntsville meeting gathered with Paine in Washington. As they discussed the circumlunar possibility, there was the strong feeling, based on intelligence information, that the revitalized Soviet program might at this very moment be preparing for such a flight. Everyone involved wanted to "beat the Russians' ass." Playing the devil's advocate, Paine reminded them that only weeks before they had been worried about man-rating the *Saturn 5* booster with its "pogo" problem, and now they proposed using it to launch men all the way to lunar orbit. Once you decide to put men on the Saturn, von Braun responded, "it doesn't matter how far you go." "There's always risk," Gilruth added, "but this is the path of less risk." "Assuming *Apollo 7* is a success, there's no other choice," Low concluded. Paine congratulated them on their daring approach, declaring himself on their side. All agreed that Webb and Mueller, at a two-week international meeting on space applications in Vienna, must be persuaded to this new course immediately so that planning could commence, and Phillips indicated he would fly to Vienna to make the case.[31]

Before he could leave, however, Mueller called him from Vienna on another matter, and Phillips used the opportunity to inform his superior. Initially unreceptive, Mueller gradually warmed a bit to the idea. He told Phillips not to come to Vienna, and to keep the possibility quiet for the time being. Paine then called Webb and informed him of what had been under way in Washington. Shocked by the proposal, Webb was inclined to say no immediately, but after talking further with Paine and then Phillips, he asked for more information.[32] Paine now gathered Phillips, Willis Shapley (whom Webb had earlier recruited from BOB for a top management support role), and Julian Scheer to draft a formal proposal for Webb. He then sent Webb a cable of information, in which he emphasized his complete support, included an item-by-item schedule of necessary actions, and set out drafts of a statement from Webb to make in Vienna and of a press release to be issued in Washington.

After discussing the proposal with Mueller, the next day Webb directed Paine to move forward and plan for the lunar orbit flight. No public announcement of this new schedule should be made, however, either in Vienna or Washington. Paine should inform the White House of the possible change in existing Apollo plans. A final decision depended on what happened with *Apollo 7*, set for October.

Whatever his reservations and conditions, Webb had said yes. Phillips met with the Houston center's leaders, bringing Webb's authorization to prepare for a launch around the moon. He noted the follow-up needed: Borman's astronaut crew assigned to the flight should be immediately trained and equipped as necessary; the launch should be scheduled for December 6; and NASA officials should continue to speak publicly of an earth orbit. He emphasized that Webb's final decision depended on what happened with *Apollo 7*, which would qualify the command module in earth orbit.

As NASA geared up, the Soviet Union gave indications of a new aggressiveness. On August 21, while Webb was still in Vienna, Soviet troops marched into Czechoslovakia to stifle the beginnings of liberalization there. A few weeks later, a new Soviet spacecraft looped the moon before returning to earth to splash down in the Indian Ocean. The flight was taken by many in NASA as proof that the intelligence they had received was sound: the Soviets, indeed pressing forward in the race, planned to have a manned circumlunar flight in the near future. Officials in NASA pressed harder than ever toward *Apollo 8*.[33]

Leveraging the Transfer of NASA Power

Although convinced that Paine, Mueller, Phillips, von Braun, Gilruth, the astronauts, and the rest of NASA could carry on toward the goal after January 20, 1969, Webb had grown increasingly concerned about the presidential transition, worried that some last-minute interference from the new administration would wreck everything. While he had done all in his power to give his team a fighting chance to succeed, he did not believe that he would be with them at the finish line. A few days after the Soviet launch, he went to the White House with a long agenda, including a report on the Vienna conference, budget matters, intelligence on Soviet capabilities and intentions, and the presidential transition. On the transition issue, the administrator made it clear to President Johnson that what mattered was the Apollo goal. NASA must be kept strong through the transition, and the agency's leadership must not become an issue of political conflict. Webb felt that if he were around on January 20, such conflict would be inevitable if Hubert Humphrey became president (he and Webb had had tensions), even more if Richard Nixon became president. If the new president removed Webb, as was likely, he might cut deeper into NASA's leadership to excise those he regarded as loyal to Webb, and, in Nixon's case, those perceived as loyal to Johnson.

NASA had to be depoliticized, in fact and in appearance. Webb thought that with Paine, a nonpolitical technocrat, in charge, even Nixon might keep the NASA leadership intact, at least until after the moon landing. If all went well with *Apollo 7* and *Apollo 8*, the lunar landing would be only months away when the new president took control. He probably would feel great pressure not to disrupt the program, if it were going well, *and* there was someone in charge who was noncontroversial in a political sense. Also, if something went wrong with Apollo—an accident—Webb "wanted to be able to defend NASA and his engineers aggressively. If he were administrator, anything he said would sound self-serving."[34]

What to do now, while Webb and Johnson could still influence events? The two arrived at a difficult reality: to influence the new president and thus assure continuity at least through the achievement of the lunar goal, Paine would have to succeed Webb sooner rather than later so he could build a record of technical success. To depoliticize the transition at NASA, the change should take place before the November election.

To Webb's complete surprise, Johnson now said, "I believe you could announce your retirement on your birthday—the logical time."[35] On October 7, Webb would be sixty-two. The two had previously broached the subject of Webb's departure in a nonserious way. Webb had at times mentioned leaving, usually after Johnson had said he would like to give Webb cabinet status if his job at NASA had not been so essential. "The only job for which I am a candidate is retirement on my sixty-second birthday," Webb would reply. And when Johnson had announced he would not run for reelection, Webb had told him, "Mr. President, the day you leave the White House is the day I will leave NASA."

But this conversation was dead serious, and Johnson was taking Webb up on his "offer" to leave early. Webb may have himself persuaded the president of the logic of the move by discussing the Paine transition strategy. Or—as some in NASA later speculated—Johnson may have had some reason, known only to himself, for wanting Webb to go. Webb may have pushed him too hard on the NASA budget or done or said something apparently innocuous but perceived by Johnson as a slight. The president was a man under extreme pressure, going without sleep, capable of behaving unpredictably. Maybe he was offended that Webb would want to leave him early, or perhaps he felt that whatever Webb might say, he would have a tough time bringing himself to resign before the lunar landing. He would certainly have agreed with Webb that if something went wrong in Apollo, Webb would be in a better position politically to defend the Apollo goal from outside NASA. Finally, Johnson always hated to have news as important as the departure of James Webb leaked to the press before he could make the announcement himself.

"Why don't we tell the press today?" he asked, less a question than a directive. "I have not had time to call Tom Paine," Webb protested. "I haven't called my wife." Johnson was not listening. He told his press secretary, George Christian, to call in the White House press corps. "Mr. Webb will be coming to your office to make an announcement." The meeting was over. Johnson said goodbye, and Webb walked down the hall to meet the press alone.

Webb did his best to collect himself. He told the press that he was going to retire on October 7, that he had spent twenty-five years in government service of one kind or another over the last forty years of his life, and it was time to move on. When reporters asked him if he was a disappointed man, he answered, "No, not at all." He said he had accepted "the decisions of government" at a time when the war and urban crisis had created pressures for economy. Always ready to speak up for NASA, he did react with feeling, however, in citing the shortcomings forced on the space program by budget reductions. "I think a good many people have tended to use the space program as a sort of whipping boy," he said at one point. He was "not satisfied" with the current space program. "What this really means is we are going to be in second position for some time to come," while the Russians "are going to have the reality and image of being out in front."[36]

On the way back to his office, Webb used the car phone to ask the vice president's secretary to convey the news to Humphrey. He reached Congressman Miller, but not Senator Anderson. Meanwhile, his wife, Patsy, was on the phone frantically calling Webb at NASA, where she spoke to Paine. She said, "Tom, Tom, what's going on down there?" as Paine later recalled. "My neighbor just called me. It's on the radio. Jim just resigned." Paine could not believe what he was hearing. "No, no, it can't be," he said. "He would have mentioned it to me." They hung up, and Paine waited for confirmation. He got it from Webb, who arrived shortly thereafter, visibly upset, and immediately called Patsy, who was quite agitated and angry that she had heard the news from a neighbor. Then Webb asked Paine to arrange a meeting where he could speak with as many of the top officials in headquarters as possible. To a group that included Paine, Mueller, Newell, and other senior people, Webb explained his rationale for leaving.[37] He said Paine would be named acting administrator, and, if Paine wished him to do so, he would remain as a consultant and help in any way he could. Come January 20, said Webb, NASA will have operated for four months with Paine at the helm. There will have been two critical launches. What the new president would see would be a "capable, nonpolitical group" in charge of NASA. As for himself, Webb said, he would have some annuities coming in after he was sixty-two and would not need to take another full-time job. "I do not intend to move away from Washington. My home is here, and so I will be available" to Paine. The aim, he emphasized, was to move NASA into a "completely nonpolitical category" during the presidential transition, which would maximize the chances for stability through the lunar landing.[38]

As word spread around the agency, skeptics asked, Why would Webb leave before the moon landing? He would be abandoning his chance for glory. Others speculated that he was "worn down" or had lost his nerve and was genuinely worried about *Apollo 8*'s failing. Some wondered if he had had a fight over money and resigned in a huff—or been fired. Some connected his leaving to an intelligence matter of great secrecy. The speculation, within NASA and outside, would continue for years. Webb stuck to his explanation, and most close observers of the space program accepted it. *Aviation Week and Space Technology,* for example, characterized the strategy behind Webb's resignation as a "sacrifice play."[39]

The president's attitude and subsequent behavior gave weight to the view that the departure was a strategic move. Johnson's science adviser, Donald Hornig, wrote Johnson on September 26, charging Webb with "unconscionable statements" in the press conference after his meeting with the president. He suggested that Johnson ask PSAC to make an "independent" assessment of where the United States and USSR stood in space and release that report to the press. Johnson replied to Hornig on the same day, "Drop it!" In a written memo, which Johnson wanted conveyed by phone, he defended Webb strongly. He had no fault with Webb's assessment of the situation and would question the "usefulness" of the office of the science adviser were it to interject itself into this matter. Johnson pointed out how much he regretted the cuts he "had had to make in Webb's budget" and said he "wanted him to succeed."[40]

As Johnson biographer Robert Dallek has pointed out, the president had "a warm feeling for Webb, who had served him so loyally for almost five years." Loyalty mattered to LBJ. He had told his wife, after the Apollo fire: "I know now why Jim was an old marine and a good one. He's got the courage. He goes through a disaster like this and he says, 'we just got to go on and do what we know is right.' . . . And he did." Johnson not only "liked Webb," wrote Dallek, but he "admired him." At this late point, also, Johnson cared very much about the historical assessment of his administration, including the space program. If he wanted Webb to succeed, he also wanted it written that *he* had succeeded in space policy. Johnson wanted Congress or the next president to get the blame for any failures, not himself.[41]

While Johnson handled the departure of Webb with almost cruel insensitivity, he most likely was doing what he thought was best for the space program—and Lyndon Johnson. And he did, after all, take Webb's advice.

As Webb's last day approached, his colleagues at NASA wanted to give him a farewell party. James Beggs recalled "that when he decided to leave he wouldn't permit us to give him a retirement party. We put the arm on him a number of times. Finally, he gave in. But there was a condition. He would give the party himself. And he did—for all his senior staff. It was held at the University Club and he paid for it himself."[42]

On the evening of October 7, Webb's last official day as administrator, Patsy gave a small dinner party celebrating her husband's sixty-second birthday, including among the guests Tom Paine, Elmer Staats, Paul Dembling, and their wives. Paine recollected "a sense of electricity in the air. As we got to the dessert, something began going on. Strangers appeared at the door. . . . Patsy held up the dessert. Then President and Mrs. Johnson came in. . . . When Johnson walked in, you knew it. He was so big, so Texan. He was obviously delighted to be there. He was bubbling over. . . . It was a birthday party."[43] The festive evening, as Paine recalled, saw plenty of byplay between the Webbs and the Johnsons. It was obvious that the two couples were comfortable with one another, and Paine felt Johnson's visit and the way the evening went were genuine compliments to Webb.

Apollo 7 was launched on October 11. As ex-administrator, Webb felt free to attend the launch rather than stay behind in Washington to mount a defense in case something went wrong. This was a critical launch—they all were now—because it was the first manned Apollo launch and used a redesigned spacecraft. A great success, the launch achieved all its goals, establishing beyond a doubt that Apollo had fully recovered from the 1967 fire. At the LBJ ranch on November 2, President Johnson honored the three *Apollo 7* astronauts—and Webb—awarding them the highest honor NASA could bestow, the Exceptional Service Medal. In handing the medal to Webb, Johnson departed from the usual paragraphs of praise and declared simply, "Jim Webb, you are the best."[44] A month later Johnson followed this up by awarding Webb the Presidential Medal of Freedom, the highest civilian honor a president can bestow on any individual.

Frank Borman, James Lovell, and William Anders were launched on *Apollo 8*—the flight around the moon—on December 21, 1968. On Christmas Eve, they turned on their television camera so millions could join them in viewing the moon below, read from the Book of Genesis, and wished the people of Earth a merry Christmas. The *Apollo 8* flight, at least for a while, lifted America's spirits. Scrapping plans to feature "the Dissenter" as its "Man of the Year," *Time* magazine substituted the three astronauts. "For the American people," *Time* wrote, "the astronauts' triumph came as a particularly welcome gift after a year of disruption and despond."[45]

For Webb, *Apollo 8* showed that the organization he had left was as able as ever, ready for the lunar landing, provided Richard Nixon's administration did not get in the way.

THE MOON AND AFTER

After his September meeting with Johnson, Webb prepared Paine to take over the agency. Paine needed little help in technical management or in planning; Webb tried to assist him most on his political role, admonishing him in particular not to take orders from White House staff. "Remember, you report to the President. Never forget it."[1]

In October when Paine took over officially, he found that Webb had left no decision "unmade or postponed . . . everything was ready for me." Webb had made NASA "a special organization. It knew how to manage large technical programs." Paine "moved people as the occasion presented itself. But I made very little change in the machine that Webb had built." Here was an organization able to "integrate government, industry, and the universities. It had found a way to use the Department of Defense. It was a partnership of equals. And Webb was able to work with very good people. I came into a very good organization."

Paine asked Webb to remain with NASA as a consultant, with an office down the hall from his own. Webb told Paine he would be available for advice and would take no full-time job. He came into Paine's office only when invited. As Paine stated, "He was very good about turning the reins over. When he left, he left."[2]

Webb used every opportunity to get word to Nixon how important it was to the success of Apollo that Paine be kept. Although he had no special connections with Nixon, he talked to individuals who had access to the president, among them Republican representative Gerald Ford of Michigan, House minority leader (who would eventually become Nixon's vice president and successor). At a dinner for *Apollo 8* astronauts, Webb told the congressman that Paine had shown his mettle by *Apollos 7* and *8*. He said the Republicans "should examine in the most responsible manner how they would supply the leadership" to fly a *Saturn 5* to the moon. Webb "got to Nixon" with his views.[3]

It was not clear what Nixon would do. He had not said anything unusual about space during the campaign and had no known space policy he wished to pursue. Once in office in 1969, he apparently looked around for a person of his own choice to be NASA administrator but was unsuccessful. In March, he turned to his secretary of defense, Melvin Laird, a former Republican congressman, for advice. Laird in turn asked Robert Seamans, his choice as secretary of the air force. Seamans replied that Nixon should keep Paine "if the President wanted to ensure the lunar landing in 1969."[4] The next day, Nixon announced that Paine would be his appointee as NASA administrator. Whatever the causal factors, Webb now had the result he had sought.

Landing on the Moon

Apollo 9 lifted off on March 3. In earth orbit, astronauts tested operations involving the lunar module. This first test of the *Saturn 5*, Apollo command module, and lunar module as a system was a complete success. In mid-May, *Apollo 10* carried three astronauts to within nine miles of the moon, a rehearsal flight in which astronauts did most of what would be necessary for the moon flight except perform the actual landing, including a close survey of the proposed landing site on the Sea of Tranquility.

On the morning of July 16, on the launch pad at Cape Kennedy, *Apollo 11* held astronauts Neil Armstrong, Edwin Aldrin, and Michael Collins. Webb and Lyndon Johnson were on hand with Patsy Webb and Lady Bird Johnson, watching with growing anticipation along with five thousand other VIPs—senators, governors, congressmen, mayors, bankers, industrialists, movie stars, athletes—all invited by NASA. The Reverend Ralph Abernathy came with a band of civil rights demonstrators to call attention to the plight of poor people in the country, especially black Americans. Nearly one million others packed the Cape Kennedy area. The media assembled in unprecedented force. Nixon watched on television, from Washington. *Apollo 11* achieved liftoff, and the astronauts headed for the moon.[5]

(The Soviet Union also sent a spaceship to the moon, but it was unmanned. Soviet leaders informed their people that the Americans would be first—if *Apollo 11* succeeded.)

Neil Armstrong stepped out of the *Apollo 11* lunar module on July 20 at 10:56 P.M. in Washington, where Webb sat at home watching television with his family. Like millions around the earth, he held his breath as Armstrong, 238,000 miles away, took his giant leap for mankind.[6] Four days later, when *Apollo 11* splashed down safely in the South Pacific, Webb felt a sense of deep, probably sublime relief. His own race to the moon was over, his mission accomplished.

Yet he did not participate in the official festivities that followed the lunar landing. On the sidelines, a private citizen, he continued to advise Tom Paine, but Paine was in a poor position to use any advice. His access to President Nixon was virtually nil, and in September 1970 he resigned. When Paine left, Webb had little reason to return to NASA. Nixon's Shuttle decision in 1972 saved manned space, but it was a far cry from the decision to go to the moon. Space was no longer a national priority, and Webb knew it.

The Apollo lunar missions ran their course. Skylab (the former Apollo Applications Program) went up May 14, 1973. On July 15, 1975, the last available *Saturn 5* launched astronauts who docked in earth orbit with a Soviet team—the Apollo-Soyuz mission. The final vestiges of the Apollo program, which had begun with U.S.-Soviet competition, ended with a symbolic voyage of cooperation. The Soviets had tried to reach the moon, as Webb had predicted, but abandoned their manned lunar quest after technical failures in the early 1970s.[7]

Now, without strong Soviet competition, much of the political impetus behind NASA disappeared. Webb did not second-guess his successors, but he later told Robert Seamans, with whom he kept in touch over the years, that he truly regretted certain choices made during the Nixon administration. Abandoning the Saturn rocket was especially unfortunate, he believed. The Shuttle decision sealed the fate of Saturn, the technological power base of manned space flight that allowed NASA to lift the equivalent of "a pair of locomotives" into "low earth orbit." "A combination of launches using Saturn could orbit a full-scale Space Station."[8] But maintaining a production line of Saturn rockets (and Apollo spacecraft) was tremendously expensive. NASA's budget in the 1970s had only one-third the purchasing power it had had at the height of Apollo in the mid-1960s.[9]

Living out the Legend

Unlike many former government leaders and policymakers, Webb did not write his memoirs, although his intellectual interest in public management continued unabated, and he advised and lectured whenever he could. In 1969, he published a book based on lectures he had given at Columbia University near the end of his tour at NASA, *Space Age Management: The Large-Scale Approach*, in which he strove to establish general administrative principles. He always had considered himself a student as well as a practitioner of management and had served as president of the American Society for Public Administration in 1966–67. He believed NASA was a model of administration, and in his book stated that what NASA (and especially Apollo) represented was a form of organization the nation needed to better understand and use to cope with its major problems. NASA had welded together government, industry, and the university into an organizational system he called the "large-scale endeavor." The nation needed a way to deal with large, complex, urgent issues, especially those with a high content of science and technology. The "large-scale approach" provided the "possibility of an important extension of management doctrine and may provide a basis for extensions of theory." He explained that "our society has reached a point where its progress and even its survival increasingly depend upon our ability to organize the complex and to do the unusual. We cannot do these things except through large aggregations of resources and power. . . . Our society desperately needs a way—an organized, proven way—to determine and judge the methods by which such aggregations of power can be applied. Certainly that way must be within the context of our free institutions. Otherwise, we may well destroy the values we are trying hardest to preserve and promote."[10]

Whether the United States, with its democratic political system, could organize large-scale endeavors to compete with nations with more authoritarian regimes Webb regarded as "the great issue of this age." America does in fact organize such efforts but has to be pushed to do so "by crisis," a wasteful, often ineffective approach, argued Webb. The NASA experience showed, he said, that large-scale endeavors can be established and successfully carried out in the United States. If we can go to the moon, we should be able to solve large-scale problems on Earth. To those who say that the aggregation of governmental power is inherently dangerous, Webb responded that "power is good or evil according to the vision that it serves."[11]

Unfortunately for Webb, his administrative philosophy did not fit the times. In 1969 the country was not looking for a statement about governmental leadership, especially one extolling administrative power. It was rebelling against such power. Distrust of public executives ran deep. The people (and intellectuals who wrote and influenced opinion) were wary of government, especially the executive branch. Lyndon Johnson was forced from office in part because he had pushed his presidential power too far. Notions implicit in *Space Age Management*—that government needed to reform complex societal institutions and forge huge political coalitions to accomplish major programs—simply were out of favor.

Moreover, Webb celebrated government-directed technology as a solution to problems, but both the 1960s counterculture and its environmental movement gathering momentum at the turn of the decade indicted technology as part of the problem. In 1970 came Earth Day with its doctrine that small (not large-scale) was beautiful. In 1971, Congress set a precedent by terminating a major technological project, the Supersonic Transport, which Webb favored. Webb preached the gospel of big technology to an indifferent or hostile congregation. With the country recoiling from Vietnam, and Nixon in the White House, a long conservative era had begun in the United States that would have little sympathy for Webb's philosophy of government. Webb was disappointed that *Space Age Management* did not get much attention in the United States. His doctrine of large-scale management was much better received, he recalled, in Japan.

Besides lecturing and writing, Webb joined the boards of a variety of companies, such as McGraw-Hill, Sperry-Rand (his former employer of the late 1930s, early 1940s), and Gannett. He was highly selective, refusing close associations with most former NASA contractors, lest he be seen as taking advantage of his governmental contacts. He turned down huge offers to become a lobbyist and lived relatively modestly in a house in northwest Washington, near the National Cathedral. Perhaps the company in which he took the greatest interest was Gannett, publisher of a number of newspapers, now including *USA Today*. The strongest and most active member of its board, Webb used his skills to steer the company deftly through a difficult and potentially explosive succession struggle. When the contest was over, the man Webb had backed took Gannett to an unprecedented level of success.[12]

But it was public service that most interested Webb, and the organization to which he devoted himself most intensively was the Smithsonian Institution, chairing its executive committee from 1970 to 1982. Webb was recruited to this position by Warren E. Burger, whom Nixon had appointed chief justice of the Supreme Court in 1969, a post that carried with it the presidency of the board of regents of the Smithsonian.

Burger looked at his role as president of the board of regents as an opportunity to strengthen the Smithsonian, chartered in 1846 for the "increase and diffusion of knowledge among men." A museum and research institution, it managed various art galleries, a zoo, an astrophysical observatory, a scientific exchange service, and, as of 1971, the Kennedy Center for the Performing Arts. In short, it was a vast and growing conglomerate.

Governing the Smithsonian was the board: in addition to the chief justice, it included the vice president, three members each of the U.S. Senate and House of Representatives, and nine private citizens appointed by joint resolution of Congress. Its full-time director was S. Dillon Ripley, considered a good entrepreneur and poor manager. The Smithsonian received an annual appropriation from Congress and raised private monies. With Congress beginning to question how the public funds were used in relation to the private funds, Burger saw potential problems. "It was critical to appoint the most sagacious analyst of major programs and institutional operations I could find to serve as Chairman of the Executive Committee of the Board of Regents," he recalled. "James Webb was the obvious choice."[13]

Hence, in 1970, Congress voted to appoint Webb a citizen regent of the board of regents of the Smithsonian, filling a vacancy. Made head of the executive committee of the board, Webb was given an office in the Smithsonian, near Ripley, which he used at least once a week. An active chair, he steered a careful course between Burger's desire to "tighten up" on the Smithsonian and Ripley's need for freedom.[14] Under the stewardship of Webb and Ripley, the 1970s proved bountiful years for the Smithsonian. In Burger's view, Webb "served with loyalty and commitment, and helped assure an effective decision-making process and a spectacular set of achievements." He noted that the Smithsonian budget almost tripled in the 1970s. Webb helped "to bring the internal management abreast of the new size and changed conditions relating to the Smithsonian."[15] Webb not only had to deal with internal problems but also had to alleviate congressional concerns.

Webb retired from the Smithsonian, in 1982, after twelve years, his leaving timed with Ripley's. He stayed around long enough to be sure that the transition to Ripley's successor, Robert M. Adams (formerly provost at the University of Chicago), would be smooth. Webb would be replaced by David Acheson, a prominent Washington lawyer and son of Dean Acheson. The key point of continuity was Phil Hughes as under secretary in charge of the administrative and financial aspects of the Smithsonian. A retired senior career official with the Office of Management and Budget (the old Budget Bureau), Hughes had been recruited by Webb.

The Smithsonian was the last major assignment. In 1975, at age sixty-nine, Webb had learned he had Parkinson's disease, a progressive disorder of the nervous system that eventually leaves its victims invalids. The news came as a devastating blow. Webb had enjoyed remarkably good health, considering all the pressures on him over the years. He made it clear he was not about to "sit back and do nothing."[16] Parkinson's was one more problem to be managed. He established a regime of regular exercise, postponing drug treatment as long as possible, lest its side effects impair his intellectual capacity. He told all the organizations on whose boards he sat that he would finish out his terms. Resting and exercising in the morning, in the afternoon he went to a small law office he maintained with his younger brother, Gorham, or to his Smithsonian office.

In September 1981, Webb was able to go to West Point to receive the Sylvanus Thayer Award, established in 1958 to honor distinguished Americans whose service and accomplishments in the national interest exemplified devotion to the ideals expressed in the U.S. Military Academy's motto, "Duty, honor, country." After accepting the award, Webb told the cadets that they, too, would one day be called on to administer large endeavors like "Apollo, based on pushing knowledge and technology to its limits, and requiring skillful leadership that takes into account social, economic, and political, as well as technical factors." They too, he said, would become part of "the large national projects in which success or failure will determine our destiny." Reporting the event, the *Washington Post* noted that Webb had not sought credit for Apollo, and thus his name had not become a household word. But among professionals concerned with government he was now "a Washington legend."[17]

By 1984, Webb was working out of his home almost exclusively. His wife devoted herself to his care. Patsy Webb had seen his rise to prominence in Sperry, his highs at BOB, his lows at State. She was by his side in Oklahoma and at NASA. Their home was always her province, and she made that home a place where Webb could rest and be renewed. Webb kept in as close touch with his children as he could. His son, Jimmy, who had an artistic temperament, ran a small company in New Jersey that produced designer tiles. His daughter, Sally, an accountant, lived in New Mexico and then California. Through Jimmy, Webb was a grandfather, and he took great delight in this fact.

Webb slowed down more and more in ensuing years, in and out of the hospital on numerous occasions but always available to friends. He kept trying new experimental treatments, and followed current events. In the hospital in 1991, having barely survived a bout with pneumonia, Webb was visited by Robert Seamans, then in his seventies. Shaking, exhausted, speaking with difficulty, Webb said his own time for action was behind him and asked Seamans to do what he could to keep alive the message of Apollo.

Webb believed that in Apollo he had found the Holy Grail of management, that America had reached a new frontier of science, technology, and government and had stepped back. He wanted people to know that the nation could still accomplish great deeds. In his last illness he remained optimistic about the future. He especially wanted young people to know that government in a democratic nation could succeed, leaders could make an impact, and the world could be changed for the better.

On March 27, 1992, at eighty-five, Webb died of a heart attack. He was buried at Arlington National Cemetery. Among those who expressed sympathy to his widow was President George Bush, who wrote of Webb:

He will always be remembered as the man who guided the newly created space agency to its extraordinary success in the 1960s, culminating in the historic walk on the Moon by an American astronaut. That single event is among this country's proudest moments. It represents one of the greatest scientific, engineering, and managerial accomplishments of the 20th century, and its success is a great tribute to Jim's leadership at NASA. The American people will always be grateful for his lasting contribution to our nation and, indeed, to the entire world.[18]

LEGACY

On May 25, 1961, with American pride and prestige at a low ebb, and the U.S. space program clearly behind that of the Soviet Union, President John F. Kennedy directed NASA to land a man on the moon and return him safely to Earth within the decade. The only human being to have flown into space at that point was Yuri A. Gagarin, a Soviet cosmonaut. The United States did not know precisely how it would get a man to the moon. NASA itself had known failure and ridicule more than success, and the U.S. Air Force was a stronger agency and an aggressive rival. The president's science adviser had earlier provided Kennedy with a report severely criticizing NASA's capability to lead the nation's space effort. In retrospect, the decision to go to the moon was not only bold, it was audacious.[1] When Apollo not only succeeded, but did so "on time and within budget," the man behind the agency—the man who built, maintained, defended, and drove NASA from 1961 to 1968—was James E. Webb.[2]

Webb's legacy is measured by Apollo, which stands today as a virtually unparalleled example of U.S. technological brilliance, as the mark of the moment when the human species took its "first journey to another world."[3] Further, in the broad sweep of history Apollo was a critical victory in the Cold War technological competition between the United States and Soviet Union. Certainly, subsequent history between the two nations would have differed greatly had Russians walked the moon, rather than Americans. Although many in the later 1960s did not believe that a race to the moon was under way, we now know that the Soviets had suffered a setback in their space program in the mid-1960s and then had regrouped and pushed forward to try to overtake the United States. After America got to the moon first, and the Soviets experienced technical failures, the USSR abandoned its lunar project in the early 1970s.[4]

Apollo also stands as an outstanding example of public management. All the ballyhoo and hucksterism aside, the fact remains that a goal was proclaimed and accomplished. The goal was technically feasible, but what is technically feasible is not usually administratively possible in large-scale government programs. The Soviets could not get the job done. John E. Pike, director of space policy at the Federation of American Scientists, pointed out that "the reason we got to the moon before they did was that they had no one to pull this all together. The critical difference was, we out-managed them."[5]

As administrator of NASA during the 1960s, Webb deserves a large measure of the credit for pulling this all together, just as he would have suffered considerable damage to his reputation if the United States had failed. Even those who cared little for the goal, who, for example, wished the money could have gone to housing or education rather than space, ought to recognize the effectiveness of NASA's administration. To be sure, NASA had many able managers and, until the latter 1960s, plenty of money. But able managers, even with money, often fail. Webb sought a group power that he could raise to the highest level of performance possible. By melding government, industry, and university talent behind a monumental goal, he showed that a democracy could best an authoritarian regime in the development of big technology.

He was not perfect. The Apollo fire revealed that he himself had lost considerable control of the Office of Manned Space Flight, as well as of the principal contractor. He may not have been fair in his treatment then of certain officials in NASA and North American. Determined to manage the information flow, he was less than forthcoming with Congress and the media during the fire inquiry. His quest to reform higher education through SUP showed the limits of his administrative power and his naiveté about the way universities work. He failed to sell a firm post-Apollo program of sufficient scale to avoid retrenchment. At the same time, certainly, he was aggressive and protective, taking on all comers in defense of NASA. He believed in active government and revealed a technocratic zeal critics found dangerous. No wonder he is controversial with those who regard government-managed technology as a threat to democracy. Apollo gave him a stage on which to play a bigger-than-life role, and he performed with gusto.

Although Webb understood the dangers of administrative power, he believed it could be controlled and wielded in the public interest. While he made money in private enterprise, he was always public-service oriented, a bureaucratic entrepreneur, a man who believed he should try to improve society through government. In the name of Apollo, he propelled NASA to advance science and technology, enhance economic development, educate thousands of graduate students, and provide geographical balance in the distribution of scientific resources. Apollo was a means, as well as an end, to move a nation to a New Frontier, a Great Society, and preeminence.

There is debate not only about whether administrative leaders make a difference, but also—when they do—if this is desirable in a democratic government.[6] For Webb, effective government *required* administrative power. Bureaucracy was a fourth branch of government, the operational part of the American system. For democracy to work, bureaucracy had to function. Democracy was more than political speeches and elections; the people had to have confidence their government could carry out policies and programs well. An administrator not only needed resources and discretion to make government work and serve democracy, but also had to be responsive to president, Congress, and the public to get those resources and be granted the necessary autonomy to succeed. Webb felt that he had found the right balance between administrative discretion and democratic responsiveness in NASA, and thus the Holy Grail of public administration. Afterward, he worried that America had pulled back from not only the new frontier of space but also the frontier of management demonstrated in getting to the moon. For Webb, it was not Apollo, but NASA as a model of administrative excellence that was his legacy. He truly believed that if a nation could put a man on the moon, it could manage its other large public problems.

Whether or not Webb had found a Holy Grail of management is conjectural. The triad, scouts, formal and informal chains of command, checks and balances within NASA and between NASA and its contractors, participation, supervision—he used these and other management schemes pragmatically to create an organizational paragon. For the most part they seemed to work, but perhaps less because of their inherent quality than Webb's ability to stay in charge and influence events. Management innovation was both a reality and public relations strategy for Webb. Above all, he understood the importance of power: its nurture, use, and loss. With this understanding he showed what a public executive with the right mix of energy, conviction, skill, wide-ranging contacts, and experience can do when conditions are ripe. He was cunning, guileful, manipulative, and hyperbolic—a lot like Lyndon Johnson. If he did not cross the line of administrative accountability, he surely edged up against it. But unlike Johnson, whose orientation was to legislation, Webb cared deeply about the effective administration of public affairs and was able to inspire those under him to new heights. He pushed a vast army of specialists in a common direction, at breakneck speed. A bold risk taker, he confronted pressures from astronauts, the president's science adviser, the air force, the defense secretary, other NASA executives, Congress, media, industry, universities, and many others, and did not flinch. Rather than break under political pressure, he used rhetorical and coalition-building techniques to impose pressures and coopt others. Organizing and reorganizing NASA as circumstances changed, using the resources at his disposal to reward and punish, he kept reign on his internal forces while orchestrating external support. Throughout, he focused on Apollo's goal and what it took to get there. If he ever questioned that goal or the country's capacity to attain it, he did not communicate such doubts to others.

Containing the Apollo fire crisis and moving NASA to recovery expended much of his own personal political capital. Still, he could not have achieved what he did as an administrator without also having been an extraordinary politician. Nor could he have been successful as a politician had he not performed well as a gifted administrator. This dual capacity sets Webb apart from the legion of others who run agencies in Washington. He could play the external and internal roles of public executive and make one strengthen the other. NASA bore his mark for many years and was synonymous with technological success up until the *Challenger* disaster of 1986, when the decline of this great organization became evident.

Webb traveled far from rural North Carolina to Washington, from the Bureau of the Budget to the State Department to NASA. A good match with the Bureau of the Budget, less so with the State Department, in NASA in the 1960s Webb had a chance to shine. Whatever his drawbacks, this formidable, dedicated, and intensely driven man used his mastery of the governmental process to lead the United States to the moon. He fought the battles in Washington, overcame bureaucratic, legislative, and industrial barriers in NASA's way, and shielded his agency when it counted most. More than a political operator or large-scale manager, Webb embodied the triumph and ambiguity of administrative leadership in America. At NASA, where he tenaciously and forcefully pursued a spectacular vision of the national interest, he indeed was the power behind Apollo.

NOTES

Introduction

1. John F. Kennedy, "Message to Congress, May 25, 1961," *Public Papers of the Presidents of the United States, January 20–December 31, 1961* (Washington: USGPO, 1962), 404.

2. John Noble Wilford, *We Reach the Moon* (New York: Bantam Books, 1969), 269.

3. Bruce Lambert, "James Webb, Who Led Moon Program, Dies at 85," *New York Times*, March 29, 1992; Richard Pearson, "James E. Webb Dies at 85; Was NASA Chief in 1960s," *Washington Post*, March 29, 1992.

4. It has been calculated that $20 billion in 1961 dollars would be $94 billion in 1990 dollars. See *Report of the Advisory Committee on the Future of the U.S. Space Program* (Washington: USGPO, 1990), 11–13. The exact figures are problematic, owing to disagreements about what should or should not be included in Apollo over the course of the program's evolution since 1961. Moreover, it is always difficult to determine the "value" of money from one decade to the next. Nevertheless, it is worth trying to give some impression of the magnitude of this endeavor. Like the Manhattan Project, Apollo stands out from other R&D endeavors in history in terms of sheer scale.

5. See Herbert Kaufman, *Time, Change, and Organizations: Natural Selection in a Perilous Environment* (Chatham, N.J.: Chatham House, 1985), and *The Administrative Behavior of Federal Bureau Chiefs* (Washington: Brookings Institution, 1981).

6. Thomas Carlyle, *On Heroes, Hero-Worship, and the Heroic in History* (1840), cited in Jameson W. Doig and Erwin C. Hargrove, eds., *Leadership and Innovation: Entrepreneurs in Government* (Baltimore: Johns Hopkins University Press, 1990), 1.

7. Fred I. Greenstein, *The Hidden-Hand Presidency: Eisenhower as Leader* (New

York: Basic, 1982); on general leadership theory, see Doig and Hargrove, *Leadership and Innovation*, 1–22.

8. James MacGregor Burns, *Leadership* (New York: Harper and Row, 1978), 4.

9. John M. Logsdon, quoted in Douglas Isbell, "James Webb, Former NASA Administrator, Dies at 85," *Space News*, April 6–12, 1992, 26; Obituary, *Aviation Week and Space Technology*, April 6, 1992, 15.

10. Clayton R. Koppes, *JPL and the American Space Program* (New Haven: Yale University Press, 1982), 143.

11. Tom Wolfe, *The Right Stuff* (New York: Bantam, 1983), 227.

12. John Mecklin, "Jim Webb's Earthy Management of Space," *Fortune*, August 1967, 87.

13. James E. Webb, *Space Age Management: The Large-Scale Approach* (New York: McGraw-Hill, 1969).

14. Mecklin, "Jim Webb's Earthy Management of Space," 83.

15. Robert L. Haught, ed., *Giants in Management* (Washington: National Academy of Public Administration, 1985), 21–34; Doig and Hargrove, *Leadership and Innovation*, 139–68.

16. Leonard Sayles, "The Unsung Profession," *Issues and Observations*, May 1984, 1.

17. Charles Sheffield, review of *Liftoff: The Story of America's Adventure in Space*, by Michael Collins, *Washington Post Book World*, June 19, 1988.

18. Wayne Biddle, "Two Faces of Catastrophe," *Air and Space*, August/September 1990, 46–49.

19. Mecklin, "Jim Webb's Earthy Management of Space," 87, 84.

20. Leonard R. Sayles and Margaret K. Chandler, *Managing Large Systems: Organizations for the Future* (New York: Harper and Row, 1971); Walter A. McDougall, *. . . the Heavens and the Earth: A Political History of the Space Age* (New York: Basic, 1985), chap. 18, "Big Operator: James Webb's Space Age America." McDougall refers to "Webb and the American technocrats" (388) and to Webb's "technocratic vision" (387); it is clear he does not share or approve of that vision.

21. Walter A. McDougall, "Big Operator," 362–73.

22. Mecklin, "Jim Webb's Earthy Management of Space," 84.

23. James M. Beggs, who worked for Webb and later became NASA administrator himself, said Webb aimed high—to create "the perfect management system." See his "James E. Webb: A Force for Excellence," the Inaugural Lecture of the Fund for Excellence in Public Administration (Washington: National Academy of Public Administration, 1983), 12; Biddle, "Two Faces of Catastrophe," 47.

24. Norton E. Long, "Power and Administration," in *Bureaucratic Power in National Policymaking*, ed. Francis E. Rourke, 4th ed. (Boston: Little, Brown, 1986), 7.

25. Wolfe, *The Right Stuff*, 226–27.

Chapter 1. The Making of a Public Executive

1. James Webb, interview by David DeVorkin and Joseph Tatarewicz, February 22, 1985, National Air and Space Museum, Washington (hereafter NASM); James Webb, interview by Robert Sherrod, April 28, 1971, NASA History Division, Reference Collection, Washington.

2. Olive Webb Wharton, interviews by Bailey Webb, August 1986–May 1, 1990, Durham, N.C.

3. Arthur S. Link and Richard L. McCormick, *Progressivism* (Arlington Heights, Ill.: Harlan Davidson, 1983), 90.

4. Woodrow Wilson, as president of Princeton, called the Bell Buckle School one of the best in the country. See Edmund Fuller, "Old Sawney's Inspiring School," *Wall Street Journal,* September 20, 1971.

5. "This Is Epochal History Making Day for Granville County," editorial, *Oxford (N.C.) Public Ledger,* March 6, 1964. The editorial praised J.F. Webb upon the dedication of a high school building in his name and said that "no man in the history of Granville County has accomplished more in public education than Mr. Webb."

6. Webb interview, April 28, 1971.

7. Fuller, "Old Sawney's Inspiring School"; Wharton interviews, August 1986–May 1, 1990.

8. Fred Webb, interview by author, June 28, 1990, Oxford, N.C.; also see Fuller, "Old Sawney's Inspiring School"; Bailey Webb, "The Family Relationships of James Edwin Webb," personal document provided the author. "Sawney was always looming in the background of the Webb family," Olive Webb Wharton said in our interview on June 28, 1990, in Durham, N.C. Matters of integrity were driven home in the Webb household, often by quoting Sawney Webb, under whom J.F. had studied. Fred Webb himself quoted Sawney—a quote he got from J.F.: "Shortly before death, when you come to the end, you realize that nothing is more important than character and what you have done for other people." Said Fred: "This is the sort of thing we always heard from father. The family really thought about this." Fred Webb interview, June 28, 1990.

9. Webb interviews, February 22, 1985, April 28, 1971; Wharton interview, June 28, 1990.

10. Wharton interviews, June 28, 1990, August 1986–May 1990.

11. Webb interviews, February 22, 1985, April 28, 1971.

12. Wharton interviews, August 1986–May 1990, June 28, 1990.

13. Webb interviews, February 22, 1985, April 28, 1971; Wharton interviews, August 1986–May 1990.

14. Link and McCormick, *Progressivism,* 85–96.

15. Wharton interviews, August 1986–May 1990.

16. Webb interviews, February 22, 1985, April 28, 1971.

17. Wharton interviews, August 1986–May 1990, June 28, 1990.

18. The article was "Reserve Pilots Active at the Local Air Fields, Nineteen Places Available in Marine and Naval Units for Air Minded Youth—Army Method Changed," *New York Times*, July 27, 1930.

19. Webb interviews, February 22, 1985, April 28, 1971.

20. Wharton interviews, August 1986–May 1990, June 28, 1990.

21. James A. Robinson, *The House Rules Committee* (Indianapolis: Bobbs-Merrill, 1963).

22. Webb interviews, February 22, 1985, April 28, 1971.

23. Franklin D. Roosevelt, letter to Edward W. Pou, October 18, 1932, Pou Papers, Division of Archives and History, North Carolina Department of Cultural Resources.

24. Wingate Lassiter, "Launching of the New Deal: Mr. Pou's Support of FDR," *Smithfield [North Carolina] Herald*, August 1971, Harvest ed.; see James E. Sargent, *Roosevelt and the Hundred Days: Struggle for the Early New Deal* (New York: Garland, 1981), 245.

25. Morrison Tucker, interview by author, December 2, 1989, Oklahoma City; Harris Hull, interviews by author, August 8, September 25, 1989, Washington.

26. Arthur M. Schlesinger, Jr., *The Coming of the New Deal* (Boston: Houghton Mifflin, 1959), 22.

27. Schlesinger, *The Coming of the New Deal*, 18.

28. Link and McCormick, *Progressivism*, 9.

29. Webb interviews, February 22, 1985, April 28, 1971.

30. Tucker interview, December 2, 1989.

31. James Webb, interview by author, September 28, 1989, Washington. When Pou died, one of his close associates recalled that "his personal life and public career were as clean as the proverbial hound's tooth. I have seen him lift his hands toward heaven and say: 'God knows these hands are clean. No tainted money has ever passed through these fingers,' and everyone who knew him believed this to be true." Wingate Lassiter, "Story of a Johnston County Lawyer: Congressman Pou and His Times," *Smithfield [North Carolina] Herald*, August 1971, Harvest ed.

32. For Lyndon Johnson as a congressional secretary, see Doris Kearns, *Lyndon Johnson and the American Dream* (New York: New American Library, 1976), 76–83, and Robert Dallek, *Lone Star Rising: Lyndon Johnson and His Times* (New York: Oxford University Press, 1991), 93–124.

33. Webb's oral history at the Lyndon B. Johnson Library indicated he did not remember meeting Johnson when they were both secretaries to congressmen. See James Webb, oral history interview by T. H. Baker, April 29, 1969, LBJ Library.

34. Allan A. Needell, "From Military Research to Big Science: Lloyd Berkner and Science Statesmanship in the Postwar Era," in *Big Science: The Growth of Large-Scale Research*, ed. Peter Galison and Bruce Hevly (Palo Alto, Calif.: Stanford University Press, 1992), 290–311.

35. Hull interviews, August 8, September 25, 1989.

36. Webb interviews, February 22, 1985, April 28, 1971.

37. Joseph L. Morrison, *Gov. O. Max Gardner: A Power in North Carolina and New Deal Washington* (Chapel Hill: University of North Carolina Press, 1971), 112, 247; Drew Pearson, "The Washington Merry-Go-Round," *Raleigh News and Observer*, February 10, 1947, North Carolina Collection Clipping File, University of North Carolina Library, Chapel Hill.

38. Morrison, *Gov. O. Max Gardner*, 144.

39. Webb interviews, February 22, 1985, April 28, 1971.

40. Roger Bilstein, *Flight in America: 1900–1983* (Baltimore: Johns Hopkins University Press, 1984), 127.

41. Morrison, *Gov. O. Max Gardner*, 146.

42. Webb interview, February 22, 1985. See also "Legislative and Administrative Activities," *Air Law Review* issues for 1932 and 1933, which reveal that considerable legislative activity on the aviation front took place during the time Webb worked for Congress.

43. Webb interview, February 22, 1985.

44. Morrison, *Gov. O. Max Gardner*, 146.

45. Ibid.

46. Paul Tillett, *The Army Flies the Mails* (University: University of Alabama Press, 1955), 60.

47. Ibid., 62; Morrison, *Gov. O. Max Gardner*, 146.

48. Morrison, *Gov. O. Max Gardner*, 147.

49. Webb interview, February 22, 1985.

50. In the nineteenth century, J. B. L. Foucault, a French scientist, gave the name to the gyroscope and demonstrated its characteristics. In 1910, the first workable gyrocompass was installed in a German warship. Sperry, who built the first automatic pilot using a gyroscope to help an aircraft on its course, in 1911 marketed the first gyrocompass in the United States. See Thomas Parke Hughes, *Elmer Sperry: Inventor and Engineer* (Baltimore: Johns Hopkins University Press, 1971).

51. "Sperry's Tar Heel Tom Morgan," *Raleigh News and Observer*, June 14, 1942, North Carolina Collection Clipping File, University of North Carolina Library, Chapel Hill.

52. Tom Johnson, "Former School Head Still Busy," *Oxford (N.C.) Ledger*, April 7, 1956; Fred Webb interview, June 28, 1990.

53. Patsy Webb, interview by author, August 2, 1990, Washington.

54. Frederick W. Taylor, *Principles of Scientific Management* (New York: Harper, 1913).

55. The Hawthorne studies carried out in the 1920s at the Hawthorne plant of the Western Electric Company in Chicago showed that the "human element" in organizations was much more complicated than Taylor implied. See William B. Eddy, *Public Organization Behavior and Development* (Cambridge, Mass.: Winthrop, 1981), 25–31.

56. Henry C. Metcalf and L. Urwick, eds., *Dynamic Administration: The Collected Papers of Mary Parker Follett* (New York: Harper and Row, 1942), 101, 248. In our interview on January 30, 1992, in Washington, Webb emphasized that Follett contributed to his early thinking about management philosophy, and he cites her as guiding his "basic philosophy" of management in other interviews; see James Webb, interview by Martin Collins, October 15, 1985, NASM.

57. Webb interview, January 30, 1992.

58. Webb, memo to Mr. Siepert, August 30, 1961, Webb Papers, Truman Library. At a time when NASA was growing, Webb explained in this memo to a management associate there how he had endeavored to raise the level of "group feeling" at Sperry and develop leadership capacities within the organization when it was growing rapidly.

59. Webb interview, February 22, 1985.

60. Hull interviews, August 8, September 25, 1989. Draper was a pioneer in advanced guidance technology for aircraft and later for missiles. A longtime professor of aeronautics and astronautics at MIT, he founded MIT's Instrumentation Laboratory in 1939 and developed various "inventions applying gyroscopic principles for World War II gun sights and for the gun sights that made possible intercontinental ballistic missiles." John Noble Wilford, "Charles S. Draper, Engineer, Guided Astronauts to Moon," *New York Times*, July 27, 1987; see also Donald MacKenzie, *Inventing Accuracy: A Historical Sociology of Nuclear Missile Guidance* (Cambridge: MIT Press, 1990). On Berkner, see Needell, "From Military Research to Big Science," 290-311.

61. David Riesman, interview by author, May 28, 1991, Cambridge, Mass.

62. As chairman of the policy committee of the association, Webb dealt with many states with aeronautics agencies, as well as with Washington, and wrote editorials for the *National Aeronautic Magazine*. Some of the letters and materials from this period are with the Webb Papers, Truman Library.

63. James Webb, interview by David DeVorkin and Joseph Tatarewicz, March 8, 1985, NASM.

64. Bailey Webb, interview by author, June 27, 1990, Durham, N.C.

65. Riesman interview, May 28, 1991. A letter from Webb to his parents states simply: "Believing that my work in helping to build up the Sperry organization to its present high level of production is accomplished, and knowing that this level of production will not only be increased but probably will be gradually decreased, I feel that it is my duty to request active duty to help the Marine Corps solve any of the technical and other problems with which I am able to assist." James Webb, letter to Papa and Mama, James Webb Personal Files, Washington.

66. Webb interview, February 22, 1985.

Chapter 2. Directing the U.S. Budget

1. James Webb, interview by David DeVorkin and Joseph Tatarewicz, February 2, 1985, National Air and Space Museum, Washington (hereafter NASM).

2. James Webb, interview by David DeVorkin and Joseph Tatarewicz, March 8, 1985, NASM.

3. James Webb, memo on visit with the president, undated, Webb Papers, Truman Library.

4. Larry Berman, *The Office of Management and Budget and the Presidency, 1921-1979* (Princeton: Princeton University Press, 1979), 38, 39.

5. Quoted in Ken Hechler, *Working with Truman* (New York: Putnam, 1982), 160.

6. Berman, *Office of Management and Budget*, 20, ix-x.

7. Harry S. Truman, *Memoirs*, vol. 2, *Years of Trial and Hope* (Garden City, N.Y.: Doubleday, 1956), 33.

8. Sam Stavisky, "People in the News," *Washington Post*, December 14, 1948.

9. Berman, *Office of Management and Budget*, 42. Appleby stayed until 1947, when he left BOB to become dean of the Maxwell School of Citizenship and Public Affairs at Syracuse University. He was replaced by Frank Pace, Jr., previously assistant to the U.S. postmaster general.

10. Staats went on to a distinguished career in government, not only in BOB, but as head of the U.S. General Accounting Office. He and Webb were lifelong friends.

11. "Joint Oral History Interview: The Truman White House," Charles Murphy, Richard Neustadt, David Stowe, and James Webb, interview by Hugh Heclo and Ann Nelson, February 20, 1980, Truman Library (hereafter cited as "Joint Oral History Interview").

12. James Webb, memo on meeting with Truman, October 28, 1946, Webb papers, Truman Library.

13. "Joint Oral History Interview"; Richard E. Neustadt, interview by author, November 15, 1991, Cambridge, Mass.

14. For a case study of this dispute, see Harold Stein, "The Foreign Service Act of 1946," in *Public Administration and Policy Development*, ed. Harold Stein (New York: Harcourt Brace, 1952), 661-737.

15. James Webb, conference notes, August 15, 1946, Webb Papers, Truman Library.

16. "Joint Oral History Interview." Webb did complain to Gardner and the president about OWMR. Webb, memo on meeting with Truman, October 28, 1946; Webb, memo on meeting with Chief Justice Vinson and Gov. Gardner, November 7, 1946, Webb Papers, Truman Library.

17. Cited in Berman, *Office of Management and Budget*, 40.

18. "Joint Oral History Interview."

19. Berman, *Office of Management and Budget*, 41-42.

20. See Richard E. Neustadt, "Presidency and Legislation: The Growth of Central

Clearance," *American Political Science Review* 48 (Sept. 1954): 641-71; and "Presidency and Legislation: Planning the President's Program," *American Political Science Review* 49 (Dec. 1955): 980-1021. See also Roger W. Jones, oral history interview by Jerry N. Hess, August 14, 1969, Truman Library.

21. Berman, *Office of Management and Budget*, 42.

22. Donald Stone, interview by author, February 16, 1991, Pittsburgh.

23. Berman, *Office of Management and Budget*, 40.

24. Donald C. Stone, "Administrative Management: Reflections on Origins and Accomplishments," *Public Administration Review* 50 (Jan./Feb. 1990): 16.

25. Through various means, this was cut down to $16 billion, still exceedingly large-scale. James E. Webb, *Space Age Management: The Large-Scale Approach* (New York: McGraw-Hill, 1969), 52.

26. Joseph Winslow, memo to file regarding Limitation on Salaries, ECA, June 7, 1948, enclosing a memo from Webb, undated, arguing for exception in case of ECA, Webb Papers, Truman Library. Webb later sought raises for government personnel at higher levels across the board. Stavisky, "People in the News," 2.

27. Stone, "Administrative Management," 16. See BOB memo, "Suggested Steps in Organizing the Economic Cooperation Administration," April 8, 1948, Paul Hoffman, letter to James Webb, April 13, 1948, and letter from Truman to Webb, April 26, 1948, Webb Papers, Truman Library. Stone later became dean of the Graduate School of Public and International Affairs, University of Pittsburgh.

28. Richard E. Neustadt, foreword to *Leadership and Innovation: Entrepreneurs in Government*, ed. Jameson W. Doig and Erwin C. Hargrove (Baltimore: Johns Hopkins University Press, 1990), viii. Webb's desire for innovation stimulated his staff to be creative and showed up in many ways. For example, he had certain functions of the budget that cut across agencies aggregated so they could be better "seen" and understood. Under his direction, the first "special analysis" of federal R&D expenditures was prepared.

29. One of Webb's many organization wars involved the National Science Foundation. Webb favored such an organization, but he influenced Truman to veto the first bill to establish this body in 1947 because he felt it was organized to be more responsive to scientists than to the president. Legislation did not pass until 1950, when Webb was no longer director of BOB. J. Merton England, *A Patron of Pure Science: The National Science Foundation Formative Years, 1945-1957* (Washington: NSF, 1982). Also, Congress in 1947 established what became known as the Hoover Commission to study the organization of the executive branch. Webb was Truman's principal liaison with the commission and infiltrated its staff with individuals who shared his view of the presidency, especially Don K. Price, later dean of the Kennedy School of Government at Harvard. The Hoover Commission—which many in the White House feared would weaken the presidency—wound up legitimating the strong institutional presidency that had evolved under Truman. Peri E. Arnold,

"The First Hoover Commission and the Managerial Presidency," *Journal of Politics* 38 (Feb. 1976): 70.

30. Clark Clifford, *Counsel to the President* (New York: Random House, 1991), 60–61; James M. Roherty, *Decisions of Robert S. McNamara* (Coral Gables: University of Miami Press, 1970), 24; Alfred Sander, "Truman and the National Security Council: 1945–47," *Journal of American History* 59 (Sept. 1972): 370.

31. Dean Acheson, *Present at the Creation: My Years in the State Department* (New York: Norton, 1969), 184–85.

32. James Webb, interview by author, March 26, 1990, Washington.

33. Francis H. Heller, *The Truman White House: The Administration of the Presidency, 1945–1953* (Lawrence: University of Kansas Press, 1980), 89. In a memo to Truman, Webb indicated he was guarding against the NSC and another proposed executive office body, the National Security Resources Board, being organized in accord with "power over" the president. Webb, memo to Truman, August 8, 1947, Webb Papers, Truman Library. See also Sander, "Truman and the National Security Council." For a relatively straightforward exposition of Forrestal's view of the military unification, see R. Gordon Hoxie, *Command Decision and the Presidency: A Study in National Security Policy and Organization* (New York: Crowell, for Reader's Digest Press, 1977), 133–41.

34. These problems were remedied in 1949 amendments to the law, which Forrestal supported. See Arnold A. Rogow, *James Forrestal: A Study of Personality, Politics, and Policy* (New York: Macmillan, 1963), 305.

35. "Joint Oral History Interview."

36. Webb contributed to the election indirectly. James Rowe, a political strategist for the Democrats who was on the outs with the White House, asked Webb to route some of his campaign ideas to Truman. Webb spoke to the president, and when they agreed that Webb's overt political role should be minimized, Webb had his aide, Richard Neustadt, give Rowe's memo to Clark Clifford. This memo, as adapted by Clifford, is regarded by many as the basis for the 1948 campaign strategy. "Joint Oral History Interview"; Clifford, *Counsel to the President*, 191.

37. Quoted in Robert J. Donovan, *Conflict and Crisis: The Presidency of Harry S. Truman, 1945–1948* (New York: Norton, 1977), 410.

38. Warner R. Schilling, Paul Y. Hammond, and Glenn H. Snyder, *Strategy, Politics, and Defense Budgets* (New York: Columbia University Press, 1962), 139; see also Steven I. Rearden, *History of the Office of the Secretary of Defense: The Formative Years, 1947–1950* (Washington: Historical Office, Office of the Secretary of Defense, 1984), 1:326–27.

39. Cited in Rearden, *History of the Office*, 327.

40. Schilling, Hammond, and Snyder, *Strategy, Politics, and Defense Budgets*, 155.

41. "Joint Oral History Interview."

42. Rearden, *History of the Office*, 345.

43. Clifford, *Counsel to the President,* 172–173. "Joint Oral History Interview." Even if Webb said nothing, others, especially Harry Vaughan, a White House assistant, did raise doubts in Truman's mind about Forrestal's loyalty during the election. See David McCullough, *Truman* (New York: Simon and Schuster, 1991), 736–37.

44. "Joint Oral History Interview"; Rearden, *History of the Office,* 350–51.

45. Schilling, Hammond, and Snyder, *Strategy, Politics and Defense Budgets,* 199; Rearden, *History of the Office,* 351.

46. Walter Millis, ed., *The Forrestal Diaries* (New York: Viking, 1951), 555. See Rogow, *James Forrestal,* for an attempt to understand this complicated and anguished man.

Chapter 3. Managing the Department of State

1. Webb wrote one of his friends: "I had hoped to come to Chapel Hill as the Dean of the School of Commerce and participate over the next 25 years or so in the development of that region served by the university." Webb, letter to Walter Brown, February 1, 1949, Webb Papers, Truman Library.

2. James Webb, interview by David DeVorkin and Joseph Tatarewicz, March 8, 1985, National Air and Space Museum, Washington (hereafter NASM).

3. Clark Clifford, *Counsel to the President* (New York: Random House, 1991), 140.

4. David S. McLellan, *Dean Acheson: The State Department Years* (New York: Dodd, Mead, 1976), 96.

5. Dean Acheson, *Present at the Creation: My Years in the State Department* (New York: Norton, 1969), 250; David McCullough, *Truman* (New York: Simon and Schuster, 1991), 753.

6. James Q. Wilson, *Bureaucracy* (New York: Basic, 1989), 155–75.

7. Webb, letter to Wilson Wyatt, January 18, 1949, Webb Papers, Truman Library.

8. McLellan, *Dean Acheson,* 97.

9. Harry S. Truman, memo for James Webb and enclosure, January 11, 1949, Webb Papers, Truman Library.

10. "How Will Acheson Appointment Affect U.S. Diplomacy?" *Foreign Policy Bulletin,* January 14, 1949, Webb Papers, Truman Library.

11. McCullough, *Truman,* 751.

12. James Webb, interview by Frank Shep, *Time,* assisted by Lloyd Lehrbas, special assistant to the under secretary, May 4, 1950 (transcript), Webb Papers, Truman Library.

13. Acheson, *Present at the Creation,* 255.

14. Richard L. Stokes, "Under Secretary of State James E. Webb in Charge of Reorganization," *St. Louis Post Dispatch,* March 27, 1949.

15. Willis Shapley, "Complete Text of Statement by Willis H. Shapley with respect to James E. Webb's contribution to management," unpublished paper, James Webb Personal Files, Washington.

16. James Webb, interview by Martin Collins, October 15, 1985, NASM. A year later, Webb reported that his system was working, and one consequence was that Acheson was having to sign off on only half as many papers, which meant he had more time for his prime responsibilities. Remarks by James Webb to annual dinner of the Granville County Chamber of Commerce, Oxford, N.C., January 27, 1950, Webb Papers, Truman Library.

17. Stokes, "Under Secretary of State."

18. James Webb, interview by author, December 12, 1990, Washington.

19. Richard E. Neustadt, foreword to *Leadership and Innovation: Entrepreneurs in Government,* ed. Jameson W. Doig and Erwin C. Hargrove (Baltimore: Johns Hopkins University Press, 1990), viii.

20. Paul Nitze, interview by author, June 6, 1991, Washington.

21. Webb interview, October 15, 1985.

22. George F. Kennan, *Memoirs, 1925-1950* (New York: Pantheon, 1967), 465.

23. David Callahan, *Dangerous Capabilities: Paul Nitze and the Cold War* (New York: HarperCollins, 1990), 70.

24. Ibid., 6.

25. James Free, "Under the Dome," *Raleigh News and Observer,* October 29, 1949.

26. Doris M. Condit, *The Test of War, 1950-53* (Washington: Office of Secretary of Defense, 1988), 15.

27. Robert J. Donovan, *Tumultuous Years: The Presidency of Harry S. Truman* (New York: Norton, 1982), 159.

28. Clifford, *Counsel to the President,* 141.

29. McCullough, *Truman,* 759; Donovan, *Tumultuous Years,* 135.

30. "Target: Acheson," editorial, *Washington Star,* March 21, 1950.

31. McCullough, *Truman,* 760.

32. Condit, *The Test of War,* 15.

33. Ibid., 8-9; McCullough, *Truman,* 765.

34. Condit, *The Test of War,* 15.

35. "Joint Oral History Interview: The Truman White House," Charles Murphy, Richard Neustadt, David Stowe, and James Webb, interview by Hugh Heclo and Ann Nelson, February 20, 1980, Truman Library (hereafter cited as "Joint Oral History Interview").

36. Ibid. There is a handwritten note in the Webb Papers, Truman Library, dated March 26, 1950, in which he mentions his communication with Truman in Key West. Webb states he went there "incognito."

37. "Joint Oral History Interview."

38. Ibid.

39. Warner R. Schilling, Paul Y. Hammond, and Glenn H. Snyder, *Strategy, Politics, and Defense Budgets* (New York: Columbia University Press, 1962), 337.

40. "Joint Oral History Interview."

41. Ibid.; also James Webb, letter to John Snyder, April 25, 1975, Webb Papers, Truman Library.

42. Webb, letter to Snyder, April 25, 1975, Webb Papers, Truman Library; McCullough, *Truman,* 777.

43. McCullough, *Truman,* 777, 779.

44. Condit, *The Test of War,* 32.

45. One of Webb's contacts in the media was Joseph Alsop, a columnist for the *New York Herald Tribune.* Alsop apparently thought highly of Webb and provided him information on Johnson's activities, including Johnson's own attempts to influence policy through leaks. Alsop, letter to Webb ("Dear Jim"), June 19, 1950, with enclosures, Webb Papers, Truman Library.

46. Carlisle Humelsine, interview by author, June 5, 1986, Williamsburg, Va.

47. Webb interview, December 12, 1990. Webb's large role in the Johnson decision is also confirmed by Acheson's personal assistant, who said, "Jim played an active role in building the fire under the White House that resulted in Johnson's being asked to resign." Lucius D. Battle, interview by author, January 18, 1990, Washington.

48. Condit, *The Test of War,* 33-34.

49. Allan A. Needell, "From Military Research to Big Science: Lloyd Berkner and Science Statesmanship in the Postwar Era," in *Big Science: The Growth of Large-Scale Research,* ed. Peter Galison and Bruce Hevly (Palo Alto, Calif.: Stanford University Press, 1992), 301. Also see Lloyd Berkner, *Science and Foreign Relations* (Washington: International Science Policy Survey Group, 1950).

50. Needell, "From Military Research to Big Science," 301-2.

51. Allan A. Needell, "Truth Is Our Weapon: Project Troy and Government/Academic Relations in the National Security State," *Diplomatic History* 17 (Summer 1993): 399-420.

52. Dean Acheson, extemporaneous remarks following his radio address at a dinner meeting of the American Society of Newspaper Editors, Washington, April 22, 1950 (unpublished transcript), Webb Papers, Truman Library. In his talk, Acheson was answering charges that State Department was infested with Communists. Webb was one of the officials he cited in refuting this allegation and drawing attention to the quality of the people in State.

53. Callahan, *Dangerous Capabilities,* 139.

54. Ibid., 138-39.

55. Webb, memo of conversation with McWilliam Pauly, May 25, 1951, Webb Papers, Truman Library.

56. Paul Nitze, interview by author, June 6, 1991, Washington; Webb interview, October 15, 1985; Webb, handwritten memo to Dean Acheson, no date, James Webb Personal Files, Washington.

57. Battle interview, January 18, 1990; Jamie McWilliams, interview by author, December 2, 1989, Oklahoma City.

58. Webb, memo to Dean Acheson, no date; David Acheson, interview by author, November 1, 1990, Washington.

59. Acheson interview, November 1, 1990; Clark Clifford writes of Nitze's subsequent career that "he was repeatedly frustrated in achieving his goal of becoming either Secretary of State or Secretary of Defense, and believed he had been denied these positions through the broken promises of Presidents and the maneuvering of his adversaries. His ambition and impatient intellect often manifested themselves in irritable peevishness and flashes of unveiled contempt for people whom he felt did not deserve the high government positions which they held." *Counsel to the President,* 489.

60. Acheson interview, November 1, 1990.

61. Harry Truman, letter to Webb ("My Dear Jim"), January 23, 1952, Webb Papers, Truman Library.

Chapter 4. The Oklahoma Years

1. One who inquired how he could help was Vannevar Bush, head of the Office of Scientific Research and Development during World War II, with whom Webb had sparred while at BOB over National Science Foundation legislation, but who subsequently became a friend. Vannevar Bush, letter to Webb, January 8, 1952, Webb Papers, Truman Library.

2. See Anne Hodges Morgan, *Robert S. Kerr: The Senate Years* (Norman: University of Oklahoma Press, 1977).

3. Daniel Seligman, "Senator Bob Kerr, the Oklahoma Gusher," *Fortune,* March 1959, 137.

4. Morgan, *Robert S. Kerr,* 37.

5. Kerr strongly supported Truman's firing of General MacArthur. Seligman, "Senator Bob Kerr," 179-80.

6. James Webb, interview by Martin Collins, October 15, 1985, National Air and Space Museum, Washington (hereafter NASM).

7. Jamie McWilliams, interview by author, December 2, 1989, Oklahoma City.

8. Morgan, *Robert S. Kerr,* 117; Clark Clifford, *Counsel to the President* (New York: Random House, 1991), 284.

9. Morgan, *Robert S. Kerr,* 106-38.

10. Duane Roller, interview by author, February 1, 1990, Oklahoma City. Roller, who was curator of the History of Science Collection at the University of Oklahoma, recalled this conversation with Webb concerning Kerr.

11. Breene M. Kerr, interview by author, November 29, 1989, Oklahoma City. Breene is Robert Kerr's son.

12. Morgan, *Robert S. Kerr,* vii.

13. McWilliams interview, December 2, 1989.

14. Webb, letter to President Truman, January 21, 1953, Webb Papers, Truman Library.

15. Morrison Tucker, interview by author, December 2, 1989, Oklahoma City.

16. McWilliams interview, December 2, 1989.

17. Ibid.

18. Ibid.

19. James Webb, interview by author and Martin Collins, October 3, 1986, NASM.

20. Kerr interview, November 29, 1989.

21. Webb interview, October 3, 1986.

22. Morgan, *Robert S. Kerr*, 211.

23. John Samuel Ezell, *Innovations in Energy: The Story of Kerr-McGee* (Norman: University of Oklahoma Press, 1979), 229, 182-83.

24. Seligman, "Senator Bob Kerr," 184.

25. Ezell, *Innovations in Energy*, 229-30.

26. Ibid., 237.

27. Elizabeth A. Zoernig, interview by author, July 3, 1990, Oklahoma City. Zoernig was secretary to Dean McGee for thirty-seven years.

28. James Webb, interview by David DeVorkin, Michael Dennis, and Joseph Tatarewicz, July 22, 1983, NASM.

29. Ibid.; James Webb, interview by David DeVorkin, Joseph Tatarewicz, and Linda Ezell, March 15, 1985, NASM.

30. Webb, letter to President Truman, January 12, 1956, Webb Papers, Truman Library.

31. James Webb, "Graduate Research Center of the Southwest" (address), November 15, 1962, NASA History Office.

32. John Kirkpatrick, interview by author, December 2, 1989, Oklahoma City.

33. Webb interview, July 22, 1983.

34. Dwight D. Eisenhower, Radio and Television Address to the American People on "Our Future Security," November 13, 1957, *Public Papers of the Presidents, Dwight D. Eisenhower, 1957* (Washington: USGPO, 1958), 234.

35. Webb interview, March 8, 1985.

36. Webb interview, October 15, 1985. Kerr is quoted in Bobby Baker, *Wheeling and Dealing* (New York: Norton, 1978), 88. On criticism of Kerr for his practices, see also Ezell, *Innovations in Energy*, 181, 230, 289, 301, 313.

37. McWilliams interview, December 2, 1989.

38. "Science, Physics Education: Two Oxford Natives Have Top Roles in Program," *Raleigh News and Observer*, December 10, 1958.

39. Ibid.

40. Kirkpatrick interview, December 2, 1989; Zoernig interview, July 3, 1990.

Chapter 5. NASA: From Appointment to Apollo

1. James Webb, oral history interview by T. H. Baker, April 29, 1969, LBJ Library.

2. James Webb, interview by David DeVorkin, Joseph Tatarewicz, and Linda Ezell, March 15, 1985, National Air and Space Museum, Washington (hereafter NASM); Jerome Wiesner, interview by author, March 15, 1985, Cambridge, Mass.

3. For a detailed overview of the political situation surrounding NASA prior to the lunar decision see John M. Logsdon, *The Decision to Go to the Moon* (Cambridge: MIT Press, 1970).

4. Webb interview, March 15, 1985; see also Webb interview, April 29, 1969.

5. Ibid. This section is based primarily on the Webb interviews of March 15, 1985, and April 29, 1969.

6. In a handwritten letter to President Truman, Webb discussed his meeting with Kennedy and how he tried but could not "get off the hook!" Of Kennedy, Webb said: "I am deeply impressed with him and believe he will make a great President." Webb, letter to Truman, February 8, 1961, Webb Papers, Truman Library.

7. Willis Shapley, interview by author, August 2, 1990, Washington.

8. Robert Rosholt, *An Administrative History of NASA, 1958-1963* (Washington: NASA, 1966), 198.

9. Tom Wolfe, *The Right Stuff* (New York: Bantam, 1983).

10. Logsdon, *Decision to Go to the Moon*, 12, 37.

11. Ibid., 38.

12. Robert Hotz, "Success and Disappointment in Space," *Aviation Week and Space Technology*, February 6, 1961, 21.

13. Naugle later concluded: "How wrong they were!!" John Naugle, *First among Equals: The Selection of NASA Space Science Experiments* (Washington: NASA, 1991), 107. He spent most of his career at NASA, rose to head its Office of Space Science, and became chief scientist of the agency before retiring in 1981.

14. Robert Seamans, interview by author, April 8, 1991, Cambridge, Mass.

15. Rosholt, *An Administrative History of NASA*, iv.

16. Ibid.

17. Logsdon, *Decision to Go to the Moon*, 71-75.

18. Robert Porter, "Ten Lessons I Learned from James E. Webb," February 19, 1985, James Webb Personal Files, Washington.

19. James Webb, interview by Martin Collins and Allan Needell, November 4, 1985, NASM. See the account of the Atlas dispute in Loyd S. Swenson, Jr., James Grimwood, and Charles C. Alexander, *This New Ocean: A History of Project Mercury* (Washington: NASA, 1966), 318-22.

20. Logsdon, *Decision to Go to the Moon*, 86-87. See also Arnold Levine, *Managing NASA in the Apollo Era* (Washington: NASA, 1982), 218-19; Webb, memorandum for the record (NASA-DOD Conf.), February 24, 1961, Webb Papers, Truman Library.

21. Logsdon, *Decision to Go to the Moon*, 79.

22. Webb interview, March 15, 1985. Ironically, several months after the Webb decision, the "thick-skinned" Atlas favored by the air force "was launched and blew up very soon after it left the pad!" Porter, "Ten Lessons."

23. Logsdon, *Decision to Go to the Moon*, 90.

24. Ibid., 91.

25. Paul Dembling, interview by author, June 12, 1990, Washington.

26. Logsdon, *Decision to Go to the Moon*, 100. Aside from asking for more money in support of a possible Project Apollo, Webb made another crucial policy decision in connection with revisions in the Eisenhower budget: to remove language in the existing budget rationale calling for $10 million cost sharing on the part of industry for demonstrating the first communication satellite. This provision reflected an Eisenhower administration policy that assumed AT&T would share the cost with NASA for this venture. However, Webb did not want to be constrained by such a provision in favor of AT&T or any specific company or technical approach. He wanted to keep communication satellites in the development stage a while longer, as he was not sure that the approach AT&T favored was the best technically, on the basis of discussions he had had with NASA people. The Eisenhower administration, on the other hand, had been anxious to transfer communication satellites from government to industry as soon as possible. These were the first practical payoffs from the civilian space program. Although AT&T was willing to help the government pay, Webb saw the company as looking for an edge in the coming communication satellite business, and he wanted to step back and see if there was a better way. Hence, his decision was to stop the policy momentum he had inherited, to give the Kennedy administration an opportunity to formulate its own communication satellite policy. This led ultimately to the creation of COMSAT Corporation and the use of a "synchronous" technical approach developed by Hughes Aircraft that virtually everyone agreed was better than the one originally proposed by AT&T. For an account of the shift in national policy from the Eisenhower to Kennedy administrations, see Roger A. Kvam, "COMSAT: The Inevitable Anomaly," in *Knowledge and Power*, ed. Sanford A. Lakoff (New York: Free Press, 1966), 271⁻92; also, W. Henry Lambright, *Governing Science and Technology* (New York: Oxford University Press, 1976), 69⁻72.

27. Logsdon, *Decision to Go to the Moon*, 101.

28. Webb, letter to Dr. J. R. Killian, March 28, 1961, Webb Papers, Truman Library.

29. James Webb, interview by David DeVorkin, Allan Needell, and Joseph Tatarewicz, April 12, 1985, NASM. For Dembling's account of Webb's anticipation of the Fulton exchange, see Paul Dembling, interview by Robert Sherrod, January 22, 1969, NASA History Office. For Dembling's later assessment of Webb as a political operator with Congress, see Dembling interview by author, June 12, 1990, Washington. Robert Seamans, who also testified at the hearings, apparently went beyond

Kennedy administration policy and drew a rebuke from the White House. Webb stoutly defended his associate and made it clear he did not take kindly to White House staff intervention. In a lengthy memo depicting the atmosphere of the hearings, he declared that "from a reading of the testimony, I believe Seamans has done an exceptionally fine job. The Chairman and the Democrats have given him little or no support." Webb, memorandum for Kenneth O'Donnell, the White House, April 21, 1961, Webb Papers, Truman Library. The full title of the House Space Committee was the House Committee on Science and Astronautics. Similarly, the Senate Space Committee was the Senate Committee on Aeronautical and Space Sciences. Most observers called them the House and Senate Space Committees.

30. Logsdon, *Decision to Go to the Moon*, 106-7.

31. The other questions were: "2) How much additional would it cost? 3) Are we working 24 hours a day on existing programs? If not, why not? If not . . . make recommendations to me as to how work can be speeded up. 4) In building large boosters should we put our emphasis on nuclear, chemical, or liquid fuel, or a combination of these three? 5) Are we making maximum effort? Are we achieving necessary results?" Charles Murray and Catherine Bly Cox, *Apollo: The Race to the Moon* (New York: Simon and Schuster, 1989), 80.

32. Ibid., 81.

33. Logsdon, *Decision to Go to the Moon*, 119.

34. Ibid., 120; Webb interview, April 12, 1985.

35. Webb interview, April 12, 1985; James M. Beggs, "James E. Webb: A Force for Excellence" (Washington: National Academy of Public Administration, 1983), 6.

36. Logsdon, *Decision to Go to the Moon*, 123.

37. Ibid., 124.

38. Robert C. Seamans, "Voyage to the Moon: A View from NASA Headquarters," unpublished monograph, no date, provided author from Seamans's personal files. Since Webb never wrote his memoirs on Apollo, and Dryden died in 1965, Seamans is the only official among the top three at NASA who wrote an account of the decision to launch and implement Apollo. Unfortunately, Seamans kept the forty-two-page document "private" and did not publish it. In Logsdon's account, the meeting at which Webb revised the decision memo for the president ended at midnight. Logsdon, *Decision to Go to the Moon*, 125. Seamans recollects the meeting as lasting until 2:00 A.M.

39. Seamans, "Voyage to the Moon."

40. Logsdon, *Decision to Go to the Moon*, 125; James Webb and Robert McNamara, memo to Vice President, and attached report, "Recommendations for Our National Space Program: Changes, Policies, Goals," May 8, 1961, NASA History Office.

41. Logsdon, *Decision to Go to the Moon*, 126.

42. Webb was made aware of the deep feelings against the manned space program in a dramatic way. The evening after Shepard's parade and address to Con-

gress (by which time the Webb-McNamara memo had gone to President Kennedy and been approved), Webb and Patsy went to a dinner at the Carnegie Institution in Washington. Webb's longtime friend Vannevar Bush saw Webb come in the door. Webb wrote: He "was so incensed at the furor [of the Shepard events] that he grabbed me by my lapels to shake me—accusing me of 'exhaltation' of a very dangerous public mood." Webb, Handwritten note, January 27, 1975, as cover to letter from Webb to Vannevar Bush, May 15, 1961, Webb Papers, Truman Library. He wrote another Apollo critic: "I am certain we must increase the capacity of our American scientific community and particularly our universities to back up our program." Webb, letter to Jerome B. Wiesner, May 15, 1961, Webb Papers, Truman Library.

43. Walter A. McDougall, . . . the Heavens and the Earth: A Political History of the Space Age (New York: Basic, 1985), 361.

44. James Webb, memo to Vice President, May 23, 1961, NASA History Office.

45. Ibid.

46. John F. Kennedy, Message to Congress, May 25, 1961, Public Papers of the Presidents of the United States, January 20–December 31, 1961 (Washington: USGPO, 1962).

47. Seamans, "Voyage to the Moon."

48. Ibid.

Chapter 6. Launching a Stronger NASA

1. James Webb, interview by David DeVorkin, Allan Needell, and Joseph Tatarewicz, April 12, 1985, National Air and Space Museum, Washington (hereafter NASM).

2. James Webb, interview by author, April 12, 1985, Washington; James Webb, interview by David DeVorkin, Joseph Tatarewicz, and Linda Ezell, March 22, 1985, NASM.

3. James Webb, interview by Martin Collins, October 15, 1985, NASM.

4. James Webb, interview by Allan Needell and Martin Collins, September 10, 1985, NASM.

5. James Webb, interview by author and Martin Collins, October 3, 1986, NASM.

6. In August 1961, Webb wrote T. Keith Glennan, his predecessor as NASA administrator, that he doubted the political honeymoon following Kennedy's decision would last long. Meanwhile: "I am finding, with some unhappiness, that I am expected to be an 'image' of an advancing, ongoing program." Although he had tried to "stay in the background," the media were insisting on personality sketches and interviews. Webb was indeed more organization man than publicity seeker. But he was finding that the nature of space precluded his being invisible. He sought to use this potential prominence to NASA's advantage by presenting an optimistic and can-do image. Webb, letter to T. Keith Glennan, August 22, 1961, Webb Papers, Tru-

man Library. He noted to a friend from Oklahoma: "This is a really tough job—with the out-in-front technological requirements, and the eyes of all the world on every move you make." Webb, letter to Edward T. Gaylord, August 24, 1961, Webb Papers, Truman Library.

7. Webb interview, October 3, 1986.

8. Ibid.

9. R. P. Young, interview by author, August 1, 1990, Washington.

10. Webb, memo for Mr. Siepert, "How to make the Dryden-Seamans-Webb group more effective on important decisions," August 28, 1961, Webb Papers, Truman Library.

11. Webb told Cox how important the president was for getting NASA's message out. The point was to show the president how the space program was helping him with his objectives. First, NASA should be "feeding" information to the president, and, second, "his words" would carry the NASA message. Webb mentioned other cabinet members who could help NASA if NASA provided them with the appropriate information. Webb, memo for Dr. Cox, December 4, 1961, Webb Papers, Truman Library.

12. Webb interview, October 15, 1985; Arthur Raymond, interview by author, November 30, 1990, Brentwood, Calif.

13. Raymond was brought aboard by Mervin Kelly, retired executive with AT&T. Along with some others they formed an informal kitchen cabinet to Webb, commenting on organizational issues and personnel problems. Kelly left after a few years. Raymond was truly used as a scout and gave Webb insights into goings on in his centers and industry—one more set of eyes and ears. Mervin Kelly, letter to Arthur Raymond, June 30, 1961, provided author from Raymond's personal files; Webb, letter to Arthur Raymond, August 1, 1961, Webb Papers, Truman Library; Webb, letter to Mervin Kelly, January 7, 1963, NASA History Office; Webb, letter to Arthur Raymond, August 12, 1963, and Raymond letter to Webb, August 14, 1963, both provided author from Raymond's personal files. Playing a different role as an informal confidant was Webb's friend Berkner, who "thought big" and shared Webb's enthusiasm for harnessing large-scale, interdisciplinary science to national problems; the two men fueled one another's visions for years. Berkner died in 1967. See Allan A. Needell, "From Military Research to Big Science: Lloyd Berkner and Science Statesmanship in the Postwar Era," in *Big Science: The Growth of Large-Scale Research*, ed. Peter Galison and Bruce Hevly (Palo Alto, Calif.: Stanford University Press, 1992), 290–311.

14. Webb interview, March 15, 1985.

15. Ibid.

16. Robert Seamans, interview by author, November 16, 1990, Cambridge, Mass.; see also Courtney G. Brooks, James M. Grimwood, and Loyd S. Swenson, Jr., *Chariots for Apollo: A History of Manned Lunar Spacecraft* (Washington: NASA, 1979), 41; Webb, letter to C. W. Perella, September 9, 1961, NASA History Office.

17. Kenneth O'Donnell, interview by Robert Sherrod, May 13, 1971, NASA History Office; Webb, memo for the president, September 14, 1961, Webb Papers, Truman Library. The memo to Kennedy came on the heels of an acrimonious telephone conversation between Webb and Gov. John Volpe of Massachusetts, who had been pressuring Webb to site the Manned Spacecraft Center in his state. Webb ended the conversation by saying that if Volpe did not watch out, Webb would be "issuing a statement to the press," and Volpe "probably wouldn't like it." Webb, memo of telephone conversation, September 12, 1961, Webb Papers, Truman Library.

18. Robert Gilruth, interview by David DeVorkin, March 2, 1987, NASM. Webb made sure Senator Byrd did not think too badly of him, informing Byrd of a $6 million expansion of the Langley Field installation. Webb, letter to Senator Harry Byrd, October 24, 1961, Webb Papers, Truman Library.

19. Charles Murray and Catherine Bly Cox, *Apollo: The Race to the Moon* (New York: Simon and Schuster, 1989), 168.

20. Ibid., 170; James Webb, interview by author, January 30, 1992, Washington. Not long thereafter, NASA and North American ran into disagreements, and by January 1963 Webb was even saying that NASA might have to "seek another contractor, even though the penalties would be very great." Webb, memo for Dr. Seamans, January 31, 1963, NASA History Office.

21. Seamans interview, November 16, 1990. The possibility of Admiral Raborn's becoming Apollo czar got into the papers, and this gave the navy time to act. Webb insisted he was "not necessarily looking for a czar but rather for a form of organization that would get our total job done." Webb, memo for Dr. Seamans, August 3, 1961, Webb Papers, Truman Library.

22. Robert Rosholt, *An Administrative History of NASA, 1958–1963* (Washington: NASA, 1966), 224–25.

23. Joseph Trento, *Prescription for Disaster* (New York: Crown, 1987), 51; see also Barton C. Hacker and James M. Grimwood, *On the Shoulders of Titans: A History of Project Gemini* (Washington: NASA, 1977).

24. Trento, *Prescription for Disaster*, 52.

25. Webb's interest in the "image aspects" extended to the name. As Gemini became the likely name, Webb asked his public affairs director to "check carefully to see that 'Gemini' does not have any unfortunate connotation which would cause trouble in some parts of the world, in mythology, or in some other area that may relate to public affairs." Webb, memo for Hiden Cox, December 19, 1961, Webb Papers, Truman Library.

26. John Simpson, interview by author, August 1, 1991, Chicago.

27. Webb, letter to Lee DuBridge, August 29, 1961, Webb Papers, Truman Library.

28. Webb interview, April 12, 1985.

29. W. Henry Lambright, *Launching NASA's Sustaining University Program* (Syracuse, N.Y.: InterUniversity Case Program, 1969), VII-2; Webb, letter to David Bell, December 6, 1961, Webb Papers, Truman Library.

30. Murray and Cox, *Apollo*, 139.

31. Ibid., 141, 143; Jerome Wiesner, interview by author, November 15, 1990, Cambridge, Mass. According to Howard E. McCurdy, after the public dispute with Wiesner Webb stood up in the front of the bus that was taking NASA and some other government officials to their next stop and declared, "Hey, we're running this show and we're going to run it." *Inside NASA: High Technology and Organizational Change in the U.S. Space Program* (Baltimore: Johns Hopkins University Press, 1993), 88.

32. John Noble Wilford, *We Reach the Moon* (New York: Bantam, 1969), 48; Wiesner interview, November 15, 1990; Seamans interview, November 16, 1990. As late as October 29, 1962, Wiesner was trying to get Webb to give him proposals from contractors associated with LOR techniques. Webb, memo for Dr. Seamans, October 29, 1962, Webb Papers, Truman Library.

33. James Webb, interview by Martin Collins and Allan Needell, November 4, 1985, NASM.

34. Hiden T. Cox, interview by author, April 10, 1990, Long Beach, Calif.; Robert Sherrod, "The Selling of the Astronauts," *Columbia Journalism Review,* May/June 1973, 16–25; Webb, memo for Robert Gilruth and Hiden Cox, March 16, 1962, and memo to Hiden Cox, March 30, 1962, Webb Papers, Truman Library. Webb also had to set guidelines for Wernher von Braun, whose outside speaking engagements (for large fees) had become excessive, in Webb's view. See Webb, memo for Wernher von Braun, December 5, 1961, Webb Papers, Truman Library.

35. Webb interview, October 3, 1986.

36. James Webb, interview by author, March 26–27, 1991, Washington.

37. Robert Seamans, interview by author, December 20, 1990, Cambridge, Mass.

38. "Reaching for the Moon," *Time,* August 10, 1962, 52–57.

39. Wilford, *We Reach the Moon,* 64; Murray and Cox, *Apollo,* 152.

40. R. P. Young, memo for the record, November 20, 1962, and see also P. T. Drotning, memos to Col. Young, November 19, 20, 1962, Webb Papers, Truman Library.

41. "Space in Earthly Trouble," *Time* 80, November 23, 1962, 15.

42. Seamans interview, November 16, 1990.

43. Webb, letter to the president, November 30, 1962, Webb Papers, Truman Library.

44. Wiesner interview, November 15, 1990.

45. Webb interview, October 15, 1985.

46. Seamans interview, November 16, 1990. Webb arranged for Holmes to go back to his former company at a salary larger than he had when he came to NASA. Holmes, however, chose to go to a new company, Raytheon, and later became its president.

47. George Mueller, interview by author, September 21, 1990, Washington.

48. Murray and Cox, *Apollo,* 158–60.

49. Ibid., 156.

50. Ibid., 160, 162.

51. Seamans interview, December 20, 1990. Webb also dealt with Secretary of Defense Robert S. McNamara and Air Force Secretary Eugene M. Zuckert. Webb, memo for Dr. Mueller, January 14, 1964, NASA History Office; George Mueller, memo for the administrator, "Utilization of Air Force Program Management Personnel," September 26, 1963, Webb Papers, Truman Library.

52. Brooks, Grimwood, and Swenson, *Chariots for Apollo*, 128.

53. Arnold Levine, *Managing NASA in the Apollo Era* (Washington: NASA, 1982), 230.

54. Ibid., 231.

55. Ibid., 231, 321; Webb, memo for Dr. Seamans, January 10, 1963, Webb, letter to Robert McNamara, January 16, 1963, McNamara, letter to Webb, September 16, 1963, and Webb, letter to McNamara, September 23, 1963, NASA History Office. Webb's characterization of McNamara's negotiation style is from my interview with Webb, January 8, 1991, Washington.

56. If Webb was uncomfortable with McNamara, McNamara was uncomfortable with Webb. The defense secretary liked meetings short and to the point. Webb talked too much for him and was too "political." Robert McNamara, interview by author, September 26, 1991, Washington. In the early period after the Apollo decision, Webb and McNamara met regularly for lunches, accompanied by aides, to facilitate coordination. At one of these lunches, McNamara lectured Webb, so offending the NASA administrator that he and Seamans walked out, and the regular lunches were discontinued. Although the two senior officials dealt with one another as little as possible thereafter, they had to cooperate to some extent for common interests. Webb used Seamans as a surrogate, and McNamara used similarly appropriate substitutes. Seamans interview, December 20, 1990. There are only a few references on space in Deborah Shapley's biography of McNamara, *Promise and Power: The Life and Times of Robert McNamara* (Boston: Little, Brown, 1993), indicating a limited interest on McNamara's part in this field compared to his other responsibilities.

57. Rosholt, *An Administrative History of NASA*, 288, 289.

58. For a case history of the Electronics Research Center decision, see Thomas Murphy, ed., *Science, Geopolitics, and Federal Spending* (Lexington, Mass.: Heath, Lexington, 1971), 225-64; Webb interview, October 15, 1985. A particular critic of the ERC decision was Joseph Karth, Democrat from Minnesota, an important member of the House Space Committee. Webb, memo for Dr. Seamans, March 20, 1962, NASA History Office. But others on the space committee also rebelled against the decision, forcing Webb to go through a new site-selection process. Webb, memo for Dr. Dryden, August 13, 1963, NASA History Office.

59. Daniel S. Greenberg, "NASA: New Fellowship Program Will Make Space Agency Biggest in Graduate Aid," *Science*, January 4, 1963, 23-24; Lambright, *Launching NASA's Sustaining University Program*, X-17, X-21.

60. One of Webb's sources was Earl "Red" H. Blaik, an executive with Avco Corporation and former West Point football coach, who warned Webb that Anderson could be "a first class obstructionist." Blaik, letter to Webb, May 17, 1963, James Webb personal files, Washington.

61. Webb interview, October 15, 1985. Reprogramming was discussed during hearings relating to the NASA authorization for fiscal year 1964. Senate Committee on Aeronautical and Space Sciences, *NASA Authorization for FY 1964* (Washington: USGPO, 1963).

62. Webb interview, October 15, 1985. Anderson frequently made Webb aware that he was watching. In October 1964, he commented to Webb somewhat casually, "I see you've issued some new patent regulations." Webb said yes, and these had been discussed with the committee and they were in accord with the policy of the White House. Anderson responded that he wondered if they were in accord with the policy laid down in the law. Webb kept stretching his authority, and Anderson kept trying to pull him in. Webb, memo for Mr. Callaghan, October 12, 1964, NASA History Office. What Webb had to help keep Anderson friendly was power to promote and support projects dear to Anderson's heart, including the NERVA nuclear rocket, a joint development effort of NASA and AEC, drawing on work by facilities in New Mexico. This long-term, long-range project was quite vulnerable to shifts in political fortune and huge in scale, well over a billion dollars for research and development. So Anderson needed Webb, much as Webb needed Anderson, and Webb did in fact try to take care of NERVA. It was folded into what became a package of post-Apollo activities, but its fate ultimately turned on the fate of NASA after Apollo, and it was canceled in 1972. Rosholt, *An Administrative History of NASA*, 254–55. W. Henry Lambright, *Governing Science and Technology* (New York: Oxford University Press, 1976), 124–27.

63. Webb interview, October 15, 1985; Margaret Chase Smith, interview by author, September 28, 1991, Hobart College, Geneva, N.Y.; Webb, memo for Paul Dembling, August 15, 1961; Webb, letter to Margaret Chase Smith, August 18, 1961; Webb, memo to Hugh Dryden, August 21, 1961, and Webb, letter to Margaret Chase Smith, April 23, 1962, Webb Papers, Truman Library; Webb, memo for the president, subject NASA activities in Maine, October 17, 1963, NASA History Office. This last memo details Webb's efforts to win Smith's support. Webb found she was especially interested in his Frontiers of Science Foundation experience, and she in fact took a delegation of Maine leaders to Oklahoma to see what had taken place there.

Chapter 7. The Struggle to Maintain Momentum

1. Lyndon B. Johnson, *The Vantage Point* (New York: Popular Library, 1971), 279.

2. Thomas Murphy, interview by author, December 21, 1990, Washington.

3. Robert B. Young, interview by Robert Sherrod, January 12, 1972, NASA History Office; "Huntsville Visit Scheduled by NASA Administrator Webb," *Marshall [Al-*

abama] Star, October 28, 1964; "Administrator Webb Visits MSFC; Cites Future Roles," Marshall Star, November 4, 1964.

4. Webb, letter to Rep. George P. Miller, May 4, 1964, NASA History Office; R. Cargill Hall, Lunar Impact: A History of Project Ranger (Washington: NASA, 1977), 254.

5. Robert Seamans, interview by author, December 20, 1990, Cambridge, Mass.

6. Ibid.; Assistant Administrator for Legislative Affairs, memo to James Webb, reply to Chairman Karth regarding difficulties with CIT, May 13, 1964, NASA History Office.

7. Webb, letter to Dr. Arnold Beckman, July 1, 1964, NASA History Office.

8. Clayton R. Koppes, JPL and the American Space Program: A History of the Jet Propulsion Laboratory (New Haven: Yale University Press, 1982), 157.

9. Webb, memo for Hugh Dryden, April 1, 1965, NASA History Office; Barton C. Hacker and James M. Grimwood, On the Shoulders of Titans: A History of Project Gemini (Washington: NASA, 1977), 254.

10. Hacker and Grimwood, On the Shoulders of Titans, 275.

11. Washington Roundup, "Moon by 1970," Aviation Week and Space Technology, March 21, 1966, 25.

12. Charles W. Mathews, interview by author, October 4, 1991, Washington.

13. Webb to Lyndon B. Johnson, November 30, 1964, LBJ files, NASA History Office, cited in Robert Dallek, "Johnson, Project Apollo, and the Politics of Space Program Planning," paper presented at NASA Conference on Presidential Leadership, Congress, and the U.S. Space Program, Washington, March 1993.

14. W. Henry Lambright, Presidential Management of Science and Technology: The Johnson Presidency (Austin: University of Texas Press, 1985), 81-84.

15. Donald Hornig, interview by author, November 16, 1990, Cambridge, Mass.

16. Walter A. McDougall, . . . the Heavens and the Earth: A History of the Space Age (New York: Basic), 307.

17. Webb, letter to Julius Stratton, January 10, 1964, cited in Laurin Henry, The NASA Memorandum of Understanding (Syracuse, N.Y.: InterUniversity Case Program, 1969), 37. In a letter criticizing a proposal for not thinking big enough, Webb wrote that "in our democracy people faced with the complex choices in voting and other forms of decision making need a 'trusted source of information.'" He felt the university could play this role if it could marry "science, technology and all the other disciplines," and he wanted evidence of an organized, institutional approach. Webb, letter to Robert V. Bartz, May 11, 1964, NASA History Office. In connection with encouraging such an approach with MIT and the New England region, including NASA's own Electronics Research Center, Webb wrote the mayor of Cambridge that he looked forward to working with MIT and the city in a joint undertaking. Webb, letter to Mayor Edward A. Crane, August 17, 1964, NASA History Office.

18. Julius Stratton, letter to James Webb, with attachments, December 16, 1964,

and Webb, memo to George Simpson, December 23, 1964, both cited in Henry, *The NASA Memorandum of Understanding*, 42.

19. Henry, *The NASA Memorandum of Understanding*, 64.

20. Charles Schultze, interview by author, February 22, 1991, Washington.

21. Henry, *The NASA Memorandum of Understanding*, 92–93. In its lifetime, SUP obligated more than $200 million for research, training, and facilities, to complement and facilitate NASA's much larger project research effort. More than 5,400 graduate students at more than 150 universities received at least one year of funding in space-related disciplines (which extended to social sciences). Of that total, more than 4,000 graduate students were completely funded at the completion of their doctorates. About 1,400 faculty members participated in research and design projects at NASA centers during the summers; thirty-seven research laboratories were built on university campuses; and more than 3,000 space-related endeavors were carried out under the research portion of SUP. See W. Henry Lambright and Laurin Henry, "Using Universities: The NASA Experience," *Public Policy* 20 (Winter 1972): 74; and Thomas Dietz, Laura Lund, and John M. Logsdon, *Evaluation of the National Aeronautics and Space Administration Predoctoral Traineeship Program*, Final Report to NASA, September 30, 1990, II-14.

22. National Aeronautics and Space Administration, *Preliminary History of NASA, 1963–1969* (Washington: NASA, 1969), II-16.

23. "Post-Apollo Lag Angers Congress," *Aviation Week and Space Technology*, March 7, 1966, 314.

24. Evert Clark, "NASA Chief Urges Space Planning Now for Post-Moon Era," *New York Times*, May 30, 1966.

25. Stuart H. Loory, "Webb Sees Soviet Pacing Moon Race," *New York Times*, October 11, 1966.

26. Donald Janson, "Webb Backs Cost of Space Program," *New York Times*, December 6, 1966.

27. Thomas Murphy, interview by author, February 22, 1991, Washington.

28. The post-Apollo budget debate between Webb and Schultze is covered well in Robert A. Divine, "Lyndon B. Johnson and the Politics of Space," in *The Johnson Years*, vol. 2, *Vietnam, the Environment and Science*, ed. Divine (Lawrence: University of Kansas Press, 1987), 217–53; see also Lambright, *Presidential Management of Science and Technology*, 141–51. Relevant documents at the LBJ Library include: Webb, memo to Johnson, August 26, 1966, White House Central File (hereafter WHCF), EX OS, Box 2; Charles Schultze, memos to Johnson, September 1, 20, 1966, WHCF, EX OS, Box 2; Joseph Califano, memo to Johnson, December 15, 1966, WHCF, EX FI 4, Box 23; Schultze, memo to Johnson, December 16, 1966, and Webb, memo to Johnson, December 14, 1966, WHCF, EX FI 4/FG 260, Box 30; Webb, memo to Johnson, December 17, 1966, WHCF, EX FI 4/FG 260, Box 30.

29. Webb, memo to Johnson, August 26, 1966, WHCF, EX OS, Box 2, LBJ Library.

30. Webb and Seamans were supported by a new associate administrator, Willis H. Shapley, who would head the Executive Secretariat. Shapley, who had joined NASA not long before from a senior career (and NASA oversight) position at BOB, was in no sense intended to fill the role left by Dryden, although he was one with whom Webb felt at ease in discussing various important issues.

31. The concept of power as "power to persuade" owes much to Webb's former BOB assistant, Richard Neustadt, *Presidential Power* (New York: Wiley, 1960).

Chapter 8. The Apollo Fire

1. Robert Sherrod, chap. 7, "The Spacecraft 012" (draft), NASA History Office, 7.

2. "Space Tragedy," *New York Times*, January 29, 1967; John Noble Wilford, *We Reach the Moon* (New York, Bantam, 1969), 95-97.

3. Lyndon B. Johnson, *The Vantage Point* (New York: Popular Library, 1971), 270.

4. Wayne Biddle, "Two Faces of Catastrophe," *Air and Space*, August/September 1990, 47.

5. Julian Scheer, interview by author, June 13, 1990, Washington.

6. Johnson, *The Vantage Point*, 284.

7. James Webb, interview by James Burke, May 23, 1979, NASA History Office.

8. Biddle, "Two Faces of Catastrophe," 47.

9. James E. Webb, oral history interview by T. H. Baker, April 29, 1969, LBJ Library.

10. Biddle, "Two Faces of Catastrophe," 47.

11. Ibid.

12. James M. Beggs, "James E. Webb: A Force for Excellence," the Inaugural Lecture of the Fund for Excellence in Public Administration (Washington: NAPA, 1983), 12.

13. "Space Program Supported," *New York Times*, January 31, 1967.

14. Wilford, *We Reach the Moon*, 99-101.

15. Robert Seamans, memo to James Webb, February 3, 1967, NASA History Office.

16. "NASA Weighs Impact of Apollo Accident," *Aviation Week and Space Technology*, February 6, 1967, 29.

17. Evert Clark, "Cause of Fire Still Unknown," *New York Times*, February 8, 1967.

18. John Noble Wilford, "NASA Engineers Criticize Test Schedule Pace," *New York Times*, February 8, 1967.

19. James E. Webb, press statement, February 25, 1967, NASA History Office.

20. "Apollo Inquest," *New York Times*, February 28, 1967.

21. S. C. Phillips, memo to G. E. Mueller, December 18, 1965, provided author by J. Leland Atwood.

22. George Mueller, letter to J. L. Atwood, December 19, 1965, provided author by J. Leland Atwood.

23. For the North American perspective, see Mike Gray, *Angle of Attack: Harrison Storms and the Race to the Moon* (New York: Norton, 1992).

24. Wilford, *We Reach the Moon*, 105.

25. Biddle, "Two Faces of Catastrophe," 48. Mondale was out in front on the Phillips report issue. But Jules Bergman had shared his information with the Senate committee's top staffer, James Gehrig, who would have told Anderson. Also, apparently, Margaret Chase Smith knew about the report from other sources. Following an off-the-record call from Bergman, Gehrig wrote a memo for the files on the conversation. Noting he would have to get the necessary "background information," he worried that "even a suggestion that the management of the Apollo program is bad could do great harm to the program." James T. Gehrig, memo to files, February 14, 1967, Margaret Chase Smith Library.

26. Biddle, "Two Faces of Catastrophe," 48.

27. Robert Seamans, interview by Robert Sherrod, June 24, 1969, Sherrod files, NASA History Office; Robert Seamans, interview by author, February 17, 1992, and by author and Martin Collins, December 16, 1988, both in Cambridge, Mass.; Paul Dembling interviews, June 20, 1991, June 12, 1990, Washington.

28. Joseph Trento, *Prescription for Disaster* (New York: Crown, 1987), 69.

29. GK/Office of General Counsel, draft memo to General S. C. Phillips, March 2, 1967, Webb Papers, Truman Library.

30. Webb, second draft memo for Col. Vogel, March 7, 1967, Webb Papers, Truman Library.

31. A.D.U. [Alan D. Ullberg], handwritten note on Phillips report, March 14, 1968, Webb Papers, Truman Library; Trento, *Prescription for Disaster*, 69.

32. Webb, handwritten note on bottom of L. W. Vogel's note to Webb, March 22, 1967, Webb Papers, Truman Library.

33. Jamie McWilliams, interview by author, December 2, 1989, Oklahoma City.

34. Hilliard Paige, interview by author, May 29, 1991, Washington.

35. William Bland, memo to Joseph Shea, November 23, 1966, NASA History Office.

36. Joseph Shea, letter to Hilliard Paige, December 5, 1966, NASA History Office; see also Charles Murray and Catherine Bly Cox, *Apollo: The Race to the Moon* (New York: Simon and Schuster, 1989), 186.

37. Paige interview, May 29, 1991.

38. Murray and Cox, *Apollo*, 216.

39. Ibid., 217.

40. Webb, handwritten note to Robert Seamans, April 1, 1967, Webb Papers, Truman Library.

41. Murray and Cox, *Apollo*, 217; Joseph Shea, letter to James Webb, March 10, 1967, Webb Papers, Truman Library.

42. Murray and Cox, *Apollo*, 219.

43. Information from Nina Scrivener, secretary to acting administrator, George

M. Low, and former secretary to James Webb, November 30, 1970, Robert Sherrod Files, NASA History Office.

44. S. Neil Hosenball, interview by author, July 17, 1990, Washington.

45. Charles W. Mathews, interview by author, October 4, 1991, Washington.

46. Webb, letter to J. L. Atwood, April 8, 1967, NASA History Office.

47. J. L. Atwood, letter to James Webb, April 8, 1967, NASA History Office.

48. Scheer interview, June 13, 1990.

49. John Noble Wilford, "Apollo Fire Review Board Finds 'Many Deficiencies'; Calls for Safety Moves," *New York Times*, April 10, 1967; see *Report of Apollo 204 Review Board* (Washington: NASA, 1967).

50. Wilford, "Apollo Fire Review Board."

Chapter 9. From Crisis to Recovery

1. Even in this time of anxiety, Webb's instincts as a teacher and institution builder came through. He had Ray Kline, who was one of Wernher von Braun's top young aides and a civil servant Webb wished to groom for a higher assignment, join headquarters. The night before the hearings he called Kline and told him to be sure to come and learn how the government operates. As this was a crisis period for NASA, and crises could recur, Webb apparently felt crisis management should be part of Kline's education. Having just arrived in Washington, Kline was astounded when he got the call. Ray Kline, interview by author, February 7, 1992, Washington.

2. John Noble Wilford, "Webb Holds Firm on Apollo Goals at House Inquiry," *New York Times*, April 10, 1967.

3. Ibid.

4. "Incompetence and Negligence," *New York Times*, April 11, 1967.

5. Webb, letter to Jack Brinkley, April 12, 1967, NASA History Office.

6. Webb, memo to Olin Teague, April 15, 1967, Webb Papers, Truman Library.

7. Evert Clark, "Effects of Apollo Fire," and "The Effect on the Space Race," *New York Times*, April 15 and 16, 1967.

8. Clark, "Effects of Apollo Fire."

9. John Noble Wilford, "Webb Is Silent on Apollo Issue," *New York Times*, April 18, 1967.

10. Frank Borman with Robert J. Serling, *Countdown: An Autobiography* (New York: Morrow, 1988), 179-80.

11. William J. Normyle, "NASA Implements Board Findings," and "NASA Revises Manned Flight Plan," *Aviation Week and Space Technology*, April 17, 1967, 30, and April 24, 1967, 29.

12. John Noble Wilford cites Hines in *We Reach the Moon* (New York: Bantam, 1969), 99; Mary McGrory, "A Niagara Falls of Words," *Washington Evening Star*, April 18, 1967.

13. Atwood's view of the dispute with Webb was that North American was being

unfairly blamed for the accident. His bitterness at the way he, Storms, and North American were treated lasted for years. The North American side is presented in Mike Gray, *Angle of Attack: Harrison Storms and the Race to the Moon* (New York: Norton, 1992). See also Atwood's own account, "Apollo Fire," November 15, 1990, which is in the NASA History Office, as are his comments on a draft of my depiction of the Apollo fire dispute from the Webb perspective.

14. Charles Murray and Catherine Bly Cox, *Apollo: The Race to the Moon* (New York: Simon and Schuster, 1989), 231.

15. John Biggs, memo for the record, "Contract Relationships with North American Aviation Inc.," April 15, 1967, Robert Sherrod Files, NASA History Office.

16. Webb, letter to J. L. Atwood, April 15, 1967, Webb Papers, Truman Library.

17. J. L. Atwood, letter to James Webb, April 18, 1967, Webb Papers, Truman Library; John Biggs, memo for James Webb, April 20, 1967, Robert Sherrod Files, NASA History Office.

18. Webb, letter to Ramsey Clark, April 25, 1967, Webb Papers, Truman Library.

19. Atwood, "Apollo Fire" documents.

20. Murray and Cox, *Apollo*, 231.

21. Joseph Trento, *Prescription for Disaster* (New York: Crown, 1987), 67–68.

22. Robert Seamans, interview by author and Martin Collins, December 16, 1988, Cambridge, Mass; Webb, draft memo to the Boeing Company, April 28, 1967, Webb Papers, Truman Library.

23. Webb, letter to J. L. Atwood, April 29, 1967, Webb Papers, Truman Library.

24. Murray and Cox, *Apollo*, 231–32.

25. J. L. Atwood, letter to James Webb, April 30, 1967, Webb papers, Truman Library.

26. J. L. Atwood, interview by Robert Sherrod, June 24, 1969, Sherrod Files, NASA History Office.

27. Webb, letter to J. L. Atwood, May 3, 1967, Webb Papers, Truman Library.

28. Robert J. Serling, *Legend and Legacy: The Story of Boeing and Its People* (New York: St. Martin's, 1992), 232–33.

29. Robert Freitag, interview by Robert Sherrod, March 17, 1971, Sherrod Files, NASA History Office.

30. "Report On Apollo Released by Ryan," *New York Times*, April 30, 1967.

31. Donald C. Winston, "NASA to Detail Apollo Fire Impacts," *Aviation Week and Space Technology*, May 8, 1967, 17.

32. Webb, letter to Margaret Chase Smith, May 8, 1967, Margaret Chase Smith Library.

33. Webb, letter to Clinton Anderson, May 8, 1967, Sherrod Files, NASA History Office.

34. William J. Normyle, "NASA Details Sweeping Apollo Revisions," *Aviation Week and Space Technology*, May 15, 1967, 24–26.

35. Thomas O'Toole, "NASA Accused of Covering Up Troubles," *Washington Post*, May 11, 1967.

36. "NASA Candor Needed," *New York Times*, May 11, 1967.

37. "Honeymoon Over," *Aviation Week and Space Technology*, May 15, 1967, 21.

38. Clark Mollenhoff, "Webb: Politics Didn't Play Part," *Minneapolis Tribune*, May 11, 1967.

39. "Pitchman for NASA's Trip to the Moon," *Business Week*, May 27, 1967, 71-77.

40. Webb interviews by author and Martin Collins, October 3, 1986, and by Martin Collins, October 15, 1985, both at National Air and Space Museum, Washington. There were those who wondered why Senator Smith was so supportive of Webb at this time. She later told a critic that it was a matter of "fairness." "The reported incident [of conflicting testimony concerning the North American award] was the only time that I found him giving conflicting statements to questions that I asked him. On all other instances, I found him not only to be honest and forthright but very cooperative with the Senate Space Committee.

"With this experience, I accepted his explanation that he had misunderstood my first question in good faith in that he thought I said 'Source Selection Board' (the higher final decision board) when I said 'Source Evaluation Board' (the subordinate recommending board)." Margaret Chase Smith, letter to Joanne Stevens, October 13, 1968, Margaret Chase Smith Library.

41. Clinton Anderson, letter to James Webb, May 15, 1966, Webb Papers, Truman Library.

42. Elmer Staats, letter to Margaret Chase Smith, June 2, 1967, NASA History Office.

43. Clinton Anderson, letter to James Webb, June 5, 1967, NASA History Office.

44. John Biggs, memo to James Webb, June 8, 1967, NASA History Office.

45. James Webb, interview by author, June 25, 1991, Washington.

46. Jack Cramer, memo for the record, briefing to the Manned Space Flight Subcommittee by George Mueller, June 13, 1967, NASA History Office.

47. Webb, letter to Olin Teague, June 20, 1967, NASA History Office.

48. Robert Seamans, memo to Floyd Thompson, June 21, 1967, NASA History Office.

49. Washington Roundup, "Bitter Pills," *Aviation Week and Space Technology*, July 24, 1967, 15.

50. Evert Clark, "Six Months after Tragedy, the Apollo Program Finds Itself Gaining, but 'Still in a Time of Testing,'" *New York Times*, July 2, 1967.

51. Buzz Aldrin and Malcolm McConnell, *Men from Earth* (New York: Bantam, 1989), 173-74.

52. Robert Hotz, "New Era For NASA," *Aviation Week and Space Technology*, August 7, 1967, 17.

53. John Mecklin, "Jim Webb's Earthy Management of Space," *Fortune*, August 1967, 87.

54. National Aeronautics and Space Administration, *Preliminary History of NASA, 1963-1969* (Washington: NASA, 1969), II-19.

55. Robert A. Divine, "Lyndon B. Johnson and the Politics of Space," in *The Johnson Years*, vol. 2, *Vietnam, the Environment, and Science*, ed. Divine (Lawrence: University of Kansas Press, 1987), 245.

56. "White House Stand Blocks NASA Budget Restoration," *Aviation Week and Space Technology*, August 28, 1967, 32.

57. President Johnson, memo to James Webb, September 29, 1967, WHCF, C.F., F.G., LBJ Library.

58. Charles Schultze, memos to Johnson, August 11, 14, 1967, WHCF, EX FI 4/FG 260, Box 30, and Webb, memo to Johnson, August 10, 1967, WHCF, EX FI 4/FG 200, Box 29, LBJ Library; Divine, "Lyndon B. Johnson," 243-44.

59. "NASA Would Take Cuts," *Washington Post*, September 29, 1967.

60. Seamans interview, December 16, 1988.

61. Robert Seamans, interview by author, August 2, 1991, Cambridge, Mass.

62. Seamans interview, December 16, 1988.

63. William Hines, "Webb Rebuts Ryan's Charge of Lack of Candor by NASA," *Washington Evening Star*, October 13, 1967.

64. Aldrin and McConnell, *Men from Earth*, 174.

65. Inside NASA, this flight was called *A.S.-501*. "A.S." stood for Apollo/Saturn, "5" for the launch vehicle, and "01" for the number of the flight. The flight that never took place because of the fire was *A.S.-204* (fourth Apollo flight of a Saturn II). *Apollo 4* was actually the first official flight of the Apollo series. See Murray and Cox, *Apollo*, 238.

66. Ibid., 246. John Noble Wilford, *We Reach the Moon*, (New York: Bantam, 1969), 135.

67. "Saturn 5 Success Quickens Apollo Pace," *Aviation Week and Space Technology*, November 13, 1967, 32; "Saturn Success Spurs U.S. Hopes," *New York Times*, November 11, 1967; Murray and Cox, *Apollo*, 250.

68. Senate Committee on Aeronautical and Space Sciences, *Apollo 204 Accident*, 90th Cong., 2d Sess., 1968, S. Rept. 956 (Washington: USGPO, 1968).

Chapter 10. *Last Hurrah at NASA*

1. Jay Holmes, Office of the Administrator, Selected Activities, January–March 1968 Report, April 22, 1968, NASA History Office.

2. James Webb, interview by author, January 30, 1992, Washington; James Webb, interview by David DeVorkin, Michael Dennis, and Joseph Tatarewicz, July 22, 1983; National Air and Space Museum, Washington (hereafter NASM).

3. John M. Logsdon, unpublished manuscript provided me by Logsdon on Space Shuttle decision, I-38.

4. Webb, memo for Mr. Magliato, January 2, 1968, NASA History Office.

5. Arnold Levine, *Managing NASA in the Apollo Era* (Washington: NASA, 1992), 7, 54-55, 160-61, 254, 327.

6. Webb, memo for distribution, January 27, 1968, NASA History Office. This memo went to ten headquarters officials, including Newell, Finger, and Mueller.

7. Charles W. Mathews, interview by author, October 4, 1991, Washington.

8. William Lilly, interview by author, July 18, 1990, Washington. Lilly was placed under Finger and purportedly headed an Office of Administration. He was in reality the agency's chief budget officer and reported directly to Webb. See Levine, *Managing NASA in the Apollo Era*, 54, 193.

9. Webb, memo for Mr. Shapley, "Problem of adding 'supervision' to the activities of top management to see that the plans made are carried out, both in the area of substance and in the area of administration," September 19, 1967, Webb Papers, NASA History Office.

10. Thomas Paine, interview by author, April 6, 1990, Los Angeles.

11. Mathews interview, October 4, 1991. Webb was drawing on a number of individuals for advice on NASA management changes at this time. He was anxious to help Paine with his entry to NASA and wrote of "introducing Dr. Paine to the right people in Washington" and needing to "establish a pattern within NASA whereby I can assign him specific duties as he becomes prepared for them and still maintain the momentum now established in our administrative procedures." Webb, letter to Raymond Bisplinghoff, February 7, 1968, NASA History Office.

12. Logsdon, unpublished manuscript, II-4. The Apollo Applications Program was the principal effort to continue the manned capability created by Apollo. As the NASA budget was constrained, other components of post-Apollo, as a package of efforts, were cut back, including the NERVA nuclear rocket R&D program, along with critical unmanned space science programs important to NASA's future. AAP, however, was the symbol of post-Apollo and its centerpiece. See W. Henry Lambright, *Presidential Management of Science and Technology: The Johnson Presidency* (Austin: University of Texas Press, 1985), 141-51.

13. George Elsey, interview by author, October 17, 1991, Washington. Webb, letter to John Foster, director of Defense Research and Engineering, May 23, 1968, Webb Papers, Truman Library; Webb, memo for Floyd Thompson, July 23, 1968, NASA History Office.

14. Logsdon, unpublished manuscript, I-35.

15. Ibid., II-4.

16. Webb, letter to Floyd Thompson, January 6, 1968, NASA History Office.

17. Logsdon, unpublished manuscript, II-5, II-8.

18. Logsdon, unpublished manuscript, II-6; W. David Compton and Charles D. Benson, *Living and Working in Space: A History of Skylab* (Washington: NASA, 1983), 102.

19. Compton and Benson, *Living and Working in Space*, 100, 102-4.

20. Ibid., 109.

21. Homer Newell, *Beyond the Atmosphere* (Washington: NASA, 1980), 397; Lambright, *Presidential Management of Science and Technology*, 142–43. On Webb and post-Apollo decision-making, see also Emmette Redford and Orion White, *What Manned Space Program after Reaching the Moon? Government Attempts to Decide: 1962–1968* (Syracuse, N.Y.: InterUniversity Case Program, 1971), and Arthur Levine, *Future of the U.S. Space Program* (New York: Praeger, 1975).

22. Charles Murray and Catherine Bly Cox, *Apollo: The Race to the Moon* (New York: Simon and Schuster, 1989), 308–9.

23. Frank Borman with Robert J. Serling, *Countdown: An Autobiography* (New York: Morrow, 1988), 185–86; Webb, letter to William Allen, president of Boeing, April 18, 1968, NASA History Office.

24. Murray and Cox, *Apollo*, 309, 313.

25. Lyndon B. Johnson, *The Vantage Point* (New York: Popular Library, 1971), 538.

26. Murray and Cox, *Apollo*, 313, 314.

27. Washington Roundup, "Post-Award Audits," and "Program Heads Urge Apollo Man-Rating," *Aviation Week and Space Technology*, April 29, 1968, 25 and 32–33.

28. Murray and Cox, *Apollo*, 316–19.

29. Compton and Benson, *Living and Working in Space*, 103.

30. Courtney G. Brooks, James M. Grimwood, and Loyd S. Swenson, Jr., *Chariots for Apollo: A History of Manned Lunar Spacecraft* (Washington: NASA, 1979), 257.

31. Buzz Aldrin and Malcolm McConnell, *Men from Earth* (New York: Bantam, 1989), 191–92.

32. Ibid., 192.

33. Ibid., 192–93.

34. Murray and Cox, *Apollo*, 322.

35. For Webb's perspective on his leaving, see James Webb, interview by author, December 12, 1990, Washington, and Transcript of Tape Recording, Mr. James E. Webb's Retirement Announcement to NASA General Management on the 16th of September 1968, in the Program Review Center at NASA Headquarters, Webb Papers, Truman Library. What Webb told me about the meeting with Johnson is consistent with what he told NASA associates immediately after the event. His lengthy remarks, contained in this transcript, include his statement of what Johnson said.

36. Carroll Kilpatrick and Thomas O'Toole, "Webb Retires Oct. 7 as U.S. Space Chief," *Washington Post*, September 17, 1968; Neil Sheehan, "Webb Quits as Head of Space Agency; Notes Soviet Lead," *New York Times*, September 17, 1968.

37. Paine interview, April 6, 1990.

38. Transcript of Tape Recording, Webb Retirement Announcement.

39. Washington Roundup, "Sacrifice Play," *Aviation Week and Space Technology*, September 23, 1968, 15.

40. Donald Hornig, memo to President Johnson, September 26, 1968, and Johnson, memo to Hornig, September 26, 1968, Hornig Collection, LBJ Library; see

Robert Dallek, "Johnson, Project Apollo, and the Politics of Space Program Planning," paper presented at NASA Conference on Presidential Leadership, Congress, and the U.S. Space Program, Washington, March 1993; also, Lambright, *Presidential Management of Science and Technology*, 149-50.

41. Dallek, "Johnson, Project Apollo."

42. James M. Beggs, "James E. Webb: A Force for Excellence," Inaugural Lecture of the Fund for Excellence in Public Administration (Washington: NAPA, 1984), 16.

43. Paine interview, April 6, 1990.

44. "National Aeronautics and Space Administration Awards," *Weekly Compilation of Presidential Documents* (week ending November 8, 1968) (Washington: USGPO, 1968), 1569. It is noteworthy that Webb's frequent critic, Senator Anderson, showed his respect by inserting praise for Webb in the *Congressional Record* at this time and also remarked: "He probably never will receive all the credit that is due him." *Congressional Record*, Senate, 90th Cong., 2d Sess., 1968, vol 114, pt. 24: 30875.

45. John Noble Wilford, *We Reach the Moon* (New York: Bantam, 1969), 205.

Chapter 11. The Moon and After

1. Thomas Paine, interview by author, April 6, 1990, Los Angeles.

2. Ibid.

3. Webb, letter to Eugene Emme, January 16, 1969, NASA History Office; James Webb, interview by author, December 12, 1990, Washington.

4. Robert C. Seamans, "Voyage to the Moon: A View from NASA Headquarters." See chap. 5, n. 38, in this work.

5. John Noble Wilford, *We Reach the Moon* (New York: Bantam, 1969), 257-60.

6. Ibid., 269.

7. Craig Covault, "Soviet Union Reveals Moon Rocket Design That Failed to Beat U.S. to Lunar Landing," *Aviation Week and Space Technology*, February 18, 1991, 58-59.

8. Joseph Trento, *Prescription for Disaster* (New York: Crown, 1987), 88.

9. Charles Murray and Catherine Bly Cox, *Apollo: The Race to the Moon* (New York: Simon and Schuster, 1989), 449. The Nixon administration also terminated DOD's Manned Orbital Laboratory.

10. James E. Webb, *Space Age Management: The Large-Scale Approach* (New York: McGraw-Hill, 1969), 15.

11. Ibid., 17, 27.

12. Al Neuharth, *Confessions of an S.O.B.* (New York: Penguin, 1992), 76, 91-93.

13. Quoted in Elmer B. Staats, "James E. Webb, Space Age Manager," in *Giants in Management*, ed. Robert L. Haught (Washington: NAPA, 1985), 29.

14. Alan Ullberg, interview by author, October 26, 1990, Washington.

15. Staats, "James E. Webb," 30.

16. Webb, letter to Bailey Webb, August 15, 1975, James Webb Personal Files, Washington.

17. Christian Williams, "James Webb and NASA's Reach for the Moon," *Washington Post*, September 24, 1981.

18. President George Bush, letter to Mrs. Webb, April 7, 1992, James Webb Personal Files, Washington.

Chapter 12. Legacy

1. John Noble Wilford, *We Reach the Moon* (New York: Bantam, 1969), 68.

2. *Report of the Advisory Committee on the Future of the U.S. Space Program* (Washington: USGPO, 1990), 13. Thanks to his "administrative discount on technical optimism," Webb was realistic about Apollo cost and schedule projections. He could also get political acceptance of realistic cost estimates in 1961. For a discussion of "optimism" and "realism" in estimating big technology programs, and their importance in selling programs and conveying the image as well as the reality of good management, see W. Henry Lambright, *Governing Science and Technology* (New York: Oxford University Press, 1976), 53-56; see also Harvey Sapolsky, *The Polaris System Developmment: Bureaucratic and Programmatic Success in Government* (Cambridge: Harvard University Press, 1972).

3. Charles Murray and Catherine Bly Cox, *Apollo: The Race to the Moon* (New York: Simon and Schuster, 1989), 459.

4. Craig Covault, "Soviet Union Reveals Moon Rocket Design That Failed to Beat U.S. to Lunar Landing," *Aviation Week and Space Technology,* February 18, 1991, 58-59; see also John M. Logsdon and Alain Dupas, "Was the Race to the Moon Real?" *Scientific American,* vol. 270, no. 6, June 1994, 36-43.

5. Quoted in Bruce Lambert, "James Webb, Who Led Moon Program, Dies at 85," *New York Times,* March 29, 1992.

6. Jameson W. Doig and Erwin C. Hargrove, eds., *Leadership and Innovation: Entrepreneurs in Government* (Baltimore: Johns Hopkins University Press, 1990); see also Larry Terry, "Why We Should Abandon the Misconceived Quest to Reconcile Public Entrepreneurship with Democracy," and Carl J. Bellone and George Frederick Goerl, "In Defense of Civic-Regarding Entrepreneurship or Helping Wolves to Promote Good Citizenship," *Public Administration Review* 53 (July/Aug. 1993): 393-95 and 396-98.

AN ESSAY ON SOURCES

Administrative Leadership

A study of James Webb is a case study in administrative leadership. The traditional emphasis in the large and growing literature on leadership and bureaucratic entrepreneurship has been on the constraints facing administrative leaders, as in Herbert Kaufman, *The Administrative Behavior of Federal Bureau Chiefs* (Washington: Brookings Institution, 1981), and James Q. Wilson, *Bureaucracy: What Government Agencies Do and Why They Do It* (New York: Basic, 1989). That is one reason why relatively few top executives in government stand out. More recently, there have been attempts to identify leaders who achieved in spite of the constraints or who found ways around the constraints, as in Jameson W. Doig and Erwin C. Hargrove, eds., *Leadership and Innovation: Entrepreneurs in Government* (Baltimore: Johns Hopkins University Press, 1990), and Eugene Lewis, *Public Entrepreneurship: Toward a Theory of Bureaucratic Political Power* (Bloomington: Indiana University Press, 1980). Still, the longstanding ambivalence about administrative leaders in government remains.

Critics cite examples of bureaucratic leaders who let power become a drug they pursued for its own sake, for instance, Robert A. Caro, *The Power Broker: Robert Moses and the Fall of New York* (New York: Random House, 1974). Finding the right balance represents an enduring theme in the political science/public administration community. The problem is democracy's healthy uneasiness with bureaucratic power. Success in government requires power, but that power must be bounded. Should the constraints on bureaucratic leaders come from external checks by other institutions or from internal checks within the administrator's own value system? How much independent authority is enough? For what ends? This ancient controversy, whose origins lie in Plato and Machiavelli, is of preeminent importance today and likely to be discussed and debated as long as democracy and bureaucracy must coexist (Norton Long, "Power and Administration"; Carl J. Friedrich, "Public Policy and the Nature of Administrative Responsibility"; Herman Finer, "Administrative Responsibility in Democratic Government," all in Francis E. Rourke, ed., *Bureaucratic Power in National Politics*, 3d ed. [Boston: Little, Brown, 1978]; also Larry Terry, "Why We Should Abandon the Misconceived Quest to Reconcile Public Entrepreneurship with Democracy," and Carl J. Bellone and George Frederick Goerl, "In Defense of Civic-Regarding Entrepreneurship or Helping Wolves to Promote Good Citizenship," *Public Administration Review* 53 [July/August 1993]: 393–95 and 396–98).

Various writers have discussed the possibilities and problems of government when "large-scale" programs with urgent deadlines are at issue. Brian Balogh noted the fusion of central state and professional expert in a "pro-administrative state" in *Chain Reaction* (New York: Cambridge University Press, 1991). Walter A. McDougall clearly finds the merger of government and technology under the leadership of "Big Operators" like Webb a concern in . . . *the Heavens and the Earth: A Political History of the Space Age* (New York: Basic, 1985). Webb himself, aware of the dilemmas, sought to find the balance in uses of modern administrative power in his own book, *Space Age Management: The Large-Scale Approach* (New York: McGraw-Hill, 1969). Leonard Sayles and Margaret Chandler analyzed Webb's NASA in *Managing Large Systems: Organizations for the Future* (New York: Harper and Row, 1971).

The Making of a Public Executive

To understand Webb's development as a public executive, one has to go back to his roots in Oxford, North Carolina. A secondary literature concerned with progressivism and its impact extends to education in North Carolina; see, for example, Arthur S. Link and Richard L. McCormick, *Progressivism* (Arlington Heights, Ill.: Harlan Davidson, 1983). This literature offers some insight into the reformist bent of Webb's father, a change-oriented educational administrator, and includes a biography of a Webb relative and source of inspiration to the Webb family in Laurence McMillin, *The School-Maker: Sawney Webb and the Bell Buckle Story* (Chapel Hill: University of North Carolina Press, 1971). Webb's letters that to a degree reveal his career at the University of North Carolina are among the personal papers in the Webb home in Washington. Concerning his initial Washington experience, with Congressman Pou, there are primary materials in the form of the Pou Papers, North Carolina Division of Archives and History. Webb's work with Gov. O. Max Gardner is illuminated by Joseph L. Morrison's *Gov. O. Max Gardner: A Power in North Carolina and New Deal Washington* (Chapel Hill: University of North Carolina Press, 1971). A considerable writing exists on the New Deal Washington of which Webb was a part and that helped shape his own attitude favoring active government, for example, Arthur Schlesinger, Jr., *The Coming of the New Deal* (Boston: Houghton Mifflin, 1959). Helpful on the airmail dispute, in which Webb played a supporting role, are Paul Tillett's *Army Flies the Mails* (University: University of Alabama Press,

1955); Roger Bilstein's *Flight in America: 1900-1983* (Baltimore: Johns Hopkins University Press, 1984); and John F. Shiner's "General Benjamin Foulois and the 1934 Air Mail Disaster," *Aerospace Historian*, December 1978, 221-30.

Webb's Sperry years are addressed by some primary sources at the Truman Library which relate mainly to Webb's "outside" role as an advocate for aviation. Other primary materials concerned with Sperry history are housed at the Hagley Museum and Library in Wilmington, Delaware, but include nothing, unfortunately, on executive decision making during Webb's time at Sperry. From interviews, we know that Webb was an avid reader of the management literature during this time and afterward, and that he became exceedingly interested in the human relations school of management theory. He was impressed with the management scholar Mary Parker Follett, who wrote extensively on issues of power and administration (Henry C. Metcalf and L. Urwick, eds., *Dynamic Administration: The Collected Papers of Mary Parker Follett* [New York: Harper and Row, 1942]).

Many other sources proved helpful in charting influences on Webb's emergence as a public executive, including material on Tom Morgan, Webb's boss as head of Sperry, located at the University of North Carolina, Chapel Hill, in its North Carolina collection; and work by Allan A. Needell on Lloyd Berkner, a scientist and close friend of Webb ("From Military Research to Big Science: Lloyd Berkner and Science Statesmanship in the Postwar Era," in *Big Science: The Growth of Large-Scale Research*, ed. Peter Galison and Bruce Hevly [Palo Alto, Calif.: Stanford University Press, 1992], 290-311). Contemporary magazine and newspaper articles were also helpful.

Absolutely critical to understanding Webb as a person were interviews with his wife, an older sister, two younger brothers, and a cousin, as well as with family friends. I also interviewed friends and associates from Webb's New Deal Washington and Sperry days.

During the Truman Administration

For Webb's years in the Truman administration, the primary sources are collected at the Harry S. Truman Library, in Independence, Missouri, where the Webb Papers are second in size only to those of Truman. The library also has extensive collections of papers of various White House aides and other members of the Truman administration and a number of useful oral histories.

The huge secondary literature on the Truman administration includes Truman's *Memoirs*, vol. 2, *Years of Trial and Hope* (Garden City, N.Y.: Doubleday, 1957), which provides background, as do the various biographies of Truman, including Robert J. Donovan's *Conflict and Crisis: The Presidency of Harry S. Truman, 1945-1948* (New York: Norton, 1977) and *Tumultuous Years: The Presidency of Harry S. Truman* (New York: Norton, 1982); and David McCullough's *Truman* (New York: Simon and Schuster, 1991).

For more detailed information on Webb's Bureau of the Budget (BOB) period,

Larry Berman's *Office of Management and Budget and the Presidency, 1921-1979* (Princeton: Princeton University Press, 1979) should be consulted. Herman Miles Somers's *Presidential Agency: OWMR* (Cambridge: Harvard, 1950) gives some flavor of the agency that was BOB's chief institutional rival when Webb became BOB director. Francis H. Heller paints a portrait of the way the Truman White House was organized and functioned in *The Truman White House: The Administration of the Presidency, 1945-1953* (Lawrence: University of Kansas Press, 1980). Some of the people who worked closely with Webb in BOB and the White House have written extensively of their experiences, among them Richard E. Neustadt, in "Presidency and Legislation: The Growth of Central Clearance," *American Political Science Review* 48 (Sept. 1954), and "Presidency and Legislation: Planning the President's Program," *American Political Science Review* 49 (Dec. 1955); Donald C. Stone, in "Administrative Management: Reflections on Origins and Accomplishments," *Public Administration Review* 50 (January/ February 1990): 3-20; Ken Hechler, in *Working with Truman* (New York: Putnam, 1982); and Clark Clifford, in *Counsel to the President* (New York: Random House, 1991).

Many books and articles deal with various issues and disputes with which Webb was involved as budget director. On the Marshall Plan are Joseph M. Jones's *Fifteen Weeks* (New York: Viking, 1955) and Theodore A. Wilson's *Marshall Plan, 1947-1951* (New York: Headline Series, Foreign Policy Association, 1977). On the postwar organization of defense, and subsequent battles to restrict the defense budget, see, for example, Paul Y. Hammond, *Organizing for Defense: The American Military Establishment in the Twentieth Century* (Princeton: Princeton University Press, 1961); Arnold A. Rogow, *James Forrestal: A Study of Personality, Politics and Policy* (New York: Macmillan, 1963); Warner R. Schilling, Paul Y. Hammond, and Glenn H. Snyder, *Strategy, Politics, and Defense Budgets* (New York: Columbia University Press, 1962); Steven I. Rearden, *History of the Office of the Secretary of Defense: The Formative Years, 1947-1950* (Washington: Historical Office, Office of the Secretary of Defense, 1984); and Walter Millis, ed., *The Forrestal Diaries* (New York: Viking, 1951).

For Webb's State Department period, general information on Dean Acheson and the State Department relationship can be found in David S. McLellan, *Dean Acheson: The State Department Years* (New York: Dodd, Mead, 1976); Dean Acheson, *Present at the Creation: My Years in the State Department* (New York: Norton, 1969); George F. Kennan, *Memoirs, 1925-1950* (New York: Pantheon, 1967); and David Callahan, *Dangerous Capabilities: Paul Nitze and the Cold War* (New York: Burlingame, 1990). For State Department–Defense Department relations, see Doris M. Condit, *The Test of War, 1950-53* (Washington: Office of Secretary of Defense, 1988). Webb's special interest in science and foreign policy is indicated by Needell's work on Berkner in this period, in "Truth is Our Weapon: Project Troy and Government/Academic Relations in the National Security State," *Diplomatic History* 17 (Summer 1993): 399-420.

In addition to these sources, contemporary magazine and newspaper accounts are exceedingly important for conveying the feeling of the time, as, for example, the Cold War passions. Interviews with many individuals associated with Webb in the Truman period—both at BOB and State—were essential, and the oral histories at the Truman Library were valuable. Webb's comments in our interviews were consistent with what he told earlier interviewers about the Truman period.

The Oklahoma Years

At the Truman Library, the primary materials on Webb's Oklahoma period relate mainly to his public service activities, such as the Frontiers of Science Foundation. Some materials relating to Webb are included among the Sen. Robert S. Kerr Papers at the University of Oklahoma, whose History of Science Collection also contains some materials on Webb and the Frontiers of Science Foundation.

Useful secondary materials include Anne Hodges Morgan's biography, *Robert S. Kerr: The Senate Years* (Norman: University of Oklahoma Press, 1977), and John Samuel Ezell's *Innovations in Energy: The Story of Kerr-McGee* (Norman: University of Oklahoma Press, 1979). Some special insights into Kerr from the vantage point of one who—like Kerr—mixed money and politics are reported in Bobby Baker's *Wheeling and Dealing* (New York: Norton, 1978).

In addition, contemporary accounts in newspapers and magazines proved helpful. Numerous interviews with Webb associates in Oklahoma were invaluable.

The NASA Years

The primary materials concerned with Webb's time at NASA are voluminous. The reason the Webb collection at the Truman Library is so huge is that Webb sent most of his NASA (and other) papers there, covering the period at least from 1928 to 1979. It is noteworthy that the Truman Library organizes its NASA materials in terms of Webb.

Primary Webb materials concerned with a particular administration and duplicated in the John F. Kennedy and Lyndon B. Johnson Libraries provide the context of individuals around Webb in the respective administrations and contain helpful oral histories from members of these administrations. The LBJ Library has an oral history by Webb that emphasizes the Webb-Johnson relation.

Extensive Webb materials are housed at the NASA History Office in Washington. Although much duplicates the Truman Library's holdings, a great deal provides organizational context for Webb activities. There are also helpful collections of BOB materials relating to NASA in the National Archives in Washington. In addition, the Margaret Chase Smith Library in Skowhegan, Maine, has documents relevant to that senator's interactions with Webb. Also, Arthur Raymond, a confidant of Webb, had a personal file of his NASA years which he allowed me to see. Webb himself had personal papers at his home he had not sent to any library, and, although most of these concerned his nonofficial life, some did touch on NASA.

The many congressional hearings on authorizations and appropriations for NASA provided a stage on which Webb held forth. Of the occasional special hearings, the most important focused on the Apollo fire.

Secondary sources on Webb's NASA era are equally abundant. Those helpful for the early period (1961–63) include the histories NASA has published on specific projects, for example: Loyd S. Swenson, Jr., James M. Grimwood, and Charles C. Alexander, *This New Ocean: A History of Project Mercury* (1966); Barton C. Hacker and James M. Grimwood, *On the Shoulders of Titans: A History of Project Gemini* (1977); and Courtney G. Brooks, James M. Grimwood, and Loyd S. Swenson, Jr., *Chariots for Apollo: A History of Manned Lunar Spacecraft* (1979). The administrative history of Webb's initial organization is presented in Robert Rosholt, *An Administrative History of NASA, 1958–1963* (1966); and, for the entire Webb tenure, see Arnold Levine, *Managing NASA in the Apollo Era* (1982). For some of the flavor of the early NASA period, see Tom Wolfe, *The Right Stuff* (New York: Bantam, 1983); Howard E. McCurdy, *Inside NASA: High Technology and Organizational Change in the U.S. Space Program* (Baltimore: Johns Hopkins University Press, 1993); and John Naugle, *First among Equals: The Selection of NASA Space Science Experiments* (Washington: NASA, 1991).

Various accounts of the Apollo decision are available. The most detailed remains John M. Logsdon's *Decision to Go to the Moon* (Cambridge: MIT Press, 1970). Also shedding light on this critical decision are John Noble Wilford's *We Reach the Moon* (New York: Bantam, 1969); Charles Murray's and Catherine Bly Cox's *Apollo: The Race to the Moon* (New York: Simon and Schuster, 1989); Walter A. McDougall's *. . . the Heavens and the Earth: A Political History of the Space Age* (New York: Basic, 1985); and Robert A. Divine's "Lyndon B. Johnson and the Politics of Space," in *The Johnson Years*, vol. 2, *Vietnam, the Environment, and Science* (Lawrence: University of Kansas Press, 1987). An extremely valuable document, unfortunately unpublished, that is useful both for the decision to go to the moon and other aspects of Webb's years at NASA is Robert C. Seamans's monograph "Voyage to the Moon: A View From NASA Headquarters."

Next to Apollo, the NASA program that became most personally associated with Webb was the Sustaining University Program (SUP). For its origins, see my *Launching NASA's Sustaining University Program* (Syracuse, N.Y.: InterUniversity Case Program, 1969). On the astronauts (in addition to Wolfe's book), see Robert Sherrod, "The Selling of the Astronauts," *Columbia Journalism Review*, May/June 1973. For accounts of NASA's locational decisions, see Thomas Murphy, ed., *Science, Geopolitics, and Federal Spending* (Lexington, Mass.: Heath, Lexington, 1971).

In addition, contemporary accounts in the newspapers and especially certain technical journals were quite helpful. Two weekly publications kept a close eye on the space program: *Aviation Week and Space Technology* and *Science*.

Webb's middle years at NASA (1964-66) are also the years when Lyndon Johnson took over from Kennedy. Accordingly, it is useful to note the material on space in Johnson's *Vantage Point* (New York: Popular Library, 1971). Also, Johnson had NASA prepare an administrative history of space during his watch: NASA, *Preliminary History of NASA, 1963-69* (Washington: NASA, 1969).

Certain programs were questioned or ran into difficulty during the 1964-66 period, as budget growth ended. For Webb's activity in connection with the Ranger controversy, see R. Cargill Hall, *Lunar Impact: A History of Project Ranger* (Washington: NASA, 1977), and Clayton R. Koppes, *JPL and the American Space Program: A History of the Jet Propulsion Laboratory* (New Haven: Yale University Press, 1982). For Webb's struggle to relate SUP to the Great Society and show the broader impacts of space, see Laurin Henry, *The NASA Memorandum of Understanding* (Syracuse, N.Y.: InterUniversity Case Program, 1969).

The third period of Webb's tenure at NASA (1967-68) was influenced by the Apollo fire, which engendered a vast literature with primary sources in the files at the NASA History Office, at the Truman Library, and elsewhere. These materials cover the NASA investigation and the legislative inquiry and contain the lengthy *Report of Apollo 204 Review Board* (Washington: NASA, 1967). Virtually all book and other accounts already mentioned that cover Apollo's history discuss the fire (e.g., Wilford, *We Reach the Moon*; Murray and Cox, *Apollo: The Race to the Moon*; Seamans, "Voyage to the Moon"). In addition, Wayne Biddle has written an insightful article comparing the political dynamics surrounding the Apollo fire with those of *Challenger*: "Two Faces of Catastrophe," *Air and Space*, August/September 1990. Also, see Joseph Trento, *Prescription for Disaster* (New York: Crown, 1987). For the North American perspective on the fire and Webb, see Mike Gray, *Angle of Attack: Harrison Storms and the Race to the Moon* (New York: Norton, 1992).

The astronaut most involved with the Apollo fire investigation and NASA's recovery effort was Frank Borman, who has provided his perspective in his book written with Robert J. Serling, *Countdown: An Autobiography* (New York: Morrow, 1988). Webb drew Boeing into the recovery activity, and the Boeing view is presented in Robert J. Serling, *Legend and Legacy: The Story of Boeing and Its People* (New York: St. Martin's, 1992). Buzz Aldrin has also given an astronaut's point of view on Apollo's recovery in his book with Malcolm McConnell, *Men from Earth* (New York: Bantam, 1989). See also the work of astronauts Alan Shepard and Deke Slayton, *Moonshot: The Inside Story of America's Race to the Moon* (Atlanta: Turner Publishing Co., 1994). In this book, Slayton comments (p. 221): "Webb was the glue that held it all together. Without him we would have lost Project Apollo after the fire."

The 1967-68 period involved Apollo's recovery, but it also embraced the continuing struggle, begun by Webb in the mid-1960s, to establish a post-Apollo program. This time, however, Webb was holding back on post-Apollo in the interest of completing Apollo. A huge manuscript deals with post-Apollo planning: Emmette

Redford and Orion White, *What Manned Space Program after Reaching the Moon? Government Attempts to Decide: 1962–1968* (Syracuse, N.Y.: InterUniversity Case Program, 1971). Arthur Levine, in *Future of the U.S. Space Program* (New York: Praeger, 1975), also deals with Webb's role in post-Apollo.

John Logsdon gave me drafts of chapters concerning post-Apollo that were planned as part of a book on the Space Shuttle decision. W. David Compton and Charles D. Benson, in *Living and Working in Space: A History of Skylab* (Washington: NASA, 1983), wrote on this difficult time in NASA's transition. Homer Newell has critical comments about Webb's inability to sell a post-Apollo program in *Beyond the Atmosphere* (Washington: NASA, 1980), and I have discussed post-Apollo decision making in *Presidential Management of Science and Technology: The Johnson Presidency* (Austin: University of Texas Press, 1985), an account that draws heavily on documents at the LBJ Library. Other works on post-Apollo decision making include Robert Dallek's "Johnson, Project Apollo, and the Politics of Space Program Planning" (paper presented at NASA Conference on Presidential Leadership, Congress and the U.S. Space Program, Washington, March 1993) and Robert Divine's "Lyndon B. Johnson and the Politics of Space."

A number of the authors of books and other writings on the history of Apollo have put forth one conjecture or another regarding Webb's leaving. The transcript of the statement Webb made to his NASA colleagues shortly after his meeting with LBJ, on file at the Truman Library, is consistent with statements he has made subsequently. Dallek's account points up the strong regard Johnson had for Webb, and LBJ's defense of Webb against an attack by science adviser Donald Hornig ("Johnson, Project Apollo, and the Politics of Space Program Planning") is documented in LBJ Library materials.

Newspaper and magazine coverage of space during this period was prodigious. The Apollo fire precipitated a torrent of media coverage, which tailed off in late 1967 only to pick up again when manned flights resumed in 1968 and moved toward the moon. Similarly, the amount of material in congressional hearings was immense, particularly in the period after the fire.

The Moon and After

The Truman Library and Webb's personal files contain primary materials on Webb's life after Apollo. I was in fact permitted to see correspondence between Webb and his cousin, Bailey Webb, a physician, that reflects Webb's final fight against the ravages of Parkinson's disease.

Relevant secondary material includes Webb's own writing, primarily *Space Age Management: The Large-Scale Approach* (New York: McGraw-Hill, 1969). Webb's role as a member of the board of the Gannett Company is dealt with by Al Neuharth in *Confessions of an S.O.B.* (New York: Penguin, 1992), and his work with the Smithsonian Institution is discussed by Elmer B. Staats, in "James E. Webb,

Space Age Manager," in *Giants in Management*, ed. Robert L. Haught (Washington: National Academy of Public Administration, 1985), as well as in unpublished documents by former chief justice Warren E. Burger. Many tributes came Webb's way in his later years, including one from a former NASA executive for whom Webb served as a mentor, who later became NASA administrator himself—James Beggs, "James E. Webb: A Force for Excellence," Inaugural Lecture of the Fund for Excellence in Public Administration (Washington: NAPA, 1984). President George Bush paid tribute to Webb in his letter to Patsy Webb, written upon Webb's death, which is in the personal files at Webb's home. Among the many other letters that went to Webb's widow, many from associates going back years, some provide insights into Webb's character and the way he significantly touched the lives of other able individuals.

The number of newspaper and magazine articles on Webb diminished once he left NASA. Although he testified before Congress occasionally and gave speeches, he faded from the attention of most observers of the space program and even students of government. One who remembered him vividly was management scholar Leonard Sayles, who wrote a glowing tribute to Webb when he died, in "James Webb at NASA," *Society*, vol. 29, no. 6, 1992, 63–68.

While this study relied on primary documents and secondary sources, I also drew on 207 interviews I conducted, as well as scores of others' interviews of Webb and NASA officials over the years. Two of these sources were especially important. First, interviews of Webb were conducted by the staff of the National Air and Space Museum, hundreds of pages of material that covers Webb's life. In addition, the museum staff interviewed Webb's associates extensively—Seamans, Mueller, and others.

The second source of invaluable interviews is Robert Sherrod, a noted writer who planned at one point to prepare the definitive history of Apollo. He worked on this project in the late 1960s and early 1970s and interviewed (it seems in retrospect) virtually everyone connected with Apollo, including Webb. Sherrod wrote some draft chapters for the Apollo book but regrettably never finished his project. He kindly granted me access to the interviews, which are held at the NASA History Office. The value of the Sherrod interviews is that they took place at the time of the culmination of Apollo, when memories of events, personalities, and conversations were fresh. Because I interviewed many of the same individuals some years after the fact, the Sherrod material provided an important check on interview validity, as did comparison of National Air and Space Museum interviews with those I conducted. What stood out was the strong agreement.

INDEX

Abernathy, Ralph, 207
Acheson, David, 67, 211
Acheson, Dean, 6, 42, 47, 211, 230 n52; feud
with Louis Johnson, 54–63; relationship with
Webb, 48–54, 64–65
Aeronautical Chamber of Commerce, 21–22, 27
Air Mail Act of 1934, 22
Aldrin, Edwin, Jr., 1, 131, 207
Allen, Bill, 176
Allott, Gordon, 121
American Society for Public Administration,
6, 209
Anders, William, 204–5
Anderson, Clinton, 80, 122, 148, 149, 151, 152,
177, 180–81, 202, 241 n62
Apollo 4, 186–88
Apollo 6, 196–97
Apollo 7, 198, 204
Apollo 8, 198, 200, 204–5, 207
Apollo 9, 207
Apollo 10, 207
Apollo 11, 1–2, 207–8
Apollo 204 fire, 143–45; executive session with
Senate Space Committee, 180–82; hearings
on, 165–70, 176–80; impact of, 183–86; inves-
tigation of, 145–47; *New York Times*'s view
of, 167; Phillips report, 151–57, 167, 176, 178,
179, 181; probable causes of, 157–58; Review
Board report, 162–64, 166

Apollo Applications Program, 139, 142, 193–96,
250 n12
Apollo program, 85–86, 96, 100, 235 n38; guide-
lines for, 98–99; schedule problems, 114–15;
support for, 102–8. See also *Apollo 4; Apollo
6; Apollo 7; Apollo 8; Apollo 9; Apollo 10;
Apollo 11; Apollo 204* fire
Apollo-Soyuz mission, 208
Appleby, Paul H., 33
Armstrong, Neil A., 1, 131, 207, 208
Associated Universities, Inc., 78
astronauts: *Apollo 8*, 204–5, 207; Gemini,
134–35; Mercury, 113–14. See also *Apollo 204*
fire
AT&T, 234 n26
Atomic Energy Commission (AEC), 43
Atwood, J. Leland "Lee," 145, 152, 153, 162, 163;
conflict with Webb, 170–75, 246 n13

Bailey, Fred, 38
Baker, Bobby, 146, 179, 180, 182
Baker, William, 78
Battle, Lucius, D., 53, 55, 67
Bay of Pigs, 94
Beckman, Arnold, 134
Beggs, James, 147, 204, 220 n23
Bell, David, 36, 91, 92, 94, 111
Bergen, Bill, 174–75
Bergman, Jules, 152, 153, 245 n25

Berkner, Lloyd, 19, 26–27, 63, 78, 82, 100
Berry, Charles, 159
Bisplinghoff, Raymond, 118
Black, Fred, 107, 146, 180, 182, 183
Blaik, Earl "Red," 241 n60
Bland, William, 157
Boeing Company, 174, 175
Boggs, Hale, 133
Bohlen, Charles "Chip," 51
Borman, Frank, 145, 150, 151, 165–66, 169, 178, 196, 204–5
Braun, Wernher von. *See* von Braun, Wernher
Brooke, Edward, 182
Brown, George, 100
Brown, Harold, 97, 127
Bruce, David, 67
Bundy, McGeorge, 99
bureaucratic leadership, 2–4, 216–17
Bureau of the Budget (BOB): changing role of, 37–43; conflicts within, 43–46; NASA's requests from, 91–93, 111, 114–16, 120–22, 132–33, 139–41, 184–85, 193, 195–96, 234 n26; Webb as director of, 30–37
Burger, Warren E., 210–11
Burns, James, 54
Burns, James MacGregor, 4
Bush, George, 213
Bush, Vannevar, 77, 78, 231 n1
Byrd, Harry, 107
Byrnes, James F., 34–35

Callaghan, Richard, 156
Callahan, David, 65
Cannon, Clarence, 121
Cannon, Howard, 170
Carlyle, Thomas, 2–3
Carmichael, Stokely, 197
Carter, Jimmy, 10
Chaffee, Roger, 143, 151. See also *Apollo 204* fire
Chandler, Margaret, 7
Christian, George, 202
Clark, Evert, 168, 183
Clifford, Clark M., 36, 47, 55, 84, 193, 227 n36, 231 n59
Collins, Michael, 1, 131, 207
communication satellites, 234 n26

COMSAT Corporation, 234 n26
Connor, John, 143, 144
Cooper, Gordon, 113, 129, 135
Cooper, John Sherman, 59
Cox, Catherine Bly, 196
Cox, Hiden T., 104

Daddario, Emilio, 182
Dallek, Robert, 203
Dawes, Charles, 33
Debus, Kurt, 106
Dembling, Paul G., 94, 104, 147–48, 154, 155, 173, 204
Dewey, Thomas, 45
Doe, Thomas, 21
Douglas, Patsy Aiken. *See* Webb, Patsy Aiken Douglas
Draper, Charles Stark, 26, 87–88, 106, 143, 224 n60
Dryden, Hugh L., 83–84, 85; as deputy administrator of NASA, 87, 88, 91, 92, 94, 97, 104, 107, 108, 116, 128, 141
DuBridge, Lee A., 78, 110, 133, 134
Dulles, John Foster, 59

Eaton, Charles, 40
Economic Cooperation Administration (ECA), 40–41
Educational Services, Inc., 80–81
Eisenhower, Dwight D., 3, 79, 86, 92
Electronics Research Center (ERC), 121
Elsey, George, 193
European Recovery Program. *See* Marshall Plan

Farley, James, 20, 22
Finger, Harold, 160, 190
Follett, Mary Parker, 24–25
Ford, Gerald, 206–7
Foreign Service Act of 1946, 35
Forrestal, James, 41–43; conflict with Webb, 42–46
Fosdick, Dorothy, 53
Foucault, J.B.L., 223 n50
Frontiers of Science Foundation, 77–79, 80, 81
Fulton, James, 93–94

Gagarin, Yuri A., 93, 135, 214
Gardner, O. Max, 20, 28, 30, 31, 35, 69; and
    Aeronautical Chamber of Commerce,
    21–22
Gaylord, E. K., 77
Gehrig, James, 245 n25
Gemini 4, 135
Gemini 12, 135
Gemini program, 109, 110, 113–14, 119–20,
    238 n25
George, Walter, 28
Gilpatric, Roswell, 90, 91, 97
Gilruth, Robert, 106–7, 109, 113, 117, 118, 143,
    148, 158, 160, 161, 194, 195, 198, 199
Glenn, John, 126
Glennan, T. Keith, 85, 105, 236 n6
Goldberg, Arthur, 143
Goldwater, Barry, 133
Graham, Phil, 84
Greene, Larry, 174, 175
Greer, Robert, 153
Grissom, Virgil, 143, 151. See also *Apollo 204*
    fire
Grumman Engineering Corporation, 113, 181

Hagerty, William, 138
Harriman, W. Averell, 61
Hechler, Ken, 166
Hickenlooper, Bourke B., 56
Hines, William, 170
Hiss, Alger, 55–56
Hoffman, Paul, 40–41
Holland, Spessard, 185
Hollomon, J. Herbert, 192
Holmes, D. Brainerd, 108, 109, 114–15, 116, 186,
    239 n46
Hoover, Herbert C., 17
Hoover, J. Edgar, 3
Hoover Commission, 226 n29
Hornig, Donald, 146, 192, 203
Hosenball, S. Neil, 155
Hotz, Robert, 184
Hughes, Phil, 211–12
Hull, Harris, 19
Humelsine, Carlisle, 55, 62, 66, 71
Humphrey, Hubert, 69, 143, 148, 154, 200, 202

Jackson, Baxter, 28
Jet Propulsion Laboratory (JPL), 133–34
Johnson, Lady Bird, 207
Johnson, Louis, feud with Acheson, 54–63
Johnson, Lyndon B., 5, 19, 82, 91, 95, 127, 130,
    190, 207; and Apollo fire, 143, 144–45, 146;
    and Sustaining University Program, 138–39;
    and U.S. space policy, 95–96, 100, 102–3,
    132–35, 184–85; and Webb's appointment as
    NASA administrator, 84, 87; and Webb's
    departure from NASA, 201–2, 204
Jonas, Charlie, 100
Jones, Roger, 36, 39

Karth, Joseph, 154, 184
Kaufman, Herbert, 2
Kefauver, Estes, 70
Kelly, Mervin, 78, 79, 237 n13
Kennan, George F., 52, 53, 54
Kennedy, Edward, 121
Kennedy, John F., 1, 5, 81; and NASA budget
    request, 92–93; problems with NASA, 83;
    and Sustaining University Program, 111; and
    U.S. space policy, 94–99, 100, 101, 102, 112–13,
    120–21
Kennedy, Robert F., 189
Kerr, Breene, 73
Kerr, Robert S., 69–70, 75, 82, 96–97, 100, 107,
    128, 180, 182–83; relationship with Webb,
    70–72, 74, 79–80, 103
Kerr-McGee Oil Industries, 5, 69, 70–71, 74–76,
    80, 180
Khrushchev, Nikita S., 93
Killian, James R., 93, 137
King, Martin Luther, Jr., 189, 197
Kirkpatrick, John, 76
Kline, Ray, 246 n1
Komarov, Vladimir, 176
Korea, crisis in, 60–61

Laird, Melvin, 207
Lassiter, R. G., 13–14, 15
leadership. *See* bureaucratic leadership
Lilienthal, David, 43
Lilly, William E., 191
Lindbergh, Charles A., 21–22

Long, Franklyn, 145
Long, Norton, 8
Lovell, James, 204-5
Lovett, Robert A., 47, 62, 108, 172
Low, George, 160, 161, 172, 198
Luedecke, Alvin, 134
lunar landing program, 112-18; Kennedy's sup-
    port of, 94-95. *See also* Apollo program

McCarthy, Joseph, 56, 123
McCullough, David, 48
McDonnell Aircraft, 69, 72, 110
McDougall, Walter, 7, 10, 100
McGee, Dean A., 71, 74, 75, 77
McGrory, Mary, 170
McKee, William F. "Bozo," 118
McLawton, Arthur, 73
McNamara, Robert S., 90-91, 97, 98, 127, 139,
    193; conflict with Webb, 119-20, 240 n56
MacVicar, Robert, 77
McWilliams, W. J. "Jamie," 70, 71-72, 76, 80, 156
Macy, John, 189, 191
Manned Orbital Laboratory (MOL), 139, 193,
    252 n9
Manned Spacecraft Center (MSC), 106-7
Marshall, Burton, 65
Marshall, George C., 39-40, 44, 45, 50, 62
Marshall Plan, 40, 43, 44
Martin, Joseph, 18
Martin Company, 107
Mathews, Charles, 191, 192
Mecklin, John, 184
Mercury astronauts, 113-14
Mercury program, 89, 110; first flight of, 95
Miller, George P., 148, 151, 181, 202
Mondale, Walter F., 6-7, 152, 153, 154, 158, 182,
    245 n25
moonshot. *See* Apollo program; lunar landing
Morgan, Thomas A., 21-22, 23, 26
Moritz, Bernie, 181, 183
Morrison, Fred W., 69
Mueller, George E., 116-18, 142, 143, 187, 188,
    194, 195, 196, 199; and aftermath of fire, 170,
    178, 181, 182; and Apollo fire, 144, 145, 148,
    151, 152-53, 154-55, 160, 161; Webb's distrust
    of, 190, 191

Mundt, Karl, 56
Municipal Manpower Commission, 81
Murphy, Charles, 36
Murray, Charles, 196

National Academy of Public Administration, 6
National Academy of Sciences (NAS) Space
    Science Board, 82
National Advisory Committee for Aeronautics
    (NACA), 85
National Aeronautic Association, 27
National Aeronautics and Space Administra-
    tion (NASA): *Apollo 11* mission, 1-2, 207-8;
    Apollo program, 102-8, 114-15, 196-200;
    beyond Apollo, 139-41; beginnings of, 85;
    budget requests, 91-93, 111, 114-16, 120-22,
    132-33, 139-41, 184-85, 193, 195-96, 234 n26;
    criticism of, following fire, 147-51, 167, 170,
    179-80; Electronics Research Center (ERC),
    121; hostility toward, 140; Jet Propulsion
    Laboratory (JPL), 133-34; Lunar Excursion
    Module, 198; Lunar Orbit Rendezvous
    debate, 112-13; Manned Spacecraft Center,
    106-7; and Mercury-Atlas test, 89-90;
    moonshot ambitions, 93, 94-95; leadership
    at, 189-92; relationship with Grumman, 181;
    relationship with North American Aviation,
    167, 168-69, 170-76, 178-79, 181, 182, 183;
    reorganizations of, 109-11, 118, 157-62;
    Sustaining University Program (SUP),
    99-100, 111, 121-22, 136-39, 243 n21; Webb as
    administrator of, 2, 4, 6-7; Webb's departure
    from, 200-205. See also *Apollo 204* fire;
    Webb, James Edwin, NASA career
National Science Foundation, 77, 226 n29
National Security Council (NSC), 42, 45. *See
    also* NSC-68 report
NATO. *See* North Atlantic Treaty Organization
Naugle, John, 86
Neustadt, Richard E., 31, 41, 52, 227 n36,
    244 n31
Newell, Homer, 111, 118, 137-38, 190, 192,
    194-95, 196
Nitze, Paul H., 52, 53-54, 57, 65, 66-67, 231 n59
Nixon, Richard M., 10, 55-56, 200, 208
North American Aviation, 107, 108, 178-79, 181,

182; and Apollo fire, 145, 146, 152–54, 155, 162, 167, 168–69; NASA negotiations with, 170–76, 183

North Atlantic Treaty Organization (NATO), 58

NSC-68 report, 57–58, 59, 64

Oak Ridge Institute for Nuclear Studies, 78

O'Donnell, Kenneth, 106

Office of Legislative Reference, 38, 39

Office of Manned Space Flight (OMSF), 108, 114, 150, 189, 215

Office of War Mobilization and Reconversion (OWMR), 31, 35

OMSF. *See* Office of Manned Space Flight

OWMR. *See* Office of War Mobilization and Reconversion

Pace, Frank, 59, 84

Paige, Hilliard, 157–58, 161

Paine, Thomas, 191–92; as deputy administrator of NASA, 192, 197, 198, 199, 250 n11; resignation of, 208; as successor to Webb, 201–2, 204, 206–7

Pauly, McWilliam, 66

Pepper, Claude, 129

Percy, Charles, 182

Phillips, Samuel C., 118, 144, 146, 152–53, 154–55, 156, 167, 176, 183, 196, 197, 198, 199

Phillips report, 151–57, 167, 176, 178, 179, 181

Pike, John E., 215

Pou, Edward W., 222 n31; Webb as employee of, 16–20

power: Follett's view of, 24–25; role of, in management, 8–9, 244 n31

Price, Don K., 226 n29

Project Troy, 63–64

Raborn, William, 108, 238 n21

Rand, Ralph, 175

Ranger 7, 134

Raymond, Arthur, 105, 237 n13

Reagan, Ronald, 147

Republic Steel, 71, 73

Republic Supply Company, 5, 71; Webb as president of, 73–74

Revenue and Expenditure Control Act, 195

Riesman, David, 27

Ripley, S. Dillon, 211

Roosevelt, Franklin D., 17–18

Rowe, James, 227 n36

Rubel, John, 97, 98

Rudolph, Arthur, 187

Rumsfeld, Donald, 166, 182

Rusk, Dean, 60

Russell, Richard, 133

Ryan, William Fitz, 176–77, 179

Salinger, Pierre, 84–85

Sayles, Leonard, 6, 7

Scheer, Julian, 104, 144, 148 199

Schirra, Walter M., 129

Schlesinger, Arthur, 18

Schultze, Charles, 141, 185

Science: The Endless Frontier (Bush), 77

Seaborg, Glenn, 97

Seamans, Robert C., Jr., 85, 86, 208, 213, 234 n29, 235 n38; and Apollo fire, 144, 145, 146, 147, 149, 153–54, 159, 167, 183; as associate administrator of NASA, 87, 88, 89, 91, 97, 98, 101, 104, 107, 108, 114, 116–17, 118; as deputy administrator of NASA, 141, 143; and negotiations with North American, 173–74; under reorganization, 109; resignation of, 185–86; as viewed by Webb, 189

Shapley, Willis H., 85, 97, 98, 199, 244 n30

Shea, Joe, 157–60, 161, 176

Shearer, Ross, 36

Shepard, Alan, 95, 97

Sidey, Hugh, 94

Silverstein, Abe, 97, 108

Simpson, George, 137, 138

Simpson, John, 110

Skylab, 139, 208

Smith, Harold D., 30, 32, 37

Smith, Levering, 108

Smith, Margaret Chase, 122–23, 177, 178, 179, 180, 181, 185, 245 n25, 248 n40

Smull, Tom, 137–38

Snelling, William, 175

Snyder, John, 30–31, 32, 34, 35, 44, 125

Sorenson, Ted, 94

Souers, Sidney, 44, 46

Soviet space program, 93, 135, 176, 208, 214
Space Age Management: The Large-Scale Approach (Webb), 209, 210
Sperry, Elmer, 23
Sperry Gyroscope Company, 5, 21, 223 n50; Webb's career at, 22–28, 224 n65
Staats, Elmer B., 33, 38, 39, 155–56, 177, 181, 204
Stafford, Thomas, 156
State Department: Acheson-Johnson feud at, 54–63; Webb's reorganization of, 48–54; Webb's waning influence at, 63–68
Steelman, John, 35, 37, 44
Stevenson, Adlai, 70
Stone, Donald C., 40, 41
Stoner, George, 176
Storms, Harrison, 152, 170, 172–73, 174, 175
Stowe, David, 36, 37
Stratton, Julius, 136–37
Sustaining University Program (SUP), 99–100, 111, 121–22, 136–39, 243 n21
Symington, Stuart, 178

Taylor, Frederick, 24
Teague, Olin E., 149, 163–64, 168, 169, 176–77, 182
Thomas, Albert, 100, 103–4, 107, 121, 134
Thompson, Floyd "Tommy," 145, 146, 150, 183, 194
Trabue, M. R., 14
Truman, Harry S., 4, 30, 125, 227 n36; and conflicts at Budget Bureau, 43–46; and Webb's role as director of Budget Bureau, 31, 32–36, 37–39; and Webb's role at State Department, 47–48, 49–50, 54–55
Tucker, Morrison, 76

U.S. Air Firce, conflict with NASA, 89–91, 193

Vandenberg, Arthur, 40
van Dolah, Robert, 150
Vinson, Fred, 28
Vogel, Lawrence, 155
Volpe, John, 238 n17
von Braun, Wernher, 108, 112, 117, 118, 127, 133, 143, 187, 195, 198, 199, 246 n1

Walker, N. W., 14
Wallace, George, 133
Warren, Earl, 143
Warren, Lindsay, 28
Webb, Gorham, 28, 29
Webb, James Edwin
—as director of Budget Bureau, 30–46
—career after NASA, 210–12
—children of, 29, 47, 72, 212
—death of, 2, 213
—early career of, 4–5; as aide to Max Gardner, 20–22; as secretary to Congressman Pou, 16–20; at Sperry Gyroscope, 22–28
—at Educational Services, 80–81
—education of, 13–14
—family background of, 11–13
—illness of, 212
—and Robert Kerr, 70–71, 74, 79–80, 103
—legacy of, 5–10, 214–17, 253 n2
—as marine aviator, 15, 16, 124
—marriage of, 23
—NASA career: administrative agenda, 99–101; administrative philosophy of, 209–10; as administrator, 2, 4, 6–7; as administrator, offered position of, 82–87; and aftermath of Apollo fire, 183–86; and Apollo fire, 142–63, 215; and Apollo fire hearings, 165–70, 176–80; and *Apollo 4*, 186–88; and *Apollo 11*, 1–2; Apollo program, 102–8, 196–200; beyond Apollo program, 139–41, 193–96; approach to management, 87–88, 105–6; and Lee Atwood, conflict with, 170–75, 246 n13; challenges to authority during, 112–18, 119–23; as consultant, 206; departure from, 200–205; and executive session with Senate Space Committee, 180–82; and Holmes, conflict with, 114–15; under Lyndon Johnson, 132–35, 200–201; as adviser to Kennedy on space program, 95–99; leadership changes, 189–92; and McNamara, conflict with, 119–20, 240 n56; reorganizations of NASA, 109–11, 118, 157–62; and Sustaining University Program (SUP), 99–100, 111, 121–22,

136–39, 243 n21; and U.S. space policy,
88–95
—in Oklahoma, 72–76; Frontiers of Science
Foundation, 76–79, 80, 81
—photographs of, 124–31
—at Smithsonian Institution, 210–11
—at State Department: Acheson-Johnson
feud, 55–63; conflict with George Kennan,
53; reorganization of, 48–54; as under secretary, 47–48; waning influence of, 63–68
Webb, James, Jr., 47, 72, 212
Webb, John, 11
Webb, John Frederick (J.F.), 11–13, 221 n8
Webb, Olive, 13, 16, 221 n8
Webb, Patsy Aiken Douglas, 23, 72, 85, 98, 202,
204, 207, 212
Webb, S. R. "Sawney," 11, 12, 221 n8
Webb, Sally, 29, 72, 212

Webb, Sarah Edwin Gorham, 11, 12–13
Wells, Herman, 137
Welsh, Edward, 92, 184
Wharton, Olive Webb. *See* Webb, Olive
White, Edward, 143, 151. See also *Apollo 204* fire
Wiesner, Jerome B., 64, 81, 82, 83, 89, 92–93, 95,
96, 111, 112, 113, 127
Wilford, John Noble, 166–67
Wilson, Woodrow, 17
Wolfe, Tom, 9, 85
Woodruff, Robert, 28
Wydler, John, 149

Young, R. P. "Rip," 104

Zuckerman, Solly, 112
Zuckert, Eugene M., 90